Micro and Macro Levels
of Analysis in Anthropology

Westview Special Studies

The concept of Westview Special Studies is a response to the continuing crisis in academic and informational publishing. Library budgets are being diverted from the purchase of books and used for data banks, computers, micromedia, and other methods of information retrieval. Interlibrary loan structures further reduce the edition sizes required to satisfy the needs of the scholarly community. Economic pressures on university presses and the few private scholarly publishing companies have greatly limited the capacity of the industry to properly serve the academic and research communities. As a result, many manuscripts dealing with important subjects, often representing the highest level of scholarship, are no longer economically viable publishing projects--or, if accepted for publication, are typically subject to lead times ranging from one to three years.

Westview Special Studies are our practical solution to the problem. As always, the selection criteria include the importance of the subject, the work's contribution to scholarship, and its insight, originality of thought, and excellence of exposition. We accept manuscripts in camera-ready form, typed, set, or word processed according to specifications laid out in our comprehensive manual, which contains straightforward instructions and sample pages. The responsibility for editing and proofreading lies with the author or sponsoring institution, but our editorial staff is always available to answer questions and provide guidance.

The result is a book printed on acid-free paper and bound in sturdy, library-quality soft covers. We manufacture these books ourselves using equipment that does not require a lengthy make-ready process and that allows us to publish first editions of 300 to 1000 copies and to reprint even smaller quantities as needed. Thus, we can produce Special Studies quickly and can keep even very specialized books in print as long as there is a demand for them.

About the Book and Editors

Arguing that there are insufficient theoretical and methodological guidelines for articulating microlevel and macrolevel analyses of sociocultural phenomena, contributors to this volume review the history of micro/macro issues in anthropology and provide a framework for a more systematic examination of potential linkages among levels. In addition, they provide empirical examples of the articulation of micro/macro theory and methods in sociocultural research that illustrate how the behavior of individuals and local communities affects and is affected by larger units and processes. These studies demonstrate that many theoretical and methodological debates in the social sciences implicitly are arguments about scale and/or level of analysis that arise from an inadequate understanding of the complementarity of analyses on different dimensions. A final essay draws together guidelines for integrating microlevel and macrolevel analyses.

Billie R. DeWalt is a professor of anthropology and rural sociology and is acting director of the Latin American Studies Program at the University of Kentucky. Pertti J. Pelto is professor of anthropology and community medicine at the University of Connecticut.

To Jennie M. DeWalt and Jenny M. Pelto

and to the memory of Harry E. DeWalt and Jaakko J. Pelto

Micro and Macro Levels of Analysis in Anthropology
Issues in Theory and Research

edited by
Billie R. DeWalt and
Pertti J. Pelto

Westview Press / Boulder and London

A Westview Special Study

Published in 1985 in the United States of America by Westview Press, Inc.;
Frederick A. Praeger, Publisher; 5500 Central Avenue, Boulder, Colorado 80301

Library of Congress Cataloging in Publication Data
Main entry under title:
Micro and macro levels of analysis in anthropology.
    1. Ethnology--Philosophy--Addresses, essays, lectures.
2. Ethnology--Methodology--Addresses, essays, lectures.
I. DeWalt, Billie R.   II. Pelto, Pertti J.
GN345.M53 1985   306'.01   85-10683
ISBN:0-8133-0251-X

Composition for this book was provided by the editors
Printed and bound in the United States of America

10 9 8 7 6 5 4 3 2 1

Contents

Tables and Figures

FIGURES

Acknowledgments

As editors, we accept full responsibility for the content of this book. Nevertheless, this volume represents the culmination of an effort that involved many different individuals. Most important has been the contribution of Sara Alexander. Her patience and forbearance in coping with multiple drafts of papers and the many details to which attention must be paid are very much appreciated. Without her efforts, this book would not have been finished.

Thanks also go to Teresa Epperson and Andrea Allen for their assistance in the typing of drafts and some of the tables, Nancy Merryman who prepared the index, and Gyulius Pauer of the University of Kentucky Cartographic Laboratory who prepared some of the figures. Our families, Saara, Gareth and Kathleen Musante DeWalt and Ari, Jon and Gretel Pelto were quite patient with us as we struggled to complete this project.

Finally, we must thank the authors of the essays presented here. Their work has served as a source of stimulation for our thinking about issues of microlevel/macrolevel linkages and we are pleased to be able to present their work in this context.

Billie R. DeWalt
Pertti J. Pelto

Contributors

Richard N. Adams is Rapaport Centennial Professor of Social Sciences at the University of Texas at Austin. He has been President of the American Anthropological Association, the Latin American Studies Association and the Society for Applied Anthropology. He has published on the subjects of power, energy, and cultural evolution. His books include Paradoxical Harvest (1982), La Red de la Expansión Humana (1978), Energy and Structure (1975) and Crucifixion by Power (1970).

John W. Bennett is Professor of Anthropology at Washington University of St. Louis, Missouri and a program associate at the Land Tenure Center of the University of Wisconsin, Madison. He has been President of the American Ethnological Society and the Society for Applied Anthropology. His publications include work on ecology and economics, communal societies, and agrarian development. His books include Of Time and the Enterprise (1982), The Ecological Transition: Cultural Anthropology and Human Adaptation (1976), Northern Plainsmen: Adaptive Strategy and Agrarian Life (1969) and Hutterian Brethren (1967).

Frank Cancian is a Professor of Anthropology in the School of Social Sciences at the University of California at Irvine. He has served as President of the Society for Economic Anthropology and has published in the areas of economic anthropology, social stratification, and peasant societies. His books include The Innovator's Situation (1979), Change and Uncertainty in a Peasant Economy (1972) and Economics and Prestige in a Maya Community (1965).

Billie R. DeWalt is Professor of Anthropology and Rural Sociology and Acting Director of the Latin American Studies Program at the University of Kentucky. His publications are in the areas of political ecology, rural development, and agricultural anthropology. His publications include Training Manual in Policy Ethnography (1985) with John van Willigen, Sistemas de Cultivo en Pespire, Sur de Honduras: Un Enfoque de Agroecosistemas (1984) with Kathleen M. DeWalt and Modernization in a Mexican Ejido: A Study in Economic Adaptation (1979).

xiii

Laura M. Montgomery is Visiting Assistant Professor of Anthropolog at Wheaton College in Wheaton, Illinois. A Ph.D. candidate a Michigan State University, her research interests include politica economy, agrarian systems, gender and development.

Pertti J. Pelto is Professor of Anthropology and Community Medicin at the University of Connecticut in Storrs. His publication include work on methodology, medical anthropology, and technolog and social change. His books include Anthropological Research: th Structure of Inquiry (1978) with Gretel H. Pelto, The Snowmobil Revolution (1973), and Technology and Social Change (1972) with Russell Bernard.

Susan C. M. Scrimshaw is Associate Professor of Public Health an Anthropology and Associate Director of the Latin American Center a the University of California at Los Angeles. She has publishe extensively in the areas of medical anthropology, culture and huma reproduction, and Latin America including A Field Guide to th Study of Health-Seeking Behavior (1984) with Elena Hurtado.

Carol A. Smith is Associate Professor of Anthropology at Duk University. She has published in the areas of political economy agrarian societies and Mesoamerican ethnography. Her publication include editing and contributing to Regional Analysis, Volumes and II (1976).

Scott Whiteford is Associate Professor of Anthropology at Michiga State University. His research interests are in political economy agrarian systems and social transformation analysis. His book include Social Impact Analysis and Development Planning in th Third World (1985) edited with William Derman, Population Growt and Urbanization in Latin America (1983) edited with John Hunte and Robert Thomas, Workers from the North: Plantations, Migran Labor, and the City in Northwest Argentina (1981), and Forgin Nations: A Comparative View of Rural Ferment and Revolt (1976 edited with Joseph Spielberg.

1
Microlevel/Macrolevel Linkages: An Introduction to the Issues and a Framework for Analysis

Billie R. DeWalt and Pertti J. Pelto

INTRODUCTION

This collection of essays grew out of an invited symposium presented at the annual meetings of the American Anthropological Association in Los Angeles. That symposium and this book arose from the increasing recognition that the social sciences have not been able to adequately explain how relatively small-scale events and processes (microlevel phenomena) are related to larger scale events and processes (macrolevel). That is, we have few theoretical and methodological guidelines for articulating the linkages between microlevels and macrolevels. While this problem is among the most vexing issues in social science research, it is also a most promising area for current research and theory building. Our hope is that this volume will help to generate productive research on micro/macro linkages by (a) bringing together the most recent thoughts on these matters from a variety of anthropologists; (b) establishing a framework within which we can begin more systematic examination of micro/macro linkages; and (c) proposing a set of methodological guidelines that can lead to more effective research in this area.

The first part of this chapter will be devoted to a brief discussion of the concepts microlevel and macrolevel and the various meanings that these terms can embody. The second part of the chapter will propose a general framework that may serve as a useful way of conceptualizing the interrelationships between micro and macro phenomena. This framework will serve as a means of introducing the works of the authors whose views are represented in this book.

MICRO AND MACRO -- AN INTRODUCTION TO THE ISSUES

The immediate reaction of most of us when "microlevel" and "macrolevel" are mentioned is to think of the one as referring to small while the other connotes large. Yet it is important to recognize that these are relational terms; micro and macro are only meaningful when used in a specific context. Thus, the scientist

1

who is interested in studying the organization of the organi
materials that make up a gene may consider the gene to be part o
the macro level. Or, from a different perspective, for the scien
tist studying the evolution of the universe, the several millio
year history of life on earth is just a moment, a micro event, i
the larger cosmic time frame.

These two examples also suggest that there are some distinc
tions that must be made in talking about micro and macro. Al
scientists study particular entities, which we can call units o
analysis, and they study processes, the series of actions or opera
tions that lead to particular results. Naturally, units of analy
sis are composed of smaller units and are themselves part of large
units. In the same way, processes are components of larger sys
tems, and contain smaller subprocesses. In addition, the scientis
may be interested only in the processes or units in the short term
or may be interested in these processes or units over much longe
periods of time. Thus, in discussing microlevels and macrolevels
at least three dimensions may be involved. These are the dimen
sions of space (the size and "geographic" location of units)
causality (processes), and time. In all of these dimensions, th
concepts "micro" and "macro" cannot be defined as absolutes bu
have meaning only in terms of the inter-relationships of the units
processes, and time frames under consideration.

THE SPATIAL SCALE OF MICRO/MACRO

Perhaps the most common formulation of micro/macro relation
ships is in terms of the size and location of the units bein
considered. Anthropologists and other social scientists are famil
iar with this issue of size in several guises.

Individuals and Aggregates

The micro/macro distinction is often formulated, especially i
social psychology and economics, in terms of the individual versu
the aggregate. Psychologists and economists (and many anthropolo
gists) must seek answers to the central issues of how individua
motives and purposes generate collective outcomes such as institu
tional, corporate, or group behavior. The various positions are
nicely summarized by Peoples (1981:384):

> One of the oldest theoretical issues in the social sciences i
> the question of how individuals are related to the socia
> groups to which they belong. Various functionalists have ar
> gued that aggregate behavior patterns can only be explained by
> the social or adaptive prerequisites of the collective organi
> zation. Those sociologists and anthropologists who adopt a
> methodological individualist approach (Blau, Homans, Barth
> have countered this view with the proposition that the attri
> butes of the collectivity can always be reduced to the strate
> gic calculations of self-interested actors.

Two recent works that specifically address this question are The Microeconomic Foundations of Macroeconomics (Harcourt 1977), and Micromotives and Macrobehavior (Schelling 1978). Both make the point that the articulation of micro and macro cannot be made through simple additive or aggregating operations.

Many people still follow Durkheim in asserting that sociological knowledge cannot be derived from the individual but must be derived from the study of "social facts" (Durkheim 1938). The anthropological phrasing of this is that culture must be explained in terms of culture (White 1949:141). More recently, anthropologists like Bennett (1969; 1976) and others have been working from a decision-making perspective that attempts to link individual behavior with larger processes. Bennett has been concerned with how the adaptive coping processes of individuals relate to the social and cultural milieu in which they exist. The contributions of DeWalt and Bennett in this volume continue their attempts to show the linkages that can be made between individual behaviors and larger sociocultural processes without resort to psychological reductionism.

While we must recognize the dangers inherent in psychological (or other forms of) reductionism, there is an equal danger in what might be called macroreductionism -- that is, the explanation of small scale phenomena through inappropriate imposition of macro-level data. Writing about the Chicago School sociologists' conceptualizations of urbanism as a way of life, for example, Cornelius stated:

> They leap from macro-societal processes of demographic change to conjecture about individual attitudes and behavior. Such inferential leaps might be justified if the results of macro-analysis could be tested against sample survey data, as they are, for example, in recent studies of population movement and voting behavior in the United States. In the absence of such data, however, there remain substantial doubts about the long-term promise of research seeking to make statements about personal political predispositions or psychological traits on the basis of aggregate data for macro units such as cities, states, or provinces (1971:110).

Levels of Organization

This is probably the most common formulation of the spatial scale in micro/macro distinctions. Anthropologists have typically focussed on local communities, or perhaps kin groups, that are ordered hierarchically in a "nesting" fashion. That is, minimal lineages are components of middle range lineages, that in turn are aggregated as maximal lineages. Similarly, villages are socially, politically, economically, and religiously linked with a regional center that is one of a number of such centers making up a state or province, that in turn is a component of a nation, continent and world.

Hierarchical systems like this are commonly encountered in anthropological research. Archaeologists have been particularly

prolific. in hierarchical (spatial) classifications. Linguistic
maps showing historical relationships among languages similarly
involve several levels of presumed degrees of affiliation of
cultural groups. The "levels" in almost all of these cases are
ever-greater agglomerations of the smaller units of analysis.

THE CAUSALITY SCALE OF MICRO/MACRO

A second important meaning that the micro/macro distinction
can take is in terms of the scale of causality. Explanation of
behavioral processes can take several different forms.

Multiple Explanations of Behavioral Processes

A good example of the need for multiple explanation of behavioral phenomena comes from an examination of why individuals
participate in civil-religious hierarchies in Mexican and Guatemalan villages (see Cancian 1965; DeWalt 1975). The proximate causes
that lead an individual to participate in the system may be the
individual's desire for prestige, or obeisance to social pressures
from the rest of the community. That is, proximate causes are the
direct mechanisms that lead to an action. On a different level, we
might distinguish the functional causes of this behavior; that is,
the way in which the actions of this individual are interrelated to
the social, religious, economic, and political systems of the
village. Often the suggested functional causes relate to presumed
maintenance of community solidarity vis-a-vis the "world outside."
At yet another level, one can focus on historical causes for the
behavior; that is, the development of the institution over time.
Here the purpose is to establish the broader processes that led to
the establishment of the system of civil-religious hierarchies (see
Rus and Wasserstrom 1980). The behavior of any individual is then
explained as a result of these historical processes. Finally, we
can try to determine ultimate causation; here, interest is in the
long-term adaptive significance of the behavior, as it affects the
survival chances of the individual and the community. We note that
these different explanations do not necessarily expand the spatial
element of what is being explained. Rather, the processes that are
used to explain the behavior are expanded in time and in terms of
supra-individual causality.

The multi-level explanation of behavioral phenomena has been
discussed most recently in anthropology by Daly and Wilson
(1983:14-19) who have used it in their sociobiological text on Sex,
Evolution, and Behavior. Their treatment of the issue is quite
similar to the one presented above. There are, however, other
ways in which this causality scale is expressed in anthropology.
One of the most important of these involves the question of whether
events are to be explained as a result of processes arising from
within the community or as a result of impinging external forces.

Local and External ✓

As a group, anthropologists, whose forte has been the study of
small-scale communities, have come under much criticism in recent
years for ignoring the linkages between local level events and the
forces operating in the larger society. There is considerable
validity to these criticisms and many anthropologists are now
pursuing theoretical strategies designed explicitly to consider the
effects of more global forces, including world wide politico-
economic systems, especially in terms of how these affect local
communities (e.g. Stavenhagen 1969; Littlefield 1978).

There is some danger, however, in the over-zealous use of such
research paradigms. It must be recognized that emphasis solely on
global or world system forces often ignores the dynamic nature of
processes in the local communities. For example, dependency theory
has been criticized because it posits only a single relation between the world system and the communities in the periphery (see
Orlove 1977 and Peoples 1978). As Smith so nicely demonstrates in
this volume, the microlevel is not passively shaped by macrolevel
forces, but reacts to these forces, often in ways that change the ✓
larger system. The clear need is for research strategies that are
able to handle the interactional nature of local and external
processes (see also Silverman 1979).

THE TIME SCALE ASPECT OF MICRO/MACROLEVEL LINKAGE

The third dimension of micro/macrolevel relationships has to
do with the time scale of explanations. That is, some research may
be designed to consider only the immediate causes and implications
of phenomena in the short run. For example, research may be
focussed on the issue of whether or not people in a particular
community or region accept or reject a particular governmental
program. Much applied anthropological research falls into this
category. On the other hand, most research in anthropology explicitly includes a longer time dimension and often includes historical
research and methods.

Ortner's review of recent anthropological theory suggests that
one of the recent major shifts in the discipline has been toward a
greater concern with diachronic analyses. According to Ortner,
there are two areas in which this shift has been reflected. The
first is research that emphasizes "microdevelopmental processes --
transactions, projects, careers, developmental cycles, and the
like." The second is "macroprocessual" or "macrohistorical" --
these are studies that pay greater attention to the externally
induced and/or internally derived developmental dynamics of societies (Ortner 1984:158).

Yet the rapprochement of anthropology with history is not
without precedent. One of the most salient ways in which the time
scale dimension has been reflected in anthropological work can be
seen in the longstanding contrast between work on cultures and
Culture.

6

Cultures and Culture

Most anthropological field work is focussed on the microlevel phenomena of a single culture within a relatively circumscribed time. In fact, a large fraction of the anthropological literature is devoted to synchronic studies of particular communities or local cultures at one moment in time. Nevertheless, anthropology has a long tradition of attempting to make sense of the long-term evolution of human Culture in general. Lewis Henry Morgan and other early evolutionist thinkers in anthropology had as their goal the creation of a general theory of how human Culture evolved. In reconstructing the evolutionary processes of human history, Morgan (1877) was one of the pioneers in the use of the "comparative method," using evidence from particular cultures to reconstruct the past stages of general cultural evolution. Thus, his macro-theory about cultural evolution was built upon the foundations of individual (microlevel) examples.

Neo-evolutionists of recent decades have built on these same foundations. In the works of many of these authors (e.g. White Service, Carneiro) the microlevel/macrolevel relationships are built up from quasi-chronological evolutionary sequences in terms of which more and more complex sociocultural systems appeared in various parts of the world. The goal of these scholars has been to determine the sequences, and more importantly, the laws according to which Culture has evolved. Many evolutionists believe that such a general theory derived from analysis of cultural evolution can eventually be applied to the study of particular cultures; that is, redirected to microlevel analysis.

Evolutionists and neo-evolutionists have sometimes been criticized for their failure to account for cultural differences among societies seemingly at the same "stage" of development. This problem led Steward (1955) to propose a different brand of evolutionism, which he called "multilinear evolution." Steward was interested in particular cultures, "...but instead of finding local variations and diversity troublesome facts which force the frame of reference from the particular to the general, it deals only with those limited parallels of form, function, and sequence which have empirical validity" (1955:19). Thus, Steward sought to improve on the evolutionists' abilities to shift between relatively more localized, microlevel phenomena and the macrolevels accounting for "parallels of form, function, and sequence." The question of how macrolevel processes can be brought down to focus on relatively short-term processes is addressed by Adams in this volume.

A FRAMEWORK FOR LINKING MICRO AND MACRO

The spatial, causal, and time dimensions of micro/macro relationships often cross-cut one another. In the examples discussed above we note that a shift to a broader theoretical framework of causality often implies changes in chronological and spatial dimensions as well. If theorists and empirical researchers were more cognizant of and more explicit about these different dimensions many of the disagreements and conflicts in social science circles could be avoided. To a considerable extent, the conflicts between microtheorists and macrotheorists arise from the fact that they are really addressing different questions with different spatial, causal and time scales. Levels of analysis suited to the explanation of certain aspects of socio-cultural phenomena may be quite unsuited to other empirical issues. Microtheory often (though not invariably) focusses on questions about relatively short-term processes in relatively circumscribed circumstances. In many cases the aim of such studies is to explain the behavior of individuals or groups in the short run, addressing such practical questions as "will the people in a particular region seek modern, rather than traditional health care?" or "how are social prestige relationships in the local community determined?". For macrotheory, on the other hand, the details about local cultural differences, social organization, and the like are not important. In the grand scale of things, it is thought that these differences are simply quaint vestigial traits that can change, intensify, or disappear without affecting the major macrolevel processes of entropy, capitalist exploitation, and the like.

Major problems arise when microlevel theorists seek to explain all behavior and all processes in terms of fundamental microprocesses such as basic human motives, genetic inheritance, or individual decisionmaking. For example, in the social science literature, some scholars have assumed that the pursuit of self-interest by individuals will lead to a maximal satisfactory solution for society as a whole (see Friedman and Friedman 1980). Yet as Schelling (1978) has shown, self-interested individual choices often lead to disastrous collective outcomes.

As we have stated earlier, there are just as many problems associated with macroreductionism as with reductionism. As Smith and Cancian show in this volume, world systems theorists have been overzealous in ignoring local responses to the expansion of capitalism. Although the larger system may impose significant constraints, local people can and do find it possible to select among a variety of alternative solutions, and utilize a variety of resources within the constraints imposed by the macrolevel processes. The obvious point is that these are not mutually exclusive domains of analysis but are complementary and, indeed, that good socio-cultural theory requires a consideration of and integration of microlevel and macrolevel approaches.

There is, alas, no magic formula for integrating the many possible levels of analysis. There is no single set of linking concepts, nor is there a particular methodological key that will unlock the doors of understanding. In this section, however, a systems framework is proposed that should serve, in conjunction with the papers in this collection, to focus debate and stimulate discussion about several aspects of micro/macrolevel approaches.

Anthropologists have established their domain of study as all aspects of human evolution and behavior at all times and in all places. Consequently the questions with which anthropologists are engaged range all the way from determining the effects of genes on behavior to the determinants of the general evolution of culture.

In a sense, anthropologists are the "systems people" in studying human behavior because they try to cope with the myriad interdependencies and interrelationships among the many systems in which humans are involved; this is what is generally meant by the concept of "holism," a major theme in anthropology.

Biological analogies in anthropology are sometimes overdrawn, but we believe that our role is much like that of the ecologists. Both have the opportunity to go beyond the narrow confines of disciplines, objects of study, and narrow theories to view the more complex whole and the integration of theories in explaining the component systems that make up that whole. A fundamental systems theory premise is especially relevant for the micro/macro problem:

> In systems terminology, ecosystems are subsystems of other systems as well as composed of subsystems. The conceptual framework of ecology is based on the assumption that there exists a series of hierarchically interacting systems from the universe to the smallest subatomic particle (Hart 1979:3).

Systems theory has had a substantial, if largely latent, impact on anthropology. Gregory Bateson and Margaret Mead were among the participants in the Macy Conference on cybernetics in the 1940s. Among the products of this conference was what came to be called general systems theory, "...a series of related theories, philosophies, and empirical inquiries related to the interdependence of parts in any natural process, including human society" (Bennett 1976:84). Buckley (1967) has written what is the most readable and cogent introduction to the topic for social scientists.

The importance of general systems analysis is not that it offers a different theoretical paradigm; indeed, there is considerable debate as to whether it is a theory at all. We tend to agree with McClelland who cautioned that "...it should be kept in mind that the general-systems approach is neither a formula nor a doctrine, but a cluster of strategies of inquiry; not a theory but an organized space within which many theories may be developed and related" (1965:271;emphasis ours). That is, general systems analysis is a framework within which concepts and theories appropriate to one system may be viewed in relation to its subsystems and the larger systems of which it is a part, as well as within which influences from smaller and larger systems can be seen to have effects. In addition to these vertical system linkages, however, there are also systems at the same level of analysis; thus we must also consider the linkages among horizontal systems.

Robert Hart's (1979) application of systems analysis has been with agricultural systems. Figure 1.1 provides an example of hierarchical and vertical relationships between some components of an agricultural system. We see that, even in this simplified system, many different kinds of specialists with their varied explanatory systems will be needed to give a picture of the patterns and processes that are occurring on an individual farm.[1] Within the local crop system, for example, we may need an expert on maize, another on beans, and another on sorghum. Within the crop

Figure 1.1 Hierarchical Relationships Between Agricultural Systems

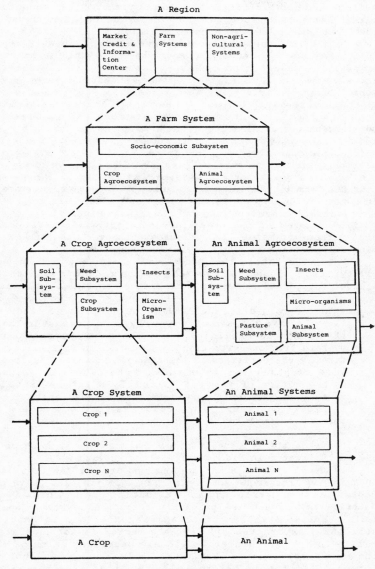

Source: Robert D. Hart, An Ecological Systems Conceptual Framework
for Agricultural Research and Development, in W.W. Shaner, P.F.
Philipp and W.R. Schmehl, eds., <u>Farming Systems Research and
Development</u> (Washington D.C.: U.S. Agency for International
Development, 1981), p. 53.

agroecosystem, we may require the explanatory skills of an agrono-
mist, a soils scientist, an entomologist, perhaps a bacteriologist,
and so on. When the farming system conception is expanded to include essential socio-economic considerations (see DeWalt n.d.),
the picture becomes even more complicated.

Hart's discussion concerning levels of analysis is similar to
Adams' framework for studying micro/macro relationships developed
in his book Crucifixion by Power. Key elements in Adams' scheme
are what he calls "operating units" -- defined as any organized
subset of the human species that tries itself out against elements
in the environment (1970:53). When these units come into contact
with one another, "....they find themselves either standing in
superordinate-subordinate positions with respect to each other, or
recognizing each other as coordinates" (1970:54). The levels at
which these operating units are found, Adams calls levels of articulation. Similar to what we have earlier referred to as the spatial scale and what others have called levels of analysis, Adams
uses the term articulation to indicate that these levels are always
in contact with one another in situations of cooperation, conflict,
integration, coordination, and the like. Figure 1.2 shows a simplified diagram of the operating units that were involved in the
events that ultimately led to the overthrow of the Arbenz government in Guatemala in 1954.

While the levels that Adams used in this diagram are ones that
are typically found in research, he has made it clear that these
are not categories that should be treated as fixed. He stated:

> It was a very distinct finding in the present study that if
> "levels" are to used effectively, it is necessary to regard
> the number as flexible, for a different number might well
> operate from one situation to another. In fact, it was speci-
> fically the variation in the number of levels that could pro-
> vide crucial indications about the nature of the society.
> ....the notion of "level" is really a set of intellectual
> categories into which articulations between units are placed
> in order to arrange them, relative to one another, in some
> sort of ordinal scale (1970:54-5).

Hart has made the same point about the openness with which levels
should be treated in biological systems research.[2]

Vertical systems and relationships are not the only important
ones in most research; horizontal linkages are also quite significant. Marvin Harris provides an outline in his book Cultural
Materialism of what are primarily horizontal systems (see Figure
1.3). Harris' division of these elements into infrastructure,
structure, superstructure, and the mental (emic) superstructure
relate to his own theoretical ideas concerning which of these is
the most deterministic of cultural behavior. We are not arguing
for or against this theoretical position here, but rather, we
present his categorization as an example of a complex set of interrelationships that will obtain among horizontal elements of any
sociocultural system.

Figure 1.2 Operating Units

LEVEL OF ARTICULATION	REVOLUTIONARY GOVERNMENT	INSURGENCY
International	Iron Curtain (arms) ———————	U.S. (cash and arms)
National	Arbenz ———————————	Castillo
Regional	Agrarian Comités —————	farmers
Local	campesinos —————————	campesinos
Family		

g >—— h g allocates power to h; g ——— h g conflicts with h
g ——→ h g exerts power over h

Source: Richard N. Adams, Crucifixion by Power (Austin: University of Texas Press, 1970), p. 63.

The purpose of introducing Adams' vertical schema and Harris' horizontal schema is to give some indication of the interdependencies that may exist among the phenomena of human behavior. We want to make it clear that no single investigator or theoretical explanatory system can possibly handle everything one would like to know about humans. The systems framework we are presenting is not a plea for overarching eclecticism that will enfold just about any explanation within its reach. We are, however, urging the realization that theories about different systems of human behavior at different levels may be potentially complementary to one another rather than directly competing explanations. Too often in anthropology and other social sciences, scholars act and write as though nearly every other social scientist is wrong and only they (or a small group of peers) have discovered "the truth." We believe that this is unfortunate.

The papers presented in this volume provide one such set of complementary theoretical positions. The following section will show that placing these within a systems framework enables us to see how they are interrelated.

PICTOGRAPHIC GRID FOR CATEGORIZING VERTICAL AND HORIZONTAL LINKAGES

The systems framework outlined above was intended to suggest that scholars approach bodies of knowledge from a perspective that encourages them to look to see how each informs the other. As one way of facilitating such an endeavor, the models that have been presented in previous pages suggest that perhaps there is a way that the search for micro/macro linkages could be facilitated through visual representation. That is, if the contents of any contribution to knowledge could be visually represented, it might

Figure 1.3 Conceptualization of Horizontal Systems

Technology of Subsistence
Techno-environmental Relationships
Ecosystems
Work Patterns
Demography
Mating Patterns
Fertility, Natality, Mortality
Nurturance of Infants
Medical Control of Demographic Patterns
Contraception, Abortion, Infanticide

INFRASTRUCTURE

Family Structure
Domestic Division of Labor
Domestic Socialization,
    Enculturation, Education
Age and Sex Roles
Domestic Discipline, Hier-
    archies, Sanctions
Political Organization,
    Factions, Clubs, etc.
Division of Labor, Taxation,
    Tribute
Political Socialization, En-
    culturation, Education
Class, Caste, Urban, Rural
    Hierarchies
Discipline, Police/military
    Control
War

Art, Music, Dance,
    Literature,
    Advertising
Rituals
Sports, Games
    Hobbies
Science

SUPERSTRUCTURE

STRUCTURE

Source: Adapted from Marvin Harris, Cultural Materialism: The Struggle for a Science of Culture (New York: Random House, 1979), pp. 51-54.

facilitate determining what other contributions are really competing explanations as opposed to potentially complementary explanations.

An interesting example of such a representation has been used
for many years by the journal Ekistics. This journal on the
"science of human settlements" includes an "ekistic grid index" in
each issue. The grid index codes the articles in each issue by the
size of settlement as well as "aspects of ekistic elements." There
are five ekistic elements (nature, anthropos, society, shells, and
networks), each divided into four subheads. In addition, each
article is described by key words, a more common procedure used by
most other major social science journals. While the specific
categories utilized by Ekistics are not very relevant for our
purposes, we felt that placing the papers in this volume into a
similar grid might be useful. We have chosen to call ours a pictographic grid, a term meant to suggest the prehistoric drawings or
paintings on rock walls. The term is also meant to suggest that
ours may be a crude first approximation and that many future
improvements on our grid may be desireable and necessary.

The horizontal linkage axis of our grid is perhaps easier to
deal with because a variety of anthropologists have proposed categorization schemes for sociocultural systems. Many such schemes
exist in the literature; these include Radcliffe-Brown's (1952)
division of the social system into social structure, ecological,
and cultural; the "functional prerequisites of a society" by Aberle
et al.(1950); the categories used by Murdock for coding cross-
cultural data in the World Ethnographic Atlas (1967); and Harris'
list presented above (Figure 1.3). Each of these taxonomies reflects the theoretical biases of the authors and it is inevitable
that any such "laundry list" will be considered "biased" in some
manner. The list used here will be solely to represent the papers
contained in this volume and are very general categories, largely
taken from the recognized subfields with which anthropologists are
concerned. The top of Figure 1.4 contains these categories. Note
that several important categories such as socialization, religion/
ritual, language, and expressive culture are not included but this
is only because these topics were not represented in the papers
included in this volume.

While the proper horizontal categories for the analysis of
human systems presents thorny problems, there are even more prickly
issues surrounding the categories for vertical systems. There are
many precedents, including Kroeber's hierarchy of body, psyche,
society, and culture (1952:118-20), as well as Adams' "levels of
articulation" (1970). It is noteworthy that Adams did not insist
on a hard and fast version of what the various levels should be.
Instead, he suggested that the definition of levels should grow out
of the data that one wishes to examine. In spite of the arbitrary
nature of defining them, we believe there are a number of levels of
analysis that are commonly used in social science analysis. We
have listed these as vertical systems in Figure 1.4. It is hardly
an exhaustive listing but we feel that it makes sense in terms of
how anthropologists have been analyzing human behavior.

Figure 1.4 A Pictographic Grid of the Papers Presented in this Volume

	Ecology/Ecosystem	Technology	Economics	Politics	Social Organization	Social Structure	Demography
Individual	D	D	D^C				Sc
Household	D	D	D^C				Sc
Community	D^W	D	M^W D^C	M^W	W		Sc
Region	D^W	D^W	M^W_C D	M^W			
Nation	D	D	M^D	M^W			Sc
World System	A^D	D	M^D	M^A		A	A
Culture	A		A	A		A	A

D = DeWalt

Sc = Scrimshaw

C = Cancian

W = Whiteford and Montgomery

A = Adams

M = Smith

Finally, we should note that it might be desirable to
clude <u>time</u> as an additional dimension in our pictographic system.
storical analysis is an important component of much anthropologi-
l research. Prime examples are the contributions of Smith and
ams in this volume (see also Ortner 1984). We have left this
mension out of the diagram because it makes portrayal of the grid
ch more difficult, and because we believe that the horizontal and
ertical systems are most important for the framework we are sug-
sting.

Before placing the papers in this volume in the grid, we must
itially make several essential qualifying statements. First, the
odes and statements that are presented here are a product of the
inking of DeWalt and Pelto and are our effort to put all of the
ork presented into a broader perspective.

Second, the articles in this volume do not cover the full
veep of sociocultural theory, as a quick look at the pictographic
rid will tell us. The various authors in this volume were chosen
ecause we felt that they had done the best extant work on micro/
acro issues. Many perspectives are missing that could also be
omplementary to the positions presented. While we will try to
how the linkages among the positions presented in this volume,
here are many more such linkages that could be made with work and
erspectives that are not represented.

A clear difference among the articles presented in this book
s in spatial scale, or the level of analysis that is the starting
oint for the research (see Figure 1.4). DeWalt and Scrimshaw, and
o some extent Cancian, remain most faithful to the micro side of
nthropological tradition -- the study of individuals and communi-
ies. They focus on the decisions of individuals or households.
eWalt is concerned with how and why farmers in southern Honduras
onvert their lands from grain cultivation to pasture. Scrimshaw
ooks at induced abortions among lower-income families in Guaya-
uil, Ecuador. Cancian wants to understand economic behavior in
ounded rural stratification systems; they may or may not be ana-
yzable in terms of class when put into a larger global context.
ank can be seen to be operating in the Honduran case as well
ecause it is medium and larger farmers who are converting their
and to pasture.

While DeWalt's research begins in a small scale community, the
analysis quickly shifts to processes affecting the southern region
of Honduras. Whiteford and Montgomery begin with the Mexicali
Valley region and eventually use one community to illustrate the
interaction between local and regional systems. Smith's analysis
is of the interaction between a region of Guatemala and the larger
national and world system.

In terms of spatial and temporal scale, Adams is the most
macro of the works presented here. His paper is focussed on human
Culture in long term perspective. He views human sociocultural
evolution within the context of the selective pressures that allow
some groups to survive and expand while others decline and stag-
nate. We should note that the stratification systems about which
Cancian is writing are one of the components of the macroframework
that humans partially construct and to which they must adapt.

Perhaps the most striking commonality among the papers in th
volume is that all of them have some degree of historical analysi
That is, in terms of the time scale of micro/macro, none of the
focusses only on short-term phenomena. Of the research presente
here, Scrimshaw's work on abortions has the shortest time frame
but even her analysis looks historically at the pattern of abor
tions and government policy in Ecuador. DeWalt looks at the recer
agrarian history of southern Honduras and Central America; thi
spans about 30 years. Whiteford and Montgomery review events c
more than 100 years duration, while Smith begins her analysis a
the opening of the colonial period in Guatemala (1521).

It is in terms of the causality scale that we can see th
greatest complementarity among the papers. Adams' conception c
the macroframework as involving hierarchy and market systems a
well as uncontrollable Nature is a theme that lies behind a numbe
of the articles. Smith talks about Guatemalan Indians who ar
becoming increasingly and successfully involved in the market sys
tem while Ladinos increasingly migrate to the city; and the peas
ants in DeWalt's analysis are caught up in a situation in whic
there is a more profitable market for beef than for grains. Thes
are all processes that may be seen within the light of Adams
argument that, in increasing concentration of power, energy, an
regulation in order to achieve control, the situation becomes mor
uncontrollable.

The reasons why the Ecuadoran squatter settlement women i
Scrimshaw's research are choosing to have induced abortions pro
vides comparisons and contrasts, for example, with Harris' (1981
view of sex, procreation and family in the United States. Larg
families in Ecuador are no longer adaptive, a change that occurre
earlier in the United States as the country moved from an agraria
to an industrial mode of production. Under these circumstances i
is understandable that there is a desire to limit family size i
Ecuador. With the lack of availability and of acceptance of con
traceptives, it is not surprising that abortion becomes the primar
resort. But even in the United States, where contraceptives ar
much more widely used and available, there are high numbers o
abortions. The reasons why abortion is chosen by many women in th
United States and Ecuador may not be as different as we woul
think.

The works presented in this volume illustrate what Bennet
believes are the most important requirements for effective study o
micro/macro relationships. As he expresses in the following chap
ter, these requirements are that systems must be seen as interac
tive and dynamic. In terms of interaction, we share with Bennet
the belief that human behavior can best be understood if we ar
able to handle the interplay among different levels. In this book
Smith, DeWalt, and Whiteford and Montgomery, beginning from dif
ferent levels of analysis, are looking at the interaction betweer
international capitalism (the marketplace) and local adaptations.
Causality is not assumed to be from the world system to the local
level, as these authors look at ways in which the local system is
modifying the influences impinging from more distant levels.

In similar ways, Scrimshaw also looks at micro/macro interac-

:ions. She is interested in a particular behavior at the local level -- the decision to undergo induced abortion. Here analysis of the behavior is placed within the context of governmental rules and regulations. Adams is operating on a more global scale, but he too is viewing the interactions of systems. What happens to human :ulture as individual societies attempt to gain greater control over resources and population is Adams' topic.

By seeing the interactions of systems, these analyses are intended to be <u>dynamic</u>. They are not snapshots of events frozen in time but are reports about events that are continuing. The authors are not giving us accounts of bounded communities and the relationships among its component parts at one period in time. Instead, their systems are units attempting to cope within an ever-changing milieu. DeWalt's epilogue about the current decline in beef prices means that, notwithstanding all of the events that have come before, Honduran farmers will have to make some difficult decisions in order to respond to these world events. The prevalence of induced abortion and apparent "demand" for safe and effective contraceptive devices that Scrimshaw documents will ultimately force changes in the health care system in Ecuador. Smith brings us right up to the present repressive and revolutionary conditions in Guatemala -- a situation that as yet does not appear to have a clear outcome. Adams is explicit in stating that whenever societies make changes in order to gain greater control, the changes themselves become a part of the macroframework over which there is little control. In all of these situations we see that there is a real dynamism in which changes at one level engender changes at other levels, which in turn create pressures and changes at higher and lower levels. Those who attempt to study the micro/macro "relational nexus" must be equipped to cope with the ever-shifting nature of their subject matter. Anthropologists will find it more and more difficult to find static, isolated communities. Analyses that seem to suggest this condition will be more difficult to defend.

Although many more linkages could be pointed out, we hope we have made the point that there is complementarity in this work, even though the starting points and the substantive interests of these authors are so diverse. Were we to review research in particular areas of the world within this framework we might find even greater complementarity. The key, it seems to us, is to have researchers sufficiently explicit concerning the dimensions of the micro/macro contrast with which they are dealing. Also researchers must be explicit about what it is they are attempting to explain.

SUMMARY

This chapter provided an introduction to issues of micro/macro interrelationships. We pointed out that micro/macro problems may be conceptualized in three separate dimensions -- spatial, causal and time. In our view, there is very considerable complementarity in many of the models and explanations of phenomena that have been used in the social sciences. To help in identifying this comple-

mentarity, we have introduced a systems framework and a pict
graphic grid. These were utilized to introduce the papers in th
book and to discuss some of the inter-relationships among them.

In the following chapter, John Bennett considers the micr
macro problem as an issue in the history of sociocultural anthr
pology. His perspective is that many anthropological concepts a
no longer adequate for addressing real world issues. Benne
places these issues within the context of a plea for anthropol
gists to become more involved in studying the central issues a
processes confronting our contemporary world.

NOTES

1. It is true, of course, that certain conceptual tools ar
theories might be used by a number of different disciplinary spe
cialists. Interdisciplinary use of genetics, "natural selection
and "evolution" come immediately to mind. Nevertheless, it i
unreasonable to expect that someone who knows about the genetics
maize will be able to also handle beans, or still less, be able t
know details of nitrogen-fixing bacteria.

2. The definition of levels in ecosystems analysis in biolog
is not any easier to determine than it is in human groups. Thi
became clear to one of us when asked for help with homework by
high school student in Honduras. As a result of a field trip, th
students were asked by their instructor to define a small, medium
and large ecosystem in the river they had just visited. The ques
tion, of course, is who is to say what constitutes the boundarie
of such systems? As Bennett (1976:85) and many others have pointe
out, how one separates one system from another is often arbitrar
and "may be resolvable only as an operational decision." We shoul
note that this applies to boundaries of both vertical and horizon
tal systems.

BIBLIOGRAPHY

Aberle, D. F., A. K. Cohen, A. K. Davis, M. J. Levy, Jr., and F. X. Sutton. 1950. "The Functional Prerequisites of a Society." Ethics 60:100-111.

Adams, Richard N. 1970. Crucifixion By Power: Essays on Guatemalan National Social Structure, 1944-1966. Austin & London: University of Texas Press.

Bennett, John W. 1969. Northern Plainsmen: Adaptive Strategy and Agrarian Life. Chicago: Aldine.

_____. 1973. "Ecosystemic Effects of Extensive Agriculture." Annual Review of Anthropology, Vol.II. Palo Alto: Annual Reviews.

_____. 1976. The Ecological Transition: Cultural Anthropology and Human Adaptation. New York & London: Pergamon Publishing Company.

Buckley, Walter. 1967. Sociology and Modern Systems Theory. Englewood Cliffs: Prentice-Hall.

Cancian, Frank. 1965. Economics and Prestige in a Maya Community. Stanford, California: Stanford University.

Cornelius, Wayne. 1971. The Political Sociology of Cityward Migration in Latin America: Toward Empirical Theory. In Francine Rabinovitz and Felicity Trueblood, eds. Latin American Urban Research. Beverly Hills, California: Sage Publications. pp. 95-147.

Daly, Martin & Margo Wilson. 1983. Sex, Evolution, and Behavior. Boston: Willard Grant Press.

DeWalt, Billie R. 1975. "Changes in the Cargo Systems of Mesoamerica." Anthropological Quarterly 48:87-105.

_____. 1979. Modernization in a Mexican Ejido: A Study in Economic Adaptation. Cambridge: Cambridge University Press.

_____. n.d. "Anthropology, Sociology and Farming Systems Research." Human Organization (in press).

Durkheim, Emile. 1938. (orig. 1895) Rules of Sociological Method. Glencoe, Illinois: Free Press.

Friedman, M. and R. Friedman. 1980. Free to Choose: A Personal Statement. New York: Avon Books.

Harcourt, G. R., ed. 1977. The Microeconomic Foundations of Macroeconomics. Boulder, Colorado: Westview Press.

20

Harris, Marvin. 1968. The Rise of Anthropological Theory. New Yor:
    Thomas Y. Crowell Company.
    _____. 1979. Cultural Materialism: The Struggle for a Scien(
    of Culture. New York: Random House.
    _____. 1981. America Now: The Anthropology of a Changin
    Culture. New York: Simon and Schuster.
Hart, Robert D. 1979. Agroecosistemas: Conceptos Basicos. Tur
    rialba, Costa Rica: CATIE.
    _____. 1981. An Ecological Systems Conceptual Framework f(
    Agricultural Research and Development. In W.W. Shaner, P.I
    Philipp and W.R. Schmehl, eds. Farming Systems Research an
    Development. Washington D.C.: U.S.A.I.D.
Kroeber, Alfred. 1952. The Nature of Culture. Chicago: Universit
    of Chicago Press.
Littlefield, Alice. 1978. "Exploitation and the Expansion of Capi
    talism: The Case of the Hammock Industry of Yucatan." America
    Ethnologist 5:495-508.
McClelland, C. A. 1965. System Theory and Human Conflict. In E. I
    McNeil ed., The Nature of Human Conflict. Englewood Cliffs
    Prentice-Hall.
Morgan, L. H. 1963. (orig. 1877) Ancient Society. E. Leacock, e(
    New York: Meridian Books, World Publishing.
Murdock, G. P. 1967. Ethnographic Atlas. Pittsburgh: Universit
    of Pittsburgh Press.
Orlove, Benjamin. 1977. Alpacas, Sheep and Men: The Wool Expor
    Economy and Regional Society in Southern Peru. New York
    Academic Press.
Ortner, Sherry. 1984. "Theory in Anthropology since the Sixties.
    Comparative Studies in Society and History 26:126-166.
Peoples, James G. 1978. "Dependence in a Micronesian Economy.
    American Ethnologist 5:535-552.
    _____. 1981. Book Review of Micromotives and Macrobehavior, b
    Thomas C. Schelling. New York & London: W. W. Norton & Co.
    1978. In Human Ecology 9(3):384-386.
Radcliffe-Brown, A. R. 1952. Structure and Function in Primitiv(
    Society. London: Oxford University Press.
Roberts, Bryan. 1976. The Provincial Urban System and the Process
    of Dependency. In Current Perspectives in Latin America
    Urban Research. Alejandro Portes and Harley L. Browning, eds
    Austin: University of Texas Press, pp. 99-131.
Rus, Jan and Robert Wasserstrom. 1980. "Civil-Religious Hierarchie
    in Central Chiapas: A Critical Perspective." American Eth-
    nologist 7(3):466-478.
Schelling, Thomas C. 1978. Micromotives and Macrobehavior. New
    York & London: W. W. Norton & Company.
Shaner, W.W., P.F. Philipp and W.R. Schmehl. 1981. Farming Systems
    Research and Development. Washington D.C.: U.S. Agency for
    International Development.
Silverman, Marilyn. 1979. "Dependency, Mediation and Class Forma-
    tion in Rural Guyana." American Ethnologist 6(3):466-490.
Stavenhagen, Rodolfo. 1969. Social Classes in Agrarian Societies.
    Garden City, NY: Doubleday.

21

Steward, Julian H. 1955. The Theory of Culture Change. Urbana:
    University of Illinois Press.
White, Leslie. 1949. The Science of Culture. New York: Grove
    Press.

2
The Micro-Macro Nexus: Typology, Process, and System

John W. Bennett

INTRODUCTION

The purpose of this paper is to consider the problem of micro/macro systems articulation as an issue in the history of anthropological ideas. This includes anthropology's increasing concern with the historical present, as well as implications for theories of anthropology and kindred disciplines. A major assumption is the necessity for anthropology to join with other social disciplines in dealing with the demanding issues of world social transition. However micro-macro articulation may be defined, it certainly refers to a set of social problems which anthropologists cannot solve alone; while they possess distinctive and important knowledge, at the same time they must depend on other fields for important contributions.

For historical purposes, I have found it useful to condense the many available topics into just three general ones: (1) "micro" and "macro" phenomena defined as different types of community, society, or culture; (2) "micro" and "macro" as referring to interactive processes of change, involving diffusion, influence, and defensive adaptation; and (3) the question of broader systemic convergence in world society: How "micro" social phenomena, and/or local communities, are being incorporated into ever-larger systems of action and control.

The generalized level of discussion in this paper precludes detailed consideration of the voluminous empirical literature pertaining to these topics in anthropology and other disciplines. This analysis will be confined to the broader theoretical issues and points of view, and even then, only those with major implications for the issues -- or at least those which are dominant in the view of the writer -- will be considered. A comprehensive review would necessarily include hundreds of references; in fact, most of the theoretical literature of anthropology and sociology bears in one way or another on the overall topic, although only a small part of this literature contains explicit reference to the micro/macro frame of reference. The descriptive literature is even more extensive and quite beyond the capabilities of a single writer. Despite this abundance, it has taken a long time for anthropologists to

23

become fully aware of the significance of the issue. Once this awareness was aroused, it became possible to establish anthropological careers on the necessary reinterpretation of the ethnological corpus, a task that has barely begun.

The high level of generalization also means that some important, but lower-level distinctions will be taken for granted. Perhaps the most obvious of these is the vagueness of the phrase, "micro/macro." This can clearly refer to at least two different things: first, the size or magnitude of the social forms and processes: "micro" in this sense means "small-scale," and "macro," "large." Secondly, the phrase may refer to "local" social forms as contrasted to "external" forms which may intervene or influence the local. Logically, this duality creates a four-fold table: one may have "small" forms with highly "local" peculiarities, but, also: "local" forms which are duplicates of the "large" and "external" forms; and so on. There is no need to elaborate the obvious. A "microcosm," which is the root form of "micro," in reality refers to a small-scale phenomenon which contains all the characteristics of the macrocosm. However, this is by no means the only empirical outcome. We shall find that one or the other pair will be found to have greater or lesser importance for one or the other of the three topics.

My choice of the word "nexus" in the title refers to an emphasis on process. I consider that the main task is to determine how the micro (or local) forms interact with the macro (or external) forms: how people solve their problems in a milieu of relationships and adaptive coping. I further consider that this problem of nexus is becoming a major theme of sociocultural anthropological research; along with history, to be dealt with later, it is the mainline anthropology of the future. And once attention turns to such issues, the ethical and ideological relevance of our work emerges in concrete and unavoidable form.

Thus, however it may be phrased, the "micro/macro" issue is a paramount one for sociocultural anthropology since it is an eternal issue in human history; and along with environmental problems, it is the most salient opportunity for anthropology to make a real contribution to public policies and affairs. In this issue anthropology faces its antecedents and its future, its scholarly fulfillment and its moral obligation to humanity. These are large words and phrases, but the writer believes them with conviction.

HISTORICAL BACKGROUND

Although "applied anthropology" had its inception in the "native races" protection issue in England in the 1840s and 1950s (Reining 1962); and in the Amerind problem of the 1880s and the formation of the Bureau of American Ethnology as a shield against mistreatment of the tribes, the full implications of the historical progression toward incorporation of indigenes in larger social systems did not become manifest until the 1950s (Hinsley 1979). The liquidation of the colonial empires subsequent to World War II meant that the national state became the dominant political frame of tribal societies. For the first time, anthropologists were required to take the nation as a system into full account; its demands on tribal populations and communities were unanswerable; political freedom meant a new conformity to law and regulation; the District Commissioner was replaced by the national bureaucracy.

Before this happened the "micro/macro" issue for anthropology was largely one of defending tribal communities against unwarranted interventions of colonial power. This meant, for example, the need to explicate the rationality and morality of tribal modes of punishment of wrongdoers in the face of insistence by administrators on adherence to Euro-American legal and moral constructs. On the other hand, no such issue was perceived by anthropologists working in European and North American rural society; the local-external relationship there was visualized as "normal": rural communities were seen as components of the total society, conducting their affairs in full awareness of their role and position in the nation. Nation was an accomplished fact; not a social problem. Change was part of "progress"; it was normalized, accepted by the rural population.

Anthropologists eventually assimilated modern rural society into the rubric of "complex society," and this was contrasted to tribal and peasant-folk communities, conceived as homogeneous, non-institutional entities. Thus the anthropological image of the world down to about 1960 was one-sided: the possibility of the existence of a general or "cross-cultural" process of micro vs. macro, local vs. external, was not seriously entertained. Awareness of such a process would emerge only when tribal or peasant communities were subjected to intervention by bureaucracies or governments whose centers of power were located at a distance from the communities' territories.

After World War II the inauguration of new national states in former colonies required a new view of the social process: the national state came to be seen as a pervasive institution, which generated problems of local-external interaction in communities everywhere, not only in the so-called "underdeveloped countries." Thus, Vidich and Bensman, in their 1958 book on a small town and its rural hinterland in New York State, made a strong case for the way the larger national society impinged on the culture and economic welfare of the community to its detriment. The present writer's mid-career paper (Bennett 1967) on macro/micro relationships in a post-frontier agrarian region in Canada was in one sense an answer to Vidich and Bensman's conclusions. In that paper I sought to show that for better or for worse, the residents of the rural region had forged their own institutions in the local-external interactive process, and found it possible to obtain the rewards and resources they needed -- as well as having to constrain certain endeavors as a result of external intervention. That is, I was trying to suggest that the process cut both ways.

Since the 1960s, anthropologists have proceeded to conceptualize the macro/micro process as general and pervasive, applicable to all societies and all national state systems. Most of the work has of course taken place in the developing countries; rural studies in Western countries are really only getting under way. Some of the specific cases, however are currently receiving close attention; an example is the "family farm" issue in North America (e.g., Williams 1981; and Bennett 1982). Much of this anthropological work on rural communities is informed by the idea that social life and production in smaller units is more effective and rewarding than life in communities with industrialized agriculture (Walter Gold- schmidt's 1947 book, As You Sow, was the pioneer statement -- twenty-five years ahead of its time). The same issue is important for new programs in Third World rural development: both the World Bank and the U.S. Agency for International Development have shown interest in traditional modes of production and community organiza- tion as a substitute for the scientized and technologized modes of production promoted by earlier development programs.

Returning to the issue of the national state as the key social frame in the modern world, the basic question was whether the state was the best means of organizing indigenous government and produc- tion in former tribal-peasant populations under colonial control. Obviously regional federations and production systems would have been more efficient, and perhaps less abusive of traditional ways. However, the adoption of the national state model was politically and perhaps economically inevitable, given the fact that most of the leaders of the new nations had been educated in Europe or North America and trained in the doctrine and practice of state politics and autonomy. The structure of the international market economy also required independent national governing bodies as the respon- sible organs for control of funds and execution of development projects. However, the shift to national states meant that the world came to be populated by dozens of new nations differing greatly in resource potential and in their capacity to make their own decisions, introducing new dimensions of inequality and politi- cal instability. It was this choice of the independent state as the model for the post-colonial world that was and is mainly re- sponsible for the difficulties and tensions of development -- granted that residues of "imperialism" and exploitation play their role as well (for studies by anthropologists, see Richard Adams 1970; Beck 1985).

However, to identify the contemporary micro/macro issue as generated exclusively by the transition from colony to new nation is historically short-sighted. As Lloyd Fallers observed in his 1974 essay on the nation-state, a discussion of the East African situation:

> This does not mean that the microcosmic, everyday lives of contemporary East Africans are for the most part still condi- tioned by precolonial ethnic cultures and social solidarities alone, nor is their more self-conscious political behavior. That ethnic gemeinschaften remain needs no emphasis, but the new states are not simply arenas for raw ethnic competition and conflict, as news reports might sometimes lead one to believe. For one thing, the precolonial societies of the region were never as discrete as would be suggested by the lines anthropo- logists are accustomed to draw on "tribal" maps. There were "international" political systems in East Africa before the

coming of Arabs and Europeans and there was much cultural
interchange. The image of Africa as a stagnant region is now
recognized for what it is: a product of Western ignorance and
prejudice. The "dark continent" has in fact been the scene of
vast population movements, of the rise and fall of countless
empires (p. 35).

Fallers goes on to sketch the complex reality of East African
politics and culture: the interaction within regional social systems; the multi-lingual accommodations; the cross-cutting loyalties
and allegiances; the constant interplay of local communities and
larger political systems. These phenomena were neglected by anthropologists for years, as Fallers implies in the quotation.
Whether this was due to sociological and political ignorance -- as
he also seems to imply -- or to the exclusive focus on tribal entities induced by ethnological theory; or by conformity to colonial
concepts and restrictions, is not a question we can answer glibly.
The problem needs historical research, and anthropologists have not
shown much interest in documenting their past failings. In my own
case, I can recall from my graduate school days that the complex
local-external relationships were acknowledged by professors, but
were considered to be the subject matter of "history" or "sociology," not anthropology. Anthropology concerned culture -- i.e.,
ethnicity -- the purer the better, although Robert Redfield seemed
to disagree: for him, the basic anthropological unit of analysis
was not "a culture." Instead it was "the little community" (1955),
a physical and institutional frame for human existence, not the
thoughts and habits of people. The significance of the distinction
was lost to Redfield's American contemporaries, and probably was
not fully appreciated by Redfield himself.

THE PROBLEMS

Thus, as tribal and peasant communities began publicly and
officially merging into national populations, anthropologists came
to discover what historians and sociologists had known for a long
time: that the social forms of the small community or any localized
demographic unit are not created in situ, but evolve in complex
relationship with the institutions of larger societies. This is a
theme that emerged first in the "peasant studies" of the 1950s
(Redfield 1956; Wolf 1957). As this awareness developed, anthropologists began changing their fundamental image of humanity: instead
of an exclusive preoccupation with a patchwork of single communal
entities, they began to perceive a world of interactive communication with localities and social units of indefinite boundedness.
The issue took a tripartite form. The first problem was an
old one: purely descriptive differences between small, relatively
isolated network-type communities on the one hand, and large,
multi-institutional, multi-group societies on the other. This
typological problem had its roots in an old tradition of European
folk sociology which had always enjoyed some influence in anthropology -- the descriptive dichotomy of the Gemeinschaft and Gesell-

28

schaft. The second problem concerned the nature of the relation
ships of local groups and communities to the external institutiona
and organizational apparatus of government, economic markets, an
political movements (this is where peasantry became crucial). Thi
problem concerned social dynamics and process, not typology. Th
third problem concerned the essential nature of large supra-sys
tems; that is, the way the local and the external combined to mak
up single large interactive entities; e.g., the nation.

When these distinctions are made, the relationships betwee
the various social disciplines become clearer. Sociology is th
study of the supra-systems as wholes; rural sociology (and som
types of agricultural economics) focus on the study of the loca
systems in contact and interaction with external entities and th
nation; general or macroeconomics resembles sociology insofar as i
posits the existence of large economic systems, as wholes, tha
pervade everything else; political science has branches in bot
camps: studies of local politics and national political system
and movements. Cultural anthropology (ethnology) was preoccupie
with the descriptive typological differences between small (local
and large (cosmopolitan) societies. All of these fields are of
course patchworks of specialized inquiries that contain differin
empirical emphases on small and large systems. Their theories
however, remain based in the dominant interests as noted above.
That is, sociological theory is "macro" on the whole; its difficulties often stem from the misapplication of societal-level theory to
local social groupings. Cultural anthropology, although now busy
with research on larger systems, nevertheless operates with theory
from the ethnological past -- theories derived from the study of
small, network, low-energy societies with a high degree of geographical and vicinal isolation. Anthropologists are beginning to
generate significant empirical generalizations -- if not theory --
appropriate to larger entities, but there are few or no anthropological studies of large systems as wholes, although a handful of
classic works come close; (e.g., studies of large African tribal
nations like Herskovits' Dahomey [1938]; Leach's book on Burmese
tribal politics [1954]; or Fallers' penultimate little book on the
Anthropology of the Nation-State [1974]).1 These productions,
however, did not spawn an anthropology of large politico-economic
systems. What general theory pertaining to such systems exists in
anthropology -- e.g., social stratification -- is on the whole derived from the other disciplines. Anthropologists moreover have
shown resistance to the acceptance of concepts and models from
other fields, lest they be accused of simply "doing sociology" (or
political science).

The question, of course, in everyone's mind is whether there
can be any such thing as a distinctively anthropological theory of
large systems. That is, are the existing theories derived from
sociology, economics, and political science the only possible
theories. There simply has not been sufficient work by anthropologists to justify a detailed appraisal of theoretical trends. Even
"urban anthropology," which is an attempt to look at large social
systems, has shown little more than a willingness to discover the
validity of urban subcultures and social groupings with distinctive

life styles. This is useful work insofar as it shows that sociologists have missed a lot, but then some of the classic studies of this kind, like Whyte's Street Corner Society (1943), were produced by sociologists.

The point is that the paradigms employed by anthropologists from the late nineteenth through most of the twentieth century were derived from the study of relatively small, isolated social groups. The concept of culture was almost entirely derived from a contemplation of shared mental products and customs in such societies, and the prestige of the paradigm was derived from extraordinarily persuasive ethnographies like Malinowski's on the Trobriands, or Margaret Mead's Pacific Island studies. The facts and speculations introduced in these productions captivated the intellect of anthropologists as well as other social scientists for two generations, and helped create additional paradigmatic creations like "functionalism," "British structuralism," or "culture and personality." Thus movement toward a wider compendium of social facts from a larger sample of human societies was delayed.

This meant that while anthropology started its empirical investigations lower in the levels of social experience than sociology, its theoretical corpus also terminated at a much lower point in the hierarchy of social magnitudes. Sociology, often showing willingness to engage in participant observation at microlevels (following anthropology's lead, in other words), has always been interested in the theoretical relevance of such studies for higher levels of societal generalization. Anthropology, however, simply lacks a block of indigenous theory dealing with the most general or pan-human theory of macrosocial functioning. It must borrow such theoretical propositions or concerns from sociology, economics, political science, social psychology and related sub-fields.

In the long run it does not matter who or what discipline produces anything - it is a question of truth and competence. The issue is crucial however, for anthropologists because for years they were unique: only they studied tribal peoples. Now that there are almost no more "tribes" -- at least in the special sense of the isolated, low-energy, interactive-network society -- anthropologists simply join the pack of social scientists of various stripes who study the modern world and its integrative social systems of large scale. What does anthropology bring to this joint and often confused effort? We shall return to this question at the end of the paper.

MICRO/MACRO AS DESCRIPTIVE TYPOLOGY: FOLK AND URBAN

Let us return to the first problem: the attempt to describe the differences between the small, interactive-network communities and the large, pluralistic societies. As already noted, this effort was influenced by the dichotomous typology that developed in German social scholarship influenced by the romantic tradition. Ferdinand Tonnies' Gemeinschaft was the type of the folk community and its presumably socially-emotionally satisfying total environment; Gesellschaft was the open, accessible, impersonal system of

large communities (Loomis-Tonnies 1940). Sir Henry Maine's sequence from status to contract was another version (1896); Durkheim's mechanical-organic still another (Simpson 1933); and a general synthesis was attempted by Howard Becker, who used sacred and
secular to denote the grand types (1950). Robert Redfield's folk-
urban dichotomy (1947) was the only full-scale anthropological
version of the tradition. It was closely related to the German
sources, via the sociologist Robert Park. All of these dichotomies
produced valuable descriptive distinctions, but were of little use
in analyzing empirical social situations. The typologies were
devoid of a concept of system or process: societies were viewed as
collections of traits and tendencies, not a matter of the continuous adaptive struggles that characterize all human communities,
large and small. Thus, social process and locus were not important
in this tradition. It was the form of the community that was the
matter of concern.

At a more empirical level, anthropologists always distinguished between bands and villages, towns and cities; this was seen
as part of the historical transition from nomadic food-collecting
to settled agricultural societies, with the concomitant increase in
population. V. Gordon Childe's various "revolutions" (food-produc-
ing; urban; industrial) represented one of the most popular versions (1942). Empirically based, these temporal typological constructs also had a background in European scholarship, and of
course in the nineteenth century Danish and continental archeological tradition. One of the most useful systematizations of the
village-cosmopolitan transition was contributed by Alfred Weber
(Eckert 1970), whose distinction between culture and civilization
was sometimes used by Redfield in his class lectures to clarify
what he meant by culture. In this conception, culture is a quality
which can vary quantitatively; i.e., some societies have more
culture than others; thus culture is a Gemeinschaftliche intimacy
and interactiveness. Civilization, on the other hand, is represented by literacy, institutions, and contractual relations. Redfield's version was ultimately expressed in his and Milton Singer's
"little tradition" and "big tradition" concepts (Singer 1958):
this preserved the Weberian notion of culture, but it anthropo-
logized civilization by acknowledging that these entities, and
especially the ancient Oriental versions, also had culture (e.g.,
universalistic religions like Hinduism). Perhaps the key underlying concept here is consensus. Societies with culture have a
high quotient of agreement as to what constitutes the traditions
and lifeways -- granting the existence of variant patterns. The
agreement is manifested by universal religious beliefs; formal
institutions, patriotism, etc.. Their fabric, however, is characterized by a variety of often incompatible subcultures based on
social stratification and other structural differentiations. Power
factors tended to be neglected in such conceptualizing.

Running through most of these typologies and distinctions was
an unstated preference for the folk way of life, as a more humane,
satisfying, committed frame for human existence. Alienation and
despair were inevitable in the urban and industrial macrosocial
systems; the problems of deviance, conformity, and inequality be-

come acute, and contribute to endemic social and political tension. These ideas were congenial to anthropologists who were eager to uphold the folk way of life since it was their trade specialization. However, around the World War II period a tougher breed of ethnologists began pointing out that tribal and peasant folk societies were rife with hostility, gossip, and the ruthless suppression of individual tendencies in their socialization rituals. The controversy over Pueblo culture, started by Benedict's apotheosis of the Apollonian style in her Patterns of Culture (1934), marks the beginning of this awareness in the 1940s.

Thus, an intellectual paradox began appearing: while the typologies had broad historical and descriptive validity, the closer one got to the real life of the folk societies, the less "folk" they seemed to be. Or put analytically, the typologies were useless as a way of handling the vicissitudes of human behavior in concrete social settings. If betrayal, hostility, deviance, alienation, impersonality, and the like were typological qualities of the Gesellschaft, then what were they doing in folk societies (e.g., Bennett 1946)?

Further ambiguity in the typologies concerned the factors of population and territorial size. Were the "micro" types concerned with small populations and territories and the "macro" with large? And if macro concepts meant institutions and organizations without definite geographical or territorial boundaries, then was the distinction really a matter of the local community vs. the diffuse external system? Implicit in the Redfield-Singer distinction between big and little traditions was the notion that the local communities replicated the big traditions, making them true microcosms of the civilizational society or macrocosm. What all this meant was that at the very least, it was necessary to distinguish between culture and society in the typologies (Miner 1955). The typological folk society may differ profoundly from the social system of the urban, but the folk might well assimilate the cultural lifeways of the urban, while preserving or generating its own unique, naive cultural patterns.

In anthropology the dominant issue was the status of the tribe as a basic unit of demographic, economic, political, and cultural analysis. Doubts about the validity of the tribal unit began surfacing in the 1940s, and flowered in the 1950s, as exemplified by Edmund Leach's examination of Burmese hill tribes as political fictions (1954). The issue did not however, become a source of theoretical reformulation until Fredrik Barth's book on ethnic boundaries and cultures appeared at the end of the 1960s (Barth 1969). To simplify: the issue centered on the increasing inability of ethnologists to find typological correlations between the various dimensions of ethnic phenomena. For generations the folk world was believed to be divided into distinct tribal entities with their own languages, cultures, politics and so on. This paradigm was probably supported mainly by the work of the Americans who found this kind of multidimensional correlation reasonably accurate in many regions of the New World. But in other parts of the world, especially Africa, tribes had been an ambiguous phenomenon due to military conquest and the existence of quasi-feudal political sys-

tems. The collapse of the colonial empires in the 1940s reveal
these tendencies in sharp outline. It became obvious that ma
"tribes" began to cultivate their tribal identity as a rationa
for asserting their control over weaker and less aggressive neig
bors. A tribe, in other words, had to be viewed in new terms, le
as a linguistic or cultural type or entity and more as a sel
conscious political faction in a nation.

As this new status emerged, tribes also entered the historica
present, usually as "peasants" (who had been there all alon
neglected by anthropologists). It is likely that the persistenc
of typological approaches in anthropology was in large part due t
the fact that anthropologists studied peoples without histories
written or articulate histories, that is (see Wolf 1982). Lackin
a sense of historical unfolding of institutions and customs, on
can only formulate types -- types of cultures, kinship systems
artifact styles, etiquette, and brands of magic and ritual. Peas
ants lack history; hence a concern for the type, "peasant" a
contrasted to "farmer;" American Indians lacked history, hence
concern for the "tribe" as a type, or the tribal cultures a
unique. The case of the Amerinds is especially significant. An
thropologists were aware for years that these people were in fac
accumulating a history, as the reservations evolved and the rela
tionships with state and federal governments, as well as citize
reform organizations, unfolded. But this history was written o
the whole by non-anthropologists. (Noteworthy exceptions ar
Joseph Jorgenson's 1978 monograph on Amerinds as part of the poli
tical and economic institutional structure of American society; an
more recently, Brian Fagan's history of Old World-New World inter
action). In any case, tribes are becoming historical all over th
world and anthropologists are beginning to pick up the challenge o
historical study.

Along with nationalization came urbanization. This proces
also presented a severe challenge to anthropologists because the
had no theory of urbanization other than the archeological (e.g.
R. Mc. Adams 1966). Even more disturbing was the fact that th
cities of the Third World began filling up with "folk" people
i.e., detribalized persons and peasants (Roberts 1978). Once agai
the social phenomena began outstripping the typologies. Peasant
had their problems in cities, but they also on occasion showe
remarkable adaptability, forging far-flung networks of mutual sup
port between village and city, and establishing poverty as a way o
life (Whitten 1969). Peasant status, for a decade the subject o
typological debate (e.g., Redfield 1956) has shifted away fro
typology and into studies of adaptive process (e.g., Halperin & Do
1977).

No formal solution to the problems of typology was available
until Talcott Parsons published The Social System (1951). Parsons
shifted the focus of classification from types of whole societies,
cultures, or communities to social interaction processes, using the
structure-function dichotomy as the key to the analysis of process.
The structural component referred to frameworks of social relationships that persisted because they performed important functions in
everyday life, and in the congeries of tasks and goals called

institutions in the older sociology. The dominant emphasis in the scheme was analytical description, and application of the concepts to empirical cases brought forth rather static portrayals of equilibrium-seeking social systems. The incapacity of the scheme to deal with change formed the basis of the extensive critiques of Parsons appearing in the 1950s and 1960s.

The most enduring aspect of the scheme, however, was the "pattern variables." These conceptual pairs, designating characteristics of social action in any and all societies, have proven continuously useful as tools of descriptive analysis. And it is these variables which came to serve as a replacement for the folk-urban categories. The original versions appear in The Social System (1951:67): (italics ours)

I. The Gratification-Discipline Dilemma
    Affectivity vs. Affective Neutrality
II. The Private vs. Collective Interest Dilemma
    Self-Orientation vs. Collectivity-Orientation
III. The Choice Between Types of Value-Orientation Standard
    Universalism vs Particularism
IV. The Choice Between "Modalities" of the Social Object
    Achievement vs. Ascription
V. The Definition of Scope Interest in the Object
    Specificity vs. Diffuseness

Parsons saw these five pattern variables as more than mere tags for some dominant "dilemmas," "choices," or "definitions" of social action. He recognized that they could become cultural descriptions insofar as there existed an "element of consistency of pattern which must run throughout a system of value-orientations in a cultural tradition" (ibid). And it was this potential for cultural description and analysis that attracted Clyde Kluckhohn to the scheme (Kluckhohn 1951). In later pages (pp. 102-05) Parsons showed how the pattern variables combine and cross-cut each other to form major vectors of social behavior and values (see Table 2.1). Universalism-Particularism are combined with Achievement-Ascription to create a four-fold table defining "major value-orientations" for a specimen social system or culture. The illustration is useful because the two pattern variable sets represent ideas important in both sociology and anthropology for a long time. Achievement and ascription appear for the first time in that terminology in Ralph Linton's Study of Man (1936); the universalism-particularism set owes much to the status vs. contract dichotomy that goes back to Sir Henry Maine and others in the nineteenth century. Some of Redfield's folk-urban criteria parallel many of the pattern variables. Max Weber dealt with most of the variables in his many works on historical sociology, and one of his conceptual pairs -- traditional vs. rational-legal -- constitutes a sixth pattern variable set if one wishes to add it to Parsons' list (see Bendix 1960, Chapter 12).

Anthropologists familiar with the Redfieldian version of Gemeinschaft-Gesellschaft typology could, if they wished, identify the universalistic and achievement variables with the "urban" pole;

TABLE 2.1
Types of Combination of Value-Orientation Components to Crea
Major Social Value-Orientations

	UNIVERSALISM	PARTICULARISM
ACHIEVEMENT	**A.** Universalistic Achievement Pattern	**B.** Particularistic Achievement Pattern
	Expectation of active achievements in accord with universalized standards and generalized rules relative to other actors.	Expectation of active achievements relative to and/or on behalf of the particular relational context in which the actor is involved.
ASCRIPTION	**C.** Universalistic Ascription Pattern	**D.** Particularistic Ascription Pattern
	Expectation of orientation of action to a universalistic norm defined either as an ideal state or as embodied in the status-structure of the existing society.	Expectation of orientation of action to an ascribed status within a given relational context.

Based on Parsons (1951:102).

and the particularistic-ascription with the "folk." Such prematur
identifications gave way immediately to the recognition that al
societies, however small or large, however isolated or accessible
have all four pattern variables, with variable tendencies or em
phases in one direction or another. In addition, the institution
associated with large, pluralistic societies will have characteris
tic forms of universalism (for example), which would not be presen
in smaller, more uniform social systems. Thus, universalism be
comes a <u>necessary</u> vector of social action when the population i
large, with diverse subcultures and social status, and with lega
requirements for conformity and obedience. Unless people ar
treated alike -- given similar opportunities, etc. -- inequalit
can lead to anomie and social collapse. Obviously the politica
orientation is an important mediating variable; democratic insti
tutions or ideology create a stronger mandate for universalisti
prescriptions. Still, beyond and beneath the level of publi
institutions, particularism flourishes in the complex societies

wherever local social systems with relatively small populations must allocate resources in accordance with traditional status and social rewards (e.g., Bennett 1982, matrix table, p.209).

The Parsonian pattern variables are now part of the history of social science. Their utility for descriptive analysis has been demonstrated and they have entered into the frame of reference of most sociocultural anthropologists as well as those of the other social-behavior sciences. Only economics, which possesses its own scheme of action pattern analysis based on the theory of utility-maximization and rational choice, has not incorporated them. We need not pursue the exposition of pattern variables further but the point should be clear. The variables offered a way around the contradictions inherent in the cultural or community-based typology. Instead of whole sociocultural system types, certain tendencies and vectors could be associated with social groupings with differing traditions, population sizes, political orientations, and so on.

In general, as societies become configured in large multi-institutional and centralized political systems, their members must learn to deal with bureaucracies and their universalistic regulations. Affectively-neutral attitudes may characterize the association of strangers. Interplay develops between self-oriented desires and collective needs for order. There appears a greater need to achieve one's position in life rather than to rely on birth status. And highly specific definitions of the situation, especially in occupations requiring efficient performance in impersonal organizations, become typical. These tendencies are those associated with "modernization," which in the last analysis is mainly the spread of the social patterns of the Euro-North American urban-industrial social systems across the world. It can be assumed they were present as well in ancient urban civilizations. Thus, abstract typologies are only a first approximation of difference and similarity; they must eventually give way to historical concreteness, and emphasis on the significance of geographical location and channels of influence and dominance.

MICRO/MACRO AS PROCESS OF INFLUENCE AND CHANGE: LOCAL AND EXTERNAL

Thus the major contemporary issues concern process and change. These are both romantic and nostalgic issues, as well as analytical ones. They concern human rights, the rewards to be found in cultural diversity vs. global cultural uniformity in the urban-industrial order, and of the loss of community freedom in the process of political centralization. How can local peoples preserve the freedom to make their own decisions, and at the same time how can social communities provide reasonable freedom for their own members, in a world of increasing pressures to produce at ever-rising levels of efficiency and output?

The first necessity in pursuing the problem of influence and change is to specify the particular geographical, historical, and social locus of the social community. That is, one cannot solve the change problem by typologizing and generalizing. The relation-

ships between micro and macro, and local and external, in Nort
America will be different than those in India -- even though his
torically, India may be moving in a highly generalized European
North American "macro" direction as her national government con
solidates its control over localities.   Concreteness is thus th
order of the day.   An ethnology of the change process must locat
its units of observation and analysis in real times, places, an
institutions.   Attention is paid both to the structural frames o
social life as well as to the mental or cultural traditions an
styles, because these can vary independently.

The second requirement of an inquiry into micro/macro
local/external change relationships is to specify the nature o
geographical and social space.   For example, in a typical Nort
American rural context, the local community may be seen to exis
within the following "spheres":

(1)   The Migration Sphere, or the geographical spread o
persons who formerly lived in the community.   This may take th
form of dispersed kinship networks, friendship, vacations, sub
scriptions to media, travel to ceremonials and so on.   Indices o
cosmopolitanism may be constructed from these descriptive data i
one wishes, but these always need to be compared to actual atti
tudes and life styles.

(2)   The Resource Allocation Sphere, or the loci of the powe
to assign rights to key resources to community members.   The bu
reaus that control government land, the organizations that contro
credit, the bureaus that assign water rights, taxation powers, an
so on.   The larger the community, the greater the tendency to hav
responsible agencies with respect to resources located in th
community; the more remote the community, the farther away thes
may be.

(3)   The Marketing Sphere.   If the community is agrarian, it
products may be distributed world wide.   The income of the commu
nity is derived from the entire geographical area in which it
products are distributed.   This can include local garden products
manufactured items serving the locality or nation, or cash crop
sent overseas.   Either local or external agencies may perform th
distribution functions.

(4)   The Local Shopping Sphere.   Commodities for productio
and consumer goods may be acquired locally, or at a distance
depending on transportation facilities and cost.   The automobil
has, of course, widened this sphere greatly, but changing costs o
operation and the condition of the local and national economy wil
tend to make the sphere contract and expand.

(5)   The Kinship Sphere.   Aside from migration of communit
members, people will move within the region for marriage, visitin
relatives, helping with chores and so on.

These five spheres are by no means the only ways to map th
geographical and social space, but they are among the most impor
tant ones for a North American agricultural community, with it
facilities for physical mobility, and intricate town-country asso
ciations.   Each sphere will produce a map of movement, socia
connections, and need-satisfaction.   The boundaries of the commu
nity will thus be flexible, depending on the particular functio

observed and the time of the observation. The mapping of spheres
is not merely a matter of analyzing the external relationships, but
will also serve to demarcate the internal territorial and time-
distance relationships; e.g., resource allocation may be a matter
of ties to the capitals of the state-provincial or federal governments, while marital ties may serve to designate mainly internal
spatial networks. The methods followed in this type of analysis
are, of course, the familiar ones developed by cultural and economic geographers, although anthropologists are likely to introduce
special techniques reflecting their disciplinary interests. For
example, mapping of kinship connections within the region may be
done so as to show any tendencies toward preferential mating or
biases in the line of descent (see Smith 1976 for an anthropological introduction to locational analysis; and Whitten & Wolf 1973
for a discussion of network analysis).

The selection of the "spheres" concept to delineate key
micro/macro issues of the North American rural community is influenced by the distinctive settlement pattern of this part of the
world -- the so-called "open-country neighborhood" system in which
agricultural producers live apart, on their own acres. Their
services are provided by specialized village and town centers,
whose populations are, in the main, composed of tradesmen and
specialists (and recently, substantial numbers of retired country-
men). If we turn to the European scene, the focus of analysis is
likely to differ. Ronald Frankenberg's studies of British rural
communities of varying sizes may provide an example (1966). Here
the village or town is the unit of settlement; farmers live in the
settlements and move out to their fields, or the individual farm-
steads are clustered into somewhat spread-out communities. In this
situation, the interest shifts from geographical spheres of interaction to social role relationships. Frankenberg carried out part
of his analysis in typological terms, but with an awareness of
process. In fact, his approach is a synthesis of the Redfieldian
folk-urban model with a sociological conception of role relationships.

His presentation is based on the proposition that in rural
society, the number of roles, when compared with urban society,
tends to be small. But the patterning of these roles is complex:
"Rural social life is built up out of a relatively small number of
role relationships -- which are arranged with great fluidity into
varied patterns. Urban life makes up for the loss of these by a
large number of role relationships and their formalization" (Frankenberg 1966, p. 283). Similarly, the "social fields" in rural
society tend to be composed of a small number of persons, while in
urban society the "number of people met by an individual...may be
large" (op.cit.; chart, p. 287). While these generalizations do
not escape completely from the ambiguity of polar typologizing,
they are focussed on dynamic social interaction rather than static
formal or cultural (mentalistic) phenomena and hence have greater
utility in analyzing influence and change.

But village or community or kin group are by no means the only
frames for human existence. There are also the large nation-tribe,
as found in southwest Asia and parts of Africa; or the regional

cooperative resource networks, uniting many villages in water
schemes, as in southeast Asia; or the sectarian agricultural com
munes in North America and Europe. These and other settlemen
types and institutional forms will have their own distinctiv
relationships with the nation-state government and its demands fc
support, order, and taxes. Nowhere is the relationship an eas
one, and it cannot be expected to improve in Third World setting
where tribes or communities remain more persuasive frames of iden
tity than shifting, and often untrustworthy national governments
The transition from medieval to modern Europe involved the conques
of the feudal nobility by the state; the conquest of much of Afric
and Asia involves the conquest of tribal and village solidarity an
autonomy by the militarized post-colonial state. Farmer revolt
will simmer in the background.

Viewing human aggregates in the context of centralized stat
government, then, requires a very different approach from th
classical ethnological study of the single demographic and/or set
tlement unit, bounded by the tribal hunting grounds, or the villag
and its fields. Some recognition of the flexibility of boundarie
was always available, because even the most isolated societies ha
a nested set of territories for different functions -- some of the
shared with other demographic, community, or social units. Th
research focus, however, was usually on the physical fact of
breeding population inhabiting a particular settlement space. Thi
focus tended to exclude the wider ties and functions. The band o
village was the main unit of analysis, its "culture" the prim
target of research.

For example, Julian Steward (1956) did not succeed in render
ing the complexity of modern Puerto Rican society in his study of
series of separate village communities, each with a differen
economic pursuit. The fact that the separate communities wer
really parts of a larger whole -- the differentiated but function
ally interdependent political economy of the island-nation -- es
caped the Steward research program and vitiated many of its conclu
sions. There was no theory of larger systems. More generally
Steward's approach to cultural ecology lacked a clear conception o
system, hence no way of determining the roles of particular part
of that system. His approach was traditional: to find the cause
of particular social forms, not to portray the dynamic adaptiv
reality of a social system.

The dynamism of these interactive systems also means that th
anthropologist must find a basis for generalization other than th
goal of presenting a static, one-time portrait of an operatin
culture. This traditional objective was suited to isolated commu
nities that changed slowly. In the modern world of national gov
ernments and market systems, the chief components are in constan
motion. Or rather, the amount or the rhythms of change must b
considered as variables. Hence one cannot produce a forever
portrait of a modern community. It is a study of one community a
a one particular time. Time must be consciously sampled, so t
speak. There needs to be a reason for studying the society at thi
particular point in time, and this temporal "reason" defines th
problems to be solved.

The second main requirement in studying the micro/macro relational nexus is to ascertain the major quantitative and qualitative dimensions of exchange. That is, what is the net outflow and inflow of goods, services, people, energy, products? Who has the power to change and direct these flows? I am not necessarily speaking here of some abstruse quantitative energy-calculus -- the data can be collected with any degree of detail the researcher selects, depending on the demands exercised by his problem. To deal with exchanges it is usually necessary to be concerned with models of behavior that derive from disciplines other than anthropology, in particular, economics, and some branches of social psychology. These models make certain assumptions for the purposes of analysis that have been a source of disagreement among anthropologists, since they tend to assume an element of rational choice and preference: people are motivated, at least in part, by the need to increase gain or profit, whether this is expressed in monetary or in qualitative terms, like status. To achieve such ends, people must make trade-offs between quantities of desired goods. If one wishes a lot of love, one may have to take less of material achievement. In a folk world, goods, commodities, and relationships might have been finite, and the means for providing them limited (Foster 1965), but in the expanding world of the nation, there are no such constants. The promises of the state to its citizens, however, tend to be larger than the market will bear; thus "poverty" emerges, and people who existed adequately with few possessions or power now desire more of both. The external exchanges thus generate new internal exchanges, and the relationships among community members are irrevocably changed because basic needs, values, and ideologies will be affected.

These processes all generate values, and the researchers themselves are not immune. In recent years, as anthropologists have participated in research on aspiration, poverty, development, and the power interplays of communities and external organizations, they have inevitably assimilated value orientations from political commentary. During the early 1970s, for example, the writings of Andre Gunder Frank (1969) were particularly influential. In such interpretations, the relationship between micro and macro is defined as one of exploitation, or as a prolongation of imperialist domination into the post-colonial world of new nations. While these views contain much truth, the anthropologist must take pains to avoid overcommitment to single ideological vectors. Residual as it may often appear in an age of revolution and transformation, the attitude of analytical neutrality continues to have its virtues. Nevertheless, the possibilities of combining or alternating committed frames of reference with dispassionate ones are considerable; the individual worker must make his own synthesis.

A third requirement, then, for the anthropological study of the interplay and change arising from micro-macro relationships concerns the need for an adaptational frame of reference. This refers to the ways the local populations have found to manipulate the external forces and agencies -- and, of course, vice versa. Although the external bureaucratic systems usually have more power to enforce their demands (whether in the benevolent interests of the communities, or against them), the local people are never devoid of capacity to modify the demands or blunt the forces of compulsion. A case of significant proportions has occurred repeatedly in African and Latin American countries in recent years as the new national governments have sought to keep food prices low so that the urban masses can buy it, and thus avoid food riots. The farmers, however, have ignored government pleas and modest incentives to increase production for markets because they consider that prices are too low. Instead, the farmers reduce crop and livestock offtake, focussing their efforts on production for their own use, and for local and regional markets. What can the governments do - shoot the farmers, tax them, construct government farms and ranches? All methods have been tried, but none work very well, or for long, and the situation is an example of the importance of economic markets in development (even in "peasant" agriculture) and simultaneously, of the considerable power residing in the hands of the unarmed (or armed!) campesinos who alone have the capacity to produce food (Wolf 1969).

Similarly, the vulnerability of the industrial nations to energy sources, like oil, has also revealed the existence of impressive sources of power in the raw-materials-producing nations even granted the fact that the industrial nations may continue to operate as "imperialist" extractors of natural substances for the benefit of their own populations and profiteers. Clearly, the world is moving toward a complex system of interdependency which will make simplistic ideological perspectives useless for analytical purposes. Anthropologists must be sensitive to these growing complexities of the adaptive world system. A special sub-science of defensive strategy analysis is beginning to emerge in development anthropology as a result.

Of equal, and perhaps even greater importance, is the growing disparity in wealth and power among the social groupings and classes in the developing countries. It is now clear that economic development -- which in almost all cases has meant an accommodation of the new national economies to the world market system -- increases disparities in income. This is linked to a sharpening of individual differences in talent and capital (social and financial), and increasing social differentiation based on the ability to seize opportunity. Mexican ejidos have tended to fall under the control of the most energetic and capable members; coffee-producing farmers in East Africa have tended to exclude their land-poor neighbors and even relatives from membership in the profitable cooperatives; rural families with members living and working in cities can set up networks of influence and exchange which give them an advantage over families without such connections; migratory pastoralists who make the transition to a form of ranching, and buy trucks, make deals with peasant farmers for forage, and so push their smaller-herd-owning relatives and tribal members off the range. The examples are legion. The failure of development to distribute its economic benefits evenly is one of the great failures of the Development Decades since the war. In general, the more interactive the relationships between the local social units and the national institutions, the greater the tendency toward increasing inequality of goods and opportunity. Accordingly, change is uneven: some societies change rapidly, keeping their traditions; others do not change at all, and their traditions wither under the influence of the New Poverty. "Culture patterns" give way to identity-seeking, localism to nationalism. The analysis of these processes is becoming the New Anthropology of the immediate future.

THE NATURE OF MICRO/MACRO SUPRASYSTEMS

And so we approach the third problem -- the nature of the very large systems of interdependency and feedback that are coming to characterize the world society. The current literature contains a number of attempts to model world systems, some of them containing definite ideological orientations, and therefore actually critical documents (e.g., Wallerstein 1974, in re. "capitalism"). The technical understanding of the emerging suprasystems is one thing. The direction the process of emergence should take is quite another.

One fundamental theoretical issue concerns the applicability of systems theory to social phenomena. A radical negative position would hold that societies are historically evolving, living organisms with sentient properties, and thus systems theory, which was devised originally for analyzing the properties of mechanical and physical power phenomena, cannot handle the dynamic qualities of the social process. A compromise position acknowledges the unique properties of social phenomena, but recognizes the use of systems theory and concepts wherever they may be of use in understanding the nature of change and interdependency among humans. "Social systems" is by now a convenient and acceptable buzz word. The best appraisal of the qualities and processes of social systems is Walter Buckley's 1967 book on the applicability of theoretical systems models in sociological analysis. "Adaptive system" is the term he uses to refer in general to social system, implying by this a process of communication and adjustment that constantly modifies the relationships among the various components, while at the same time preserving certain process mechanics. This accords well with traditional anthropological ideas of the resistance of microcultural and social phenomena (like symbols and kinship relations) in the face of sweeping transformations of macrostructure -- a situation commonly encountered in the change processes associated with economic and social development in the Third World, as well as in such distinctive microsocial cases as the Hutterian Brethren of North America.

To theorize about large systems in terms of their abstract properties, as indicated in the previous paragraph, is one of two ways to conceive of the social magnitudes and processes involved. The second method is to view suprasystems as Immanuel Wallerstein does, as concrete historical entities, held together by ideologies, economics, and politico-military force, and conditioned by population magnitudes. Size of systems in this second perspective is then measured not so much by social space or social complexity, but by geographical space and the exercise of economic and politi-

cal power, differentially sorted by advantage and opportunity into
"cores" and "peripheries". The essential criterion of a suprasystem, then, would be certain broad patterns of conforming behavior
over large geographical areas, this conformity conferring some sort
of advantage on certain groups in large, well-endowed populations.
One gets very close to Marxian concepts here. In a sense, Fernand
Braudel (1981), Wallerstein and some others in this historical
school are modernizing and certainly broadening Marx. Above all,
they are opening up the doctrine to accept sources of dominance, or
dominant thematic content other than "capitalism" or economic phenomena exclusively. For Wallerstein, however, economics does play
a crucial role, and it is fair to say that economic institutions
may constitute the most effective means of forging what he calls a
"world system."

The unity of the two approaches -- the analytic-abstract (AA)
and the historical-concrete (HC) approaches to suprasystem theory
-- can be seen when a particular problem is researched. The current best example of a world suprasystem is the international
market economy, sometimes called the "capitalist system." (The
latter term is ambiguous because nation-states whose internal economic systems are not capitalist can participate in the international market.) This market system -- again setting aside the
ideological strictures from the left for purposes of discussion --
can function without necessarily resorting to major politico-military measures to force nations and societies to surrender their
political autonomy. "Co-optation" is used in place of or in preference to force. That is, the term "empire," in its old sense of
an existing monopoly of force over a large geographical territory
including many socio-political entities, has not been essential to
the existence of the market system. In fact, the present world has
more politically independent entities than ever before. The market
system seems to have acted as one of the liberating forces, helping
to dissolve the old colonial empires.

One can resort to AA principles to help explain this HC situation. Systems theory crossed with adaptational theory holds that
systems are built up, basically, of component sub-systems that
interact with each other on the basis of mutual advantage. Such
advantage, of course, is a dynamic process and the balance constantly shifts. When it turns against the advantage of one of the
component subsystems, adaptive manipulation or countervailing force
is exerted. Examples are familiar enough. By borrowing very large
sums of capital from government and private sources in the First
World, Third World countries do not merely accumulate debts, they
come to own the banks -- so to speak. Foreclosure is impossible,
because it would be equivalent to bankrupting the lending sources.
At the socio-political level, one perceives constant shifting of
alliances in order to exert leverage. The contemporary Middle East
is an excellent example. By such combinations, countervailing
power is exerted in order to permit the suprasystem processes to
function. In the terms of this essay, the microsocial entities
combine, separate, and combine again in order to defend their
interests and perpetuate or redress the shifting balance of advantage. In this sense, the current world strategic military or arms

control situation is another case in point. "Independence" and "freedom" of nations and societies is thus relative to the stakes in the world system that each unit may have at any given time.

Social responsibility is one of the chief issues in the present international market system. Capital gains can be more readily achieved on the basis of a large number of quasi-independent nations than on the basis of a politico-military empire. This appears to be the case because in the empire, the central political power becomes responsible for the maintenance of welfare or profitability in the component subsystems. In the present multi-national market system, the separate subsystems or nations, regional trading organizations, economic market alliances, etc., must bear that responsibility, thus liberating capital. As the previous remarks concerning the international loan system suggest, however, this may be really a matter of deferring deficits. Ultimately the piper shall have to be paid. We shall see. This is a point where AA theory escapes us, and HC actualities take over.

The sociological tradition was focussed largely on the question of social class. Tribes, cultures, communities were seen as secondary in importance. The social class, defined as a group of people with similar opportunities or deprivations, was considered to be the basic social unit of analysis for large systems. This distinction between autonomous, culturally- or geographically-based social units on the one hand, and politico-economic advantage-deprivation groups on the other, constitutes the basic cleavage between the traditional ethnological and the traditional sociological-political approach in the social sciences. The resolutions of the theoretical and methodological problems arising from this distinction were impossible so long as the issue was conceived as purely theoretical. History was the only final court of appeal. Taking the problem at the highest level of generality -- the HC "world systems" approach -- there seems no doubt that the course of recent history under the influence of the market system and all associated trends, has seen the progressive emergence in all countries of class phenomena as increasingly assertive over against culture, ethnicity, and geography. I do not mean to imply that the cultural or ethnic phenomena are irrelevant or nonexistent. On the contrary, as countervailing forces they are currently a revitalizing force. However, increasing numbers of people in all countries seek advantage on the basis of their relationship to the political economy. Peasants in Latin America and Africa move rapidly into cash-crop production; they are willing to surrender their vicinal isolation and some of their cultural peculiarities in order to achieve a favorable place in the market system. This is true also of Quebec at the moment of writing. This is not a theoretical process, but a concrete reality; it is "world system" phenomena. It does not mean that Marx was right and the ideological theory of history wrong, only that currently, class, however defined, is a very important tool for seeking redress and advantage.

All this can be very stimulating. However, this historically-based and analytically-clarified suprasystems theory can be neglectful of the physical dimension of present world systems -- that is, of the impact of current events on world ecosystems and the

state of the resource base. Population, food production and co
sumption, land degradation, environmental poisons and the like ha
their own rhythms, and these appear to be increasing, often at
exponential rate. While the world suprasystem tends to fluctuate
the basis of adaptive power principles, the ecosystem appears to
running down. Malthusian processes operate in complex ways -- n
necessarily on the basis of some simple ratio of population magni
tudes to available resources, but as an equation with flexib
terms. It is population size plus effective demand plus the scie
tific capacity to enhance, as well as exploit, resources.

More useful, though less intellectually intriguing, is t
synthesis of both sociological and ecological data for significa
subsistence economies associated with particular world regions a
biomes. I have suggested the term socionatural system for the
entities (Bennett 1981). A recent study by an anthropologist mak
an interesting empirical attempt to analyze one, the Mormon fro
tier in Arizona (Abruzzi 1981). A socionatural system brin
together the relevant physical resources, social resources, tec
nology, and human needs and wants into a system of productio
These systems are illumined by human values. That is, they a
defined not by some environmental value, but by human purpose
This may be a fatal flaw. However, if the concept of sustaine
resource yield can be introduced as a check against resource abus
this defect can be handled. The difficulty is that all such co
trol systems are referred ultimately to human demands that a
virtually unchallengeable in most political systems, democratic
authoritarian.

Put another way, the world ecosystem (including humans
course) cannot seem to be brought under control because the micr
units or subsystems seek to maximize gain and gratification, and
the world fills up, this can be done only at the expense of othe
subsystems. Frequently, however, means are found through scien
and technology to modify impacts or make a given quantity of re
sources yield at a higher rate or level. This ambiguity or flu
tuation in the Malthusian equation, while productive of human nee
want gratification, also makes planning and control of resourc
use-abuse extremely difficult. Thus, controls are decisively ex
erted over the process only when crises of one kind or anothe
emerge, and present human needs are jeopardized. Meanwhile, th
thinking public tends to be whipsawed between prophets of Mal
thusian doom like Paul Ehrlich (1974), and prophets of Cornucopia
optimism like Julian Simon (1981).

Suprasystems are not confined to world systems. Reverting t
AA-type theory, there are no absolute magnitude or complexit
constants for defining something as a big system or as a littl
component. This is a relative matter, depending on the data and th
problem. It is here where anthropological issues become critical
The criticism of ethnological work that mounted during the ideolo
gical battles of the 1960s and early 1970s was mainly concerne
with the traditional acceptance of the colonial framework of triba
life, and its almost total neglect in the ethnological reconstruc
tion of tribal culture. That is, the micro entity, a tribal commu
nity, was presented devoid of its systemic interconnections wit

larger politico-economic systems of control. This battle has largely been won by the critics, but their victory was not so much an ideological conquest as the result of inevitable historical changes. The liquidation of colonial empires after World War II simply abolished the isolated tribal society and ethnologists really had no alternative but to broaden their scholarly horizons.

Cultural ecology may be used again as an illustration. In place of the classic monographs concerning single tribal or peasant communities, cultural ecologists are beginning to produce studies of traditionally-based economic systems covering larger geographical areas, as these systems are being modified by increasing involvement of the economic and socio-political development nexus in market economies. If the single-community frame of reference is preserved, the locality is carefully selected as a type case of some larger systemic process. Robert Netting's recent book on a Swiss agricultural community (1981) is an interesting hybrid of the old and new. While a single community study, the presentation includes hard data on population and economic trends derived from large-system economic and historical documentation, so that the published monograph contains implications beyond the immediate confines of the village. That is, it becomes a study of how a representative central European society survives in an interconnected world.

When anthropologists use world-systems concepts in their research, the frame of reference changes radically from the community-centered approach. One starts with a large systemic entity, defines it cross-culturally, then examines a particular local case to see how participation in the system has modified, benefited, or disadvantaged the local society. A case in point is the international cooperative movement. This "movement" is an organizational template originating in the Rochdale experiment in England in the late nineteenth century (Worsley 1971). That is, while indigenous cooperation as a social interaction pattern is of course as old as Homo sapiens, the modern institutionalized cooperative, found in all countries and introduced by European colonial regimes as well as the development agencies in the recent period, is a distinctive system of management and production that requires adaptation to local conditions (Bennett 1983).

The institutional cooperative contains a general ideology of mutual advantage derived from sharing scarce goods, thereby making them more readily available, or more equitably distributed. This ideology is, of course, usually modified in execution, and the cooperative organization can be adapted to agricultural societies with marked inequality of ownership of productive resources. Thus, the co-op does not necessarily solve structural problems. Indeed, like other development interventions, it may worsen them. For those groups who can benefit from cooperative organization, however, the instrumentality produces distinct gains. Cooperative organization also contains strong universalistic, rational-legal and functionally-specific elements, requiring accurate record-keeping, appropriate distribution of surpluses, equitable distribution of necessary factors of production, and intelligent dealings with outside agents of the market system. On the other hand,

because the cooperative is also a local organization, it also ca
serve to protect indigenous cultural patterns and values agains
invasion by alien perspectives and practices. Such processes con
stitute the focus of the growing anthropological interest in co-op
in developing countries. It constitutes a good example of the us
of world-system constructs to guide anthropological research o
micro/macro issues.

THE ANTHROPOLOGICAL CONTRIBUTION

An underlying question in this essay has been the value of th
contribution anthropologists might make to the micro/macro problem
given the fact that much of the relevant theory has already bee
furnished by the institutional social sciences. Must anthropolog
simply borrow this theory? And if it does, can anthropology retai
its professional distinctiveness? The question is meaningless o
scientific grounds. If anthropology has nothing to offer beyon
available sociological, political-science or economic concepts
then so be it. Social theory, however, is not finite. It is a
intellectual exercise that can be informed by many different in
sights and views of reality. Thus, anthropology's traditiona
focus on intimate social situations, and its emphasis on the menta
life of people in communities ("culture"), may provide valuabl
perspectives and concepts.

The most important of these insights concerns the adaptationa
nexus -- how local people cope with external influences, and how
they may strive to modify these forces in Third World countries
The rate of failure of development projects is substantial, and
most of these failures can be attributed to the failure of planner
and technical aid specialists to understand the full context of
local responses to intervention. Economic thinking is based on
assumptions of cross-cultural universality of certain reactions,
like the desire for more return on one's labor. The possibility
that this is not always appreciated or envisaged, or that local
social arrangements might be jeopardized by its achievement, has
been seriously neglected. Although the point is often understood
by the development planners, they must officially ignore it because
the plan, or the country government objectives, take precedence.
Anthropologists have begun to research the need for more local
participation and autonomy in development planning (e.g., Ralston
et.al. 1981 -- a study commissioned by USAID).

Individual motives, or the motives of people in social systems, rarely conform to simple paradigms of social behavior. The
tendency to assume they do is a proclivity of technical experts in
urban-based institutions without first-hand knowledge of local
communities and their cultures. This failing is itself a macro/
micro issue, and it deserves independent study by anthropologists.
Contributions to this problem have been made by development anthropologists, and these constitute one of the genuine achievements of
applied anthropology, a contribution not fully appreciated by the
academic fraternity. More often than not, however, these contributions have issued from critiques of the development process, rather

than as products of intimate participation by anthropologists in
the projects. It has been difficult to incorporate anthropological
work in development, largely for practical reasons. The amount of
time required to perform an adequate anthropological study of local
sociocultural conditions affecting project acceptance is often
longer than the organizational time-frame of the project itself.
In addition, the recommendations made by the anthropological team-
member are often couched in elliptical and qualified language; they
are not specific enough to permit incorporation in a specific
project design. Anthropologists need to learn how to make more
carefully-focussed and sharply-worded studies of intervention and
its social matrix. They also need to be more specific about cause-
and-effect sequences in human behavior.

In addition to the study of sociocultural factors influencing
project acceptance there is need for anthropological work on the
problem of effective size or magnitude of productive processes.
Attempts to merge local production systems in larger market-based
entities, based on Euro-American models, have also not met with
outstanding success, and development specialists have shown considerable interest in recent years in alternative arrangements that
preserve the smaller, indigenous technology systems. These systems
have proven to be remarkably efficient users of available physical
and social resources, even though their productive magnitudes are
not always in conformity with externally-set standards and goals.
Anthropologists have begun doing research on the technical dimensions of these local systems. "Cultural ecology" is giving way to
more sophisticated studies of energy utilization and productive
efficiency under substantively-rational conditions. These can
function as a needed corrective to the formal-rational - and unrealistic - goals of the development programs.

Aside from these practical dimensions, the anthropological
inquiry into micro/macro relationships has a scholarly importance.
Rural sociology, which grew up under the aegis of the North American and European agricultural establishment, has never fully understood the need for an examination of the rich social matrix of
local-external relationships in the developed societies, let alone
the emerging national societies of the Third World. A new "rural
anthropology" is needed and both sociologists and anthropologists
can supply this need. There are some models. Bruno Benvenuti's
study of rural life in the Netherlands (1962) is an outstanding
exception to the rather perfunctory research carried on by most
rural sociologists. Benvenuti's approach shows a profound appre-
ciation of the cultural aspects of rural-urban interaction, and the
influence of the market system. In broader perspective, S. H.
Franklin's studies of European "peasantry" in transition to a new
pan-European market agriculture (1969) illustrate the profitable
results that can be obtained when one views the agriculturalists of
a continent as intelligent beings who cope with changing macrosocial forces and are willing to make trade-offs with their own
institutions in the process. Anthropologists are entering this
field of study, in the "applied" fields of economic and development
anthropology.

Franklin's work is really history. Its illuminating qualities derive from the historical approach, and history becomes a second mode in which anthropologists may find a new productive role. To an extent greater than any other modern anthropologist, Eric Wolf has explored the relevance of historical approaches. History was always an important mode of endeavor in cultural anthropology although the excessive empiricism of the "historical approach" of the Boasians, and the grandiose universalist generalizing of the Kroeberian school prevented work on true history. The growing attention given historical writings by anthropologists is a good sign. In essence, this means the attempt to identify social and cultural forms in societies with recorded history and in societies "without history" (Wolf 1982). The Braudel influence is crucial, because he offers a method of writing history at the level of cultural patterns, institutions, and everyday structures of life. Above all, it is in the anthropological analysis of recorded historical events that answers to some of the issues of microsocial and macrosocial interaction can be found.

REPRISE

I wish to return to two themes advanced in the introductory section. The first concerns a comparison of anthropology and sociology with respect to the absence in anthropology of a block of macrolevel societal theory. We also noted, however, that anthropology can contribute a need and method for detailed microlevel investigations to sociology. At this point we can now be more specific, and suggest that the most important missing theory segment in anthropology concerns the macro/micro nexus of relationships. Sociology has no significant version of this nexus. It must rely on propositions about community power structure, socio-political theories of exploitation and dominance, graphic and empirical studies of taxation, political representation, and the like. These are a bag of sub-paradigms lacking a general focus. Sociology cannot theorize about micro/macro relations except politically (which of course is not at all bad). But nevertheless, anthropology has a significant opportunity to look for empirical phenomena, like adaptive coping, that have received less attention than they deserve.

The essential feature of a theoretical paradigm is the recognition of the need for considering the will, purposes, and needs of local-level people in the bureaucratic institutions that govern and regulate the world. This has to be more than a purely descriptive or anecdotal plea for such consideration. The approach developed by Cultural Survival and the Anthropology Resource Center, while useful and important, is a value-guided holding operation, not really a scholarly exposition. The case for the preservation of genetic diversity can be made by biologists with relevance and empirical cogency. The material consequences of loss of variant strains can be described in detail. No such convincing scientific case has yet been made by anthropologists for the preservation of locally-variant strains of lifeways, and perhaps it cannot and should not be made. I believe, however, that the problem is susceptible to theoretical development. The loss to innovativeness of

variant cultural expressions could probably be measured and presented in historical detail, if anthropologists would gird their
loins for the task.   It requires a new way of thinking for anthropologists. Their major hypotheses and problems must be recast in
socially relevant terms, and related to the historical present and
the immediate future.

The second theme concerns moral obligations to humanity, and a
self-examination of anthropology by anthropologists in order to
find their role in the world. At one time, that role was predeter-
mined.   The scholarly need to recover the facts of passing tribal-
ism required no formal justification, only money. But times have
changed. Anthropologists are now _in_ the world, not outside looking
on. They study people whose lives will be affected by their work
and its results. And whatever they do, it has inevitable practical
and policy relevance, because the people they study are also _in_ the
world. Thus the moral obligation is not a matter of choice. It is
necessity, thrust on anthropologists by their participation in a
changing society, and their decision to join "history."

This requires a close look at some of the underlying conven-
tions of anthropological thought, if not specific theories. I have
already written (Bennett 1976) on the tendency to oppose Nature to
Culture. This is a distinction embedded in anthropological thought
from the late eighteenth century and perhaps earlier, and now one
with a quaint ring in light of the desperate need for a socionatural synthesis.   The Culture-Nature distinction is archaic for two
reasons. First, it is arrogant, a product of excessive human-
centered thought of the Age of Reason and the triumphant imperial
capitalism of the nineteenth century.   Second, it is increasingly
false, insofar as Culture - that is, ourselves - constantly trans-
forms Nature into "resources," and thus moves toward total appropriation of the physical environment. The ultimate consequences of
this great transition are unknown. Its current stages do not
generate optimism.

Ecology is not, however, our main theme. More important in
the present context are the implications that intense human- or
culture-centeredness hold for our fellow humans. If the world is
divided into cultures, as anthropologists once held (and perhaps
still do -- or at least they have not formally disavowed the doctrine), then these cultures can be picked off one by one, just as
"tribes" were in fact created, segregated and disciplined by colo-
nialists. The romantic notion of separate cultures in some degree
denies common humanity and brotherhood. And classifications of
cultures, like "folk" and "urban," while well-intentioned, served
to perpetuate stereotypes with inferior-superior -- or as it was
usually put, "simple and complex" -- connotations. Anthropology
for generations emphasized differences between humans. This emphasis is sadly out of date, as the world's populations rapidly merge
into one interdependent society, and "ethnicity" becomes a conscious doctrine of identity, rather than naive, sheltered culture.
Thus, micro and macro are simply one more case of splitting and
emphasis on difference (Cohen 1974). Still, for analytical purposes the micro/macro distinction is hard to avoid, and anthropologists will not relinquish it, nor should they. The age is one of

transition. The world is not yet a fully interdependent entity
and as it moves toward inevitable fusion, haltingly and with con
flict, there is real need for analysis of the relationships betwee
the local and the external -- a political need if no other.

The point is that we are witnesses to a great contradictio:
As the world order emerges, the State intensifies its autonomy.]
is this desperate attempt of nation-states, perhaps especially th
more recent ones, to assert their dominance over territory -- ar
their own subjects -- that creates the spreading internal protes!
revolution, and terror. This is a process made even worse, or a
least more callous, by the increasing disregard for human life in
world with too many people for its resource utilization systems
As noted earlier in the paper, there has been a persistent transfe
of "culture" to the nation-state, as it seeks to forge a distinc
identity in a world society of increasing uniformity. This proces
can only lead to vast abuses of what we call human rights. This i
the apotheosis of the micro/macro problem. How are anthropologist
to deal with it?

In the final reckoning, all concepts are historically tran
sient. Culture and cultures was a fair paradigm for an older, les
interrelated world, but has proved inadequate for the new society
Anthropologists need to face up to the historical nature of thei
theories and constructs. The occasional effusions about scientifi
laws of culture are misplaced and are of no real utility in solvin
the pressing problems of modern society. Anthropologists, in a
age of transition and rapid transformation (the final end of th
Middle Ages), should devote their efforts to understanding what i
happening, not theorizing about minutiae, or propounding grand
scale general theory applicable only to trivial phenomena. This i
the final significance of the micro/macro frame. It focusses ou
attention on what is really going on in the world -- the incorpora
tion of communities into larger and larger systems, a process tha
needs research at both the micro level, to determine what it i
doing to people and their groups, and also at the macro level, t
find out how these enormous human constructions are being pu
together. We know little about either end of the continuum, an
even less about the nexi that tie the ends together.

NOTES

1. I suppose the national cultural character studies of Mea
and Benedict should also be included. The tradition did not per-
sist.

BIBLIOGRAPHY

bruzzi, W. 1981. Mormon Colonization of the Little Colorado River Basin. Doctoral Dissertation. Binghamton, New York: Department of Anthropology, State University of New York.

dams, Richard N. 1970. Crucifixion by Power: Essays in Guatemalan Social Structure. Austin: University of Texas Press.

dams, Robert McC. 1966. The Evolution of Urban Society. Chicago: Aldine Publishing Company.

arth, Fredrik. 1969. Ethnic Groups and Boundaries: The Social Organization of Culture Difference. London: George Allen & Unwin.

eck, Lois. 1985. The Quashqa'i Confederacy. New Haven, Yale University Press.

ecker, Howard. 1950. "Sacred and Secular Societies." Social Forces 28:361-376.

endix, Reinhard. 1960. Max Weber: An Intellectual Portrait. New York: Doubleday & Company.

enedict, Ruth. 1934. Patterns of Culture. New York: Houghton Mifflin Company.

ennett, John W. 1946. "The Interpretation of Pueblo Culture: A Question of Values." Southwestern Journal of Anthropology 2:361-374.

_____. 1967. "Microcosm-Macrocosm Relationships in North American Agrarian Society." American Anthropologist 69:441-454.

_____. 1976. The Ecological Transition: Cultural Anthropology and Human Adaptation. New York and London: Pergamon Publishing Company.

_____. 1981. "Social and Interdisciplinary Sciences in U.S. Man and the Biosphere Program." In E. Zube (editor), Social Sciences, Interdisciplinary Research, and the U.S., Man and the Biosphere Program. U.S. MAB, Department of State, and the University of Arizona, Tucson.

_____. 1982. Of Time and the Enterprise: North American Family Farm Management in a Context of Resource Marginality. Minneapolis: University of Minnesota Press.

_____. 1983. "Agricultural Cooperatives in the Development Process: Perspectives from Social Science." Studies in Comparative International Development 18:3-68.

Benvenuti, Bruno. 1962. Farming in Cultural Change. Assen, Netherlands: Van Gorcum Company.

Buckley, Walter. 1967.Sociology and Modern Systems Theory. Englewood Cliffs, New Jersey: Prentice Hall Incorporated.

Braudel, Fernand. 1981. The Structures of Everyday Life: Civilization and Capitalism: 15th-18th Century. New York: Harper & Row Publishers. (and other volumes.)

Childe, V. Gordon. 1942. What Happened in History. Harmondsworth: Penguin Books.

Cohen, Abner. 1974. Two Dimensional Man. Berkeley: University of California Press.

Eckert, Roland. 1970. Kultur, Zivilization, und Gesellschaft: Die Geschichts-theorie Alfred Webers, seine Studie zur Geschichte der deutschen Soziologie. Tubingen: J.C.B. Mohr.

Ehrlich, Paul R. and Anne H. 1974. The End of Affluence: A Blueprint for Your Future. New York: Ballantine.

Fagan, Brian M. 1984. Clash of Cultures. New York: W.H. Freeman.

Fallers, Lloyd A. 1974. The Social Anthropology of the Nation-State. Chicago: Aldine Publishing Company.

Foster, George. 1965. "Peasant Society and the Image of Limited Good." American Anthropologist 67: 293-315.

Frank, Andre Gunder. 1969. Capitalism and Underdevelopment in Latin America. New York: Monthly Review Press.

Frankenberg, Ronald. 1966. Communities in Britain. Harmondsworth: Penguin Books.

Franklin, S.H. 1969. The European Peasantry: The Final Stage. London: Methuen.

Goldschmidt, Walter. 1947. As You Sow. New York: Harcourt Brace & Company.

Halperin, Rhoda and James Dow. 1977. Peasant Livelihood. New York: St. Martin's Press.

Herskovits, Melville J. 1983. Dahomey. (2 volumes). New York: J.J. Augustin.

Hinsley, Curtis M. Jr. 1979. "Anthropology as Science and Politics: Dilemmas of the Bureau of American Ethnology, 1879-1904." In W. Goldschmidt (editor), The Uses of Anthropology. Washington: The American Anthropological Association, Special Publication Number 11.

Jorgenson, Joseph G. 1978. "A Century of Political Economic Effects on American Indian Society, 1880-1980." Journal of Ethnic Studies 6:1-82.

Kluckhohn, Clyde. 1951. "Values and Value-Orientations in the Theory of Action." In T. Parsons and E. Shils (editors), Toward a General Theory of Action. Cambridge: Harvard University Press.

Leach, Edmund R. 1954. Political Systems of Highland Burma. Boston: Beacon Press.

Linton, Ralph. 1936. Study of Man. New York: D. Appleton-Century Company.

Loomis, Charles (translator) and Ferdinand Tonnies. 1940. Fundamental Concepts of Sociology: Gemeinschaft und Gesellschaft. New York: American Book Company.

Maine, Sir Henry J.S. 1896. Ancient Law: Its Connection with the
    Early History of Society, and its Relations to Modern Ideas.
    London: John Murray.
Miner, Horace. 1955. "The Folk-Urban Continuum." In P.F. Lazars-
    feld and M.Rosenberg (editors), The Language of Social Re-
    search. Glencoe, Illinois: The Free Press.
Netting, Robert Mc. 1981. Balancing on an Alp: Ecological Change
    and Continuity in a Swiss Mountain Village. New York: Cam-
    bridge University Press.
Parsons, Talcott. 1951. The Social System. Glencoe, Illinois: The
    Free Press.
Ralston, Lenore, James Anderson and Elizabeth Colson. 1981. Volun-
    tary Efforts in Decentralized Management. Project on Managing
    Decentralization, Institute of International Studies, Univer-
    sity of California, Berkeley.
Redfield, Robert. 1947. "The Folk Society." American Journal of
    Sociology 52:293-308.
_____. 1955. The Little Community: Viewpoints for the Study
    of a Human Whole. Chicago: University of Chicago Press.
_____. 1956. Peasant Society and Culture: An Anthropological
    Approach to Civilization. Chicago: University of Chicago
    Press.
Reining, Conrad. 1962. "A Lost Period in Applied Anthropology."
    American Anthropologist 64:593-600.
Roberts, Bryan. 1978. Cities of Peasants: The Political Economy of
    Urbanization in the Third World. London: Edward Arnold.
Simon, Julian L. 1981. The Ultimate Resource. Princeton: Princeton
    University Press.
Simpson, George. 1933. Emile Durkheim on the Division of Labor in
    Society. New York: MacMillan Company.
Singer, Milton. 1958. "Traditional India: Structure and Change."
    Journal of American Folkore 71:No. 281.
Smith, Carol A. (editor) 1976. Regional Analysis. New York: Aca-
    demic Press (two volumes).
Steward, Julian. 1956. The People of Puerto Rico. Champaign: Uni-
    versity of Illinois Press.
Vidich, Arthur J. and J. Bensman. 1958. Small Town in Mass Society.
    Princeton: Princeton University Press.
Wallerstein, Immanuel. 1974. The Modern World System: I: Capitalist
    Agriculture and the Origin of the European World Economy. New
    York: Academic Press (and other volumes).
Whitten, Norman. 1969. "Strategies of Adaptive Mobility in the
    Columbian-Ecuadorian Littoral." American Anthropologist
    71:238-242.
Whitten, Norman & A. Wolfe. 1973. "Network Analysis." In J. Honig-
    mann (ed.). Handbook of Social and Cultural Anthropology.
    American Anthropologist 71:238-242.
Whyte, William F. 1943. Street Corner Society. Chicago: University
    of Chicago Press.
Williams, Anne S. 1981. "Industrialized Agriculture and the Small-
    Scale Farmer." Human Organization 40:306-312.

Wolf, Eric R. 1957. "Closed Corporate Peasant Communities in Meso-america and Java." _Southwestern Journal of Anthropology_ 13:1-18.

_____. 1969. _Peasant Wars of the Twentieth Century_. New York Harper & Row Publishers.

_____. 1982. _Europe and the People Without History_. Berkeley, University of California Press.

Worsley, Peter (editor). 1971. _Two Blades of Grass: Cooperatives in Agricultural Modernization_. Manchester: Manchester University of Press.

3
Regulation and Natural Selection in the Micro/Macro Perspective

Richard N. Adams

INTRODUCTION

The thesis of this paper is that the distinction between macro- and micro-phases of societal experience derives from the fact that much of society has blended with processes of natural selection. We think of those areas where we consider we have some controls as existing within a larger realm over which we have no control. The argument consists of two parts. The first (and longer) is an introduction to the processes that comprise the macroframework. The second concerns processes of regulatory expansion through which human society deals constantly with natural selection.

PROCESSES COMPRISING THE MACROFRAMEWORK

The micro-macro distinction usually contrasts events observed in a large temporal-spatial scope or plane with those occurring within a small scope and as part of a larger picture. In fact, the relation between events in broad and narrow planes may be quite obscure, such as that between pill bugs eating up your garden and the international arms race. To pose the micro/macro contrast, however, is to propose that there is a relation between these two sets of events. (Thus one might argue that pill bugs are due to the fact that population growth has increased gardening, providing pill bugs with a great resource; and that the population growth is a result of the industrial, capitalist world expansion that also involves an arms race). If such a relationship is one-way, such as the arrival of energy from the sun, there is little that it can tell us of interactions between the two planes. However, if it can be shown that there is feedback in the system, and better, that the resultant interactions have some deterministic consequences, it is more interesting. It becomes even more intriguing if the interactions can be shown to comprise a self-organizing structure. While I do not have much of a clue about the feedback between pill bugs and the arms race, there is certainly some suggestive self-organization between highly mutant virus forms and cockroaches on the one hand and the human environment created for each of them on the other.

It is broadly accepted that highly complex systems are quite indeterministic; but some people -- including myself -- would hold that if we operate within a macro/micro framework, we may anticipate some determinism to be inherent in the whole, and delineating determinisms is a major objective of science.

The micro/macro framework is usually conceived of as a "vertical" dimension, and while there is some unfortunate cultural baggage in that metaphor, we will use it for convenience here. It is useful to recall, however, that there has long been a kind of micro/macro framework used with respect to "horizontal" relations (i.e., the notion of segmentation, stemming back at least to Spencer, still is useful to describe relationships that are complementary to those operating in the vertical dimension). Much of the development of models of diffusionism and functional interrelations was occasioned by an interest in large-scale horizontal relations.

Attention to the vertical slice makes possible a more profound exploration of the processes at work in segmentation under the socioecological constraints that have affected increasing numbers of human beings for many millenia. When segmentation, in the sense of the budding off of growing populations into new community segments, became stifled, circumscribed by other peoples and constricted habitats, vertical expansion into hierarchy was the only long-term solution (see Carneiro 1970; Adams 1975; Cohen 1977). The emergence of societal hierarchies was a human invention (although presumably various insects had independently invented it long before) to solve problems associated with population growth beyond the available controls and resources. It was dependent, of course, on the same symbolic abilities that enabled the species to devise ecologically diverse adaptations.

Hierarchy, then, can be seen as one evolutionary solution to the problem of competition for resources. Societies under excessive tensions are more vulnerable to processes of natural selection. The emergence of hierarchy was first the emergence of a new, allegedly superior, regulatory device. The survival of all societies depends on the presence of internal regulative processes that successfully cope with the external forces that collectively comprise natural selection. Hierarchy cleverly constructed more controlled environments for groups under their control. Thus, social hierarchy was a regulatory strategy created to cope with the forces of natural selection.

"Natural selection classically has been used by biologists, following Darwin, to refer specifically to the process by which different genetic materials survive relative to each other. Darwinian fitness, the specific measure of successful natural selection, is measured for a life form by "the proportion of its genes left in the population gene pool" (Pianka 1978: 10); and natural selection operates "only by differential reproductive success" (Ibid.: 9). Without denying the now hallowed right of biologists to use "natural selection" in this very specific way, there is also a natural process of selection that also goes on with respect to organisms, to cultural forms, and even to rocks and

minerals. Everything that has the quality of energy is subject to
potential energy loss and its own dissipation, a process that
permanently and irredeemably changes the form itself. While the
biologist has every reason to focus on the reproduction of genetic
material, it does not alter the fact that nature is composed of
many other kinds of material, including smaller components than the
genetic material itself, and larger components, sometimes incorporating genetic material. All these forms, living and non-living,
confront the issue of continuity and/or replication, avoiding
changes in their relations with the environment that would damage
their equilibrium status.

In the following I appropriate the term "natural selection" to
refer to the process whereby the environment affects and changes
any form, natural and cultural. I must reject the distinction made
by Cavelli-Sforza and Feldman (1981) between "cultural selection"
and "natural selection" whereby the first refers to the survival of
cultural things and the second to relative reproductive success of
genetic material. I think selection must be seen as a general
process and not limited to certain kinds of materials. Moreover, I
cannot accept the notion that culture is not natural, and that
nature has set aside one special process to handle genetic material
and something else to handle cultural material. I repeat that I do
not challenge the biologist's usage for their purposes, but the
present problem is a different one, and for it the term "natural
selection" is unquestionably the most appropriate and will be used
in this much more general sense. By way of a more formal definition of this new usage, I tentatively propose the following:
Natural selection comprises processes whereby energy forms maintain
or change their equilibrium status with respect to the environment;
the measure of relative success is the degree to which a form
maintains its equilibrium status. Elsewhere (Adams ms) I explore
the subject in greater detail.

All existing life forms are dissipative structures (Prigogine,
Allen and Herman 1977) that have survived by meeting two conditions. (1) They must provide their own energetic input needs --
i.e., the biochemical needs of the individual organisms comprising
the society. (2) They must provide for the reproduction and care --
i.e., housing, etc. -- of the organisms to successfully continue
the society. This consists of maintaining the steady states of the
organisms, and a steady or expanding state of the collectivity.

Natural selection is a finite process that concentrates events
that tend to reduce the equilibrium status of the society and
dissipate it. It is not the case, as has often been asserted, that
life was an attempt to fight off the Second Law of Thermodynamics.
Rather life was a way of conforming to the Second Law by building
bigger structures to increase the flow of energy. Natural selection, as Lotka (1922) observed, favored those forms of life that
found ways of increasing their consumption of natural resources.
Survival of life has not always been, as is asserted by some ecologists, a search for stability. It has been a search for activity
that could reinstitute the energy expended in a dissipative process
that constituted life on the one hand, and control the activities
that constituted natural selection on the other.

The new regulative processes introduced by hierarchy enabled societies to enjoy greater flows of energy for both purposes under more centralized controls. Whereas a human foraging band could put only a few individuals in the field to fight, a chiefdom could mobilize hundreds or thousands, and kingdoms, empires and nations could expend thousands and millions. Thus a central feature of hierarchy was to miniaturize or centralize the triggers that control activity directed towards the survival of the society. Of course, by the same token, the greater centralization of control could yield a greater catastrophe if it worked badly -- if the individuals making decisions were unwise or insufficiently aware of the nature of the events confronting them. For example, a society that expended energy to control natural selection processes could only expect success if it correctly judged the energy available for control.

Natural selection works on human society; but human society is also a part of the natural selection process, affecting many other phases of nature as well as itself. Human society also selects things to steer natural selection in its favor. The micro/macro framework is a way of seeing the efforts of human beings, individually and collectively, trying to control events that are in large part determined by events beyond their control. The history and evolution of human society describes the differential success of finding ways to control natural selection. The macroframe is the totality of events that act as selective processes; microevents are the activities of human societies trying to effect their own selection, their controls.

In the process of trying to enhance their own selection, culture gave human species the potential for attempting many different strategies. La Barre (1955:89-91) and Hall (1976:Chapter 2) suggest that the technology really consists of extensions of human eyes, ears, hands, arms, legs and brains. In creating and exercising these extensions it was necessary to draw on materials and additional energy sources from the environment. Thus what might have been implements of natural selection against human survival were drawn within the circle of things used by human beings to favor their own selection.

Social organization is an adaptive device used by human beings to enhance their own survival. Cooperative efforts allow individuals to benefit by using skills held by others, and to accomplish tasks beyond the physical capacity of a single individual. Competition allows some to survive at the expense of others. The invention and emergence of social hierarchies combined cooperation and competition in a single bundle. It coordinated efforts that benefited the whole collectivity, by institutionalizing the collective or competitive advantage of a few over all the rest. The social hierarchy was an emergent extension of human capacities just as much as were technological tools. While the latter helped to harness non-human materials and non-human energy into the service of human beings, hierarchies enabled human beings to more effectively harness each other in larger numbers.

The growth of technological and sociological extensions affected the natural selection of human societies. By bringing greater

control over the environment into the hands of a disproportionately
few of the society's members -- i.e. specialists in technology and
politics -- it created a human macrostructure that seemed to insert
itself between the individual and the forces of natural selection.
In a way, human societies that built social hierarchies opted to
shift from what the ecologists have called an opportunistic toward
a more equilibrium selection process (Pianka 1978:120-113), from r
selection to K selection. Some members of the species made a
strategic survival choice and were betting on the advantages of
large societies over small societies. Large societies, however,
could only exist if they did so by reinforcing their own macro-
structures to coexist with the extrahuman forces of natural selection.

    Returning to the macro/micro framework, it is now apparent
that we can distinguish analytically some different components of
the macroframe. There are, at the outset, the forces of natural
selection; potentially infinite, but finite for any particular
case. The hierarchization of society differentiates the picture so
that while the microelement continues to be the acts of discrete
individuals or small groups, the separation of a subset of individuals from the larger group, invested with superior controls, con-
fronts the individual with a double macroframe -- non-human natural
selection and human natural selection -- while those with superior
controls must now cope with both the non-human forces and the
larger mass of individuals. This allows us to distinguish, apart
from the natural environment, two sectors of the human population
-- a regulatory sector and a substantive work sector. Of course,
further elaboration and differentiation of the social hierarchy
simply compounds these differentiations into what have been var-
iously conceived of as levels, strata, classes, etc.

    The discussion thus far has omitted an essential additional
process. To deal with this, let us return for a moment to the
nature of culture. The core processes that may be said to constitute an operating culture is a collectivity of people who arbi-
trarily assign shared meanings concerning events (see Adams 1975).
This implies the presence of a social relational system that maintains and changes these meanings and the things to which they are
assigned. It is this last to which I now refer. These devices are
primarily retained in particular cultural forms, the most obvious
of which are language and speech, ritualized behavior and objects,
ceremonialized performances, dogma, revelation, and the range of
recursive and complex meanings that Geertz (1973) has seen as
requiring a "thick" description, and that Bateson (1979) has characterized as the operation of "mind". All the technological and
sociological activities just discussed operate through overt and
covert processes that, at some point, require speech and performance. Their description, however, requires that our models specify the covert, mental phase of human activity. Thus our colleagues speak of mental models, rules, premises, themes, values,
cognitive systems, cognized environment, ethos, etc., all trying to
get at one or another aspect of culture that exists within the
collectivity of human nervous systems.

    An aspect of these mental processes to receive special atten-

60

tion in recent years is where the arbitrary meaning seems to re-
verse themselves very rapidly. This kind of change is illustrated
by the high price sought when one is a seller, but low price when
becoming a buyer, of shifting from cooperative behavior within a
group to competitive behavior when moving outside the group, or the
change that a cordial faculty colleague undergoes when he or she
becomes a distant and calculating dean, or the change from a humble
peasant to violent revolutionary. Changes such as these have
usually been described in terms of changes in position in the
society, changes that indicate power reversals at one level and
symbolic inversions at another (Turner 1969; Adams 1975).

Some of these reversals occur in contexts that are easily
identified in terms of hierarchy -- such as that of the professor
who becomes a dean or the peasant turned revolutionary. Some are
related to group segmentation, such as the suspicion inherent
between groups in contrast to the gemeinschaft existing within a
group. However, some, specifically that between buyer's and seller's prices, hinge not only on the positional differentiation of
the individuals, but on the fact that, as Marx argued, the individual's position is changed by virtue of the fact that the things
being symbolized also have position. My things should have a high
price, whereas other peoples' should have a low price.

Because the human species exists not as a single community,
but as a series of separate societies, as quasi-species (Catton
1980), natural selection shows dual faces, operating differently
within groups than it does between groups. The faces are dual
because intersocietal relations include both the threats of one
against another, but also their interdependency. While some dependency problems are delineated and resolved by hierarchy, there also
continue, both within and between societies, to be immense differences in control over resources and skills necessary for survival.
One solution to this has always been solved through exchange --
exchange within a small, intimate group. But exchange between
groups is rarely intended to strengthen the other group. As a
consequence, exchange between individuals of different groups has,
in principle, always been self-serving; the object has been to help
oneself, not the other.

As societies grew physically larger, internal segmentations
were accompanied by the growth of exchange based on self-concern of
the segments, not concern for the society as a whole. Just as
hierarchy was a social extension, so did exchange become a social
-- or, if you prefer, an economic -- extension of the individual
human being's adaptation. As hierarchies became elaborated in
extraordinarily diverse forms -- bureaucracies, coalitions, confed-
erations, alliances and, above all, nation states and international
blocs -- so did self-serving exchange -- market exchange -- become
elaborated into what has been called the world capitalist system
(Wallerstein 1974). The emergence of long distance trade, and
later of industrial production, pushed segmentation to the point of
isolating some individuals so that they became independently cate-
gorized not in terms of social position, but in terms of where they
stood with respect to exchange and control.

Market exchange comprises adaptive devices used by individuals to favor self-selection no matter where they operate in the social whole. It is a third analytical component of the macroframe, a complex relational system that simultaneously works for and against the selection of individuals and social segments, favoring some and increasing the dissipation and degradation of others. Thus individuals may start anywhere in the social hierarchy and, by finding a favorable spot in the market, can enhance their own position. By the same process, others may lose favorable positions. Market exchange is, then, also an extension of the ability of the individual to survive. Of course, it is also used by collectivities in dealing with individuals or other collectivities, but its great salience in continuing human survival is that it can be used by anyone who can find the favorable position from which to operate. The role of market exchange as a component of the macroframe rests on the same conditions as does the emergence of hierarchy. It becomes a major extension of human action when the amount of goods, the amount of non-human material and energy, expands to a degree where control over it becomes a significant factor in natural selection. Thus as the sheer quantity of things increase, helping oneself to control things becomes increasingly important, not for their direct use, but for changing one's own position in the market and hierarchy, in enhancing one's own life chances. Market exchange is clearly a uniquely cultural process because it requires the ability to instantly change meanings of things. These meanings always, of course, operate in a context of contrasting meanings, so there must always also be a context of meaning continuity within which the change takes place.

Market processes are separable from hierarchical processes only analytically. In the event, they operate as an interwoven, indeed a single, assemblage of choices. Control in the market may be used directly to manipulate the hierarchies, and hierarchies rapidly emerge in the market. As with other hierarchies, these provide unequal advantages for confronting natural selection. Similarly, positions in hierarchies may depend on controls that give advantages in market operations. In hierarchies, individuals can inhibit some of these. When markets are unstructured by their own hierarchies, individuals can always act in behalf of their selves or their own gemeinschaft. In a sense, human societies contrast with insect societies by having market processes. They may be suppressed or diverted by hierarchies, but they can always reappear when such suppression is released. Hierarchy intentionally constricts and narrows control; the market constantly presents new opportunities for individual control. Both are processes used in coping with natural selection, both provide ways for societies to expand. In the expansion of society, however, the two processes also expand so that they combine in the event to form the larger macrostructure of human activity that always favors some and thwarts others. Hierarchies offer some advantages to societies in more stable environments; market activity offers advantages where the environment is unstable and changing. Hierarchies try to obtain the advantages of the ecologist's equilibrium, or K selection; market activity is opportunistic and seeks the selective advantages of opportunism, or r selection. In the larger picture,

human societies seem to become dispensable segments experimentin
with natural selection, and the species thus far has found i
profitable to keep both kinds of strategies going.

The fact that contemporary human societies find it useful t
favor one of these rather than another merely means that the regu
latory components of the society believe one way to be more suc
cessful than the other in dealing with the forces of natural selec
tion. Every society is a prisoner of ideology; but in hierarchica
societies, ideologies become public myths rationalizing preference
of regulators. All regulators want the macrostructure to favo
them. Capitalists are constantly trying to manipulate governments
and socialist societies are constantly trying to control free
wheeling market forces. Each, in fact, also uses the other to th
hilt. The ideologies spawned are no more or less realistic i
substance than those prevalent about the natural environment; the
are made up of misinformation and desire, isolated facts and fears

PROCESSES OF REGULATORY EXPANSION

If the macroframe is partly non-human and beyond direct control, and partly under control, then an important aspect of micro/
macro relations is the issue of how a hierarchy continues to expand
controls.

The problem stems from the far-from-equilibrium status of
complex dissipative structures (Prigogine, Allen and Herman 1977).
Such structures naturally and necessarily fluctuate. The more
energy they consume, the greater the fluctuation, and therefore the
greater is the imperative of control. In an expanding social
structure the imperative is met by differentiation of regulatory
activities. However, this differentiation may lead, in turn, to
increasing amounts of energy being used for regulation itself.
This, in turn, means that the very structure of regulation itself
increasingly fluctuates and calls for further control. The actual
historical process has been to expand and allocate power to higher
levels of centralization, or to capture or take-over various domains, thereby creating higher levels. The argument here is that
the very quantity of energy flow in regulatory activity itself
makes effective regulation problematic. For this, let us examine
communication in an expanding social structure.

All living, energy consuming, structures have a work function
and an information-giving function. That is, any energetic activity both expends energy in what is technically called "doing work"
(yielding a product), and also inflicts some perturbation in the
environment, leaving some trace or imprint. In fact, of course,
both components do work and regulate and give information. Human
societies, however, tend to deal with events by differentiating one
of these aspects from the other, and focusing on one as opposed to
the other. Social hierarchies differentiate on the principle that
the regulatory component specializes in the informational aspect,
whereas the rest of the society specializes in doing work. This
tendency to see things as important either because of their work
capacity, or because of the information they provide is reinforced

by general systems and engineering theory that systematically regards information and energy as two quite different kinds of inputs, thus obscuring their common base.

When the amount of energy -- or work -- increases in a society's regulatory sector, it becomes increasingly impossible to ignore it because of the increase in fluctuations, in uncontrollable
activity, already described. The regulation itself must now be
controlled if the structure's control system is to work. To para-
phrase Marshall McLuhan (1967), the media itself becomes a message.
In communication terms, the work of regulatory activities now
carries metacommunication that can be more important than the
message content. We are all familiar with this in the form of
contemporary commercial television in the United States where the
concern of the network is merely that people should watch; what
they watch is less important. The same characteristic has emerged
in the tourist industry where the issue is that people should
travel, and where is of little consequence. The book publication
industry, taken as a whole, is no better in this regard, nor is the
film industry. In the question of storage, the processes of packaging are, again, the issue, and what is packaged has become secondary.

All the above may be obvious to residents in the United
States; but what of nations where public broadcasting, film, television and publishing are not controlled by private enterprise?
Here the situation is parallel. One of the first objectives of a
new socialist revolutionary government is to make the entire population literate because whatever else reading allows, it is very
important politically. A socialist country, like any country, requires the participation of the people, and this cannot be achieved
without continual communication with them. While there are messages in this communication, the real purpose is the metacommunication to obtain political participation. In Mexico, the PRI, the
dominant national political party, is less concerned with how
people vote (because that can be fixed) than with the fact that
they vote. Participation is the means necessary for control over
participants. Mass organizations of all kinds have the same goal
(Adams 1979). The costs of political campaigns, of regulatory
agencies, bureaucracies, businesses, of all the various components,
increases and obviously requires further regulation. The increase
in regulation can be well documented in the amount of human energy
that is dedicated to political hierarchical and market activities.
This has increased from usually less than five percent to between
fifteen and twenty percent over the past century (Adams 1982).

Another way of looking at this is that high energy societies
require more energy to be expended in achieving a common culture.
What Sapir (1924) called "spurious" culture, and Levi-Strauss
(1963:366) has termed "unauthentic" culture, and Hall (1976:Chapter
7) has referred to as "low context" culture all require much greater non-human energy costs, because for them to communicate it is
necessary to create a common mental context into which the messages
may fall. The ritualization that so intrigues anthropologists
about low energy societies has a high energy counterpart that is
crucial to the regulatory process, and that is particularly mani-

fest in the communication system.

The effect of the increasing energy in the regulatory process questions Bateson's position that there is no way "to equate information and difference with energy" (1979:100). Bateson clearly recognized the relation of triggers to substantive flow: "In life and its affairs, there are typically two energetic systems in interdependence: One is the system that uses its energy to open or close the faucet or gate or relay; the other is the system of whole energy that 'flows through' the faucet or gate when it is open" (1979:102). What we must argue, however, is not that information is equivalent in any simple sense with energy, but that the two are merely aspects of <u>energy forms</u>, and that the amount and kind of energy that comprises an energy form that is used as a trigger -- or that yields information -- can have a definite influence on the work that the energy form can do, and vice versa. Information that itself requires great expenditure of quantities of energy also requires more elaborate controls.

Let us now return to the role of regulation in natural selection. A major difference between high and low energy societies is that in the former control over the energy required for regulation is much more concentrated. In low energy societies, most regulation is decentralized in the nervous systems of the members; in high energy societies a whole sector is dedicated to decisions that ultimately direct not only those individuals, but also trigger the expenditure of a great deal of non-human energy. This means that there is a large amount of energy at work in the regulatory process. This has two consequences. One is a greater inherent tendency to fluctuate. It is simply much more difficult for the discrete parts of a complex system, each dependent on its own triggers and energy sources, to perform in perfect harmony. Moreover, the mistakes in such a system are as likely to be amplified through positive feedback as they are to be dampened by negative feedback. Second, the vertical hierarchical extensions mean that regulation must operate through many more separate psychological linkages, that new information must be created at every step of the process; thus, noise or error can increase at every point. Local interaction will necessarily create autonomous authentic cultures. The increase in terrorism and aimless violence in high energy societies are such manifestations. The more controls over controls, the more triggers that depend on other triggers, the more problematic becomes overall control.

It may be argued that societies that specialize in hierarchies over market processes have a relatively superior capacity to achieve such extensive controls. But they are equally subject to the inevitable "errors" that will accompany dependency on large energy flows required for the system. Russian and American space adventures are equally vulnerable to these problems; and it might be recalled that the term "hooliganism" was borrowed by the Russian press to characterize problems of that society.

It should be recalled that natural selection is composed of a finite but unknown and unpredictable set of factors at any point in time. One reason that many of these factors have not been brought under controls exercised by the hierarchy and market processes is

that they are not understood. Another is that many elements
thought to have been brought within human control have, in fact,
lodged in the hierarchical and market macroframe. This macroframe
is itself, so far removed from the individuals who act within it
that it has effectively merged with the non-cultural forces of
natural selection. For the individual, the shift of controls from
an uncontrollable nature to an uncontrollable hierarchy and market
does not make things necessarily better. Things lodged in a macroframe are, by definition, beyond immediate control. The germs of
this process exist in the first emergence of hierarchy in society.
The moment that the functions of regulation and substantive work
were differentiated into specialties, the first step had been taken
in disassociating individuals from their own regulation. Every
expansive phase thereafter marginalized members of the society
further from the regulators, and each increasingly became unpredictable to the other. The unpredictablity was not merely a problem of different cultures, but also one of growing inabilities to
keep regulation in hand at all. From the standpoint of any single
social sector, the other components of human society merge with the
non-cultural forces of natural selection.

CONCLUSION

     The micro/macro framework is useful because culture has
enabled human beings to create social hierarchies. It is not the
social hierarchies in themselves that constitute the macroframe,
but rather their blending with the still uncontrolled forces of
natural selection. As observers we analytically differentiate
subsystems -- ecological, market, political and so forth -- but in
actual process these analytical components operate through unitary
events. The real dynamics lie in the fact that they are merely
aspects and phases of a very large living, energetic, social dissipative structure that survives only by constantly and increasingly
exploiting its environment, and sloughing off its own parts into
that environment. It is a structure that is, in Simon's terms
(1969:99-108), nearly decomposable, and therefore one which constitutes part of the environment for each of its members. This is the
core of the relationship between the macroframe and the microframe.
For the individual and the small collectivity, for the small event,
everything else constitutes a part of the natural selection process.

66

Adams, Richard N. 1975. Energy and Structure. Austin: University of
Texas Press.
_____. 1979. The structure of participation: A commentary. In
Political Participation in Latin America, Vol. II: Politics
and the Poor. Mitchell A. Seligson and John A. Booth, editors.
New York and London: Holmes & Meier Publishers, Inc. pp.9-17.
_____. 1981. "The dynamics of societal diversity: Notes from
Nicaragua for a sociology of survival." American Ethnologist
8(1):1-20.
_____. 1982. The emergence of regulatory society. In The
Future of Social Control, Jack Gibbs, ed. Los Angeles: Sage
Publishing Company. In press.
_____. ms. The Eighth Day: Society as the Self Organization of
Energy Process.(in preparation).
Bateson, Gregory. 1979. Mind and Nature. New York: E.P. Dutton.
Carneiro, Robert L. 1970. "A Theory of the Origin of the State."
Science 169(3947):733-738.
Catton, William R., Jr. 1980. Overshoot: The Ecological Basis of
Revolutionary Change. Urbana: The University of Illinois
Press.
Cavelli-Sforza, L.L. and M.S. Feldman. 1981. "Cultural Transmission
and Evolution: A Quantitative Approach." Monographs in Popula-
tion Biology 16. Princeton, New Jersey: Princeton University
Press.
Cohen Mark N. 1977. The Food Crisis in Prehistory. New Haven:
Yale University Press.
Geertz, Clifford. 1973. The Interpretation of Cultures. New York:
Basic Books.
Hall, Edward T. 1976. Beyond Culture. Garden City, New York:
Anchor Press/Doubleday.
La Barre, Weston. 1955. The Human Animal. Chicago: The University
of Chicago Press.
Levi-Strauss, Claude. 1963. Structural Anthropology. New York:
Basic Books, Inc.
Lotka, Alfred. 1922. "Contribution to the energetics of evolution."
Proceedings of the National Academy of Sciences 1(8):147-151.

McLuhan, Marshall and Quentin Fiore. 1967. The Medium is the Message. New York: Random House.

Pianka, Eric R. 1978. Evolutionary Ecology. Second edition. New York: Harper & Row, Publishers.

Prigogine, Ilya, Peter M. Allen and Robert Herman. 1977. Long term trends and the evolution of complexity. In Goals for a Global Community: The Original Background Papers for Goals for Mankind, Ervin Laszlo and Judah Bierman, editors. New York: Pergamon Press.

Sapir, Edward. 1949. Culture, genuine and spurious. In Selected Writings of Edward Sapir. David G. Mandelbaum, ed. Berkeley: University of California Press.

Simon, Herbert A. 1969. The Science of the Artificial. Cambridge, Mass.: The M.I.T. Press.

Turner, Victor W. 1969. The Ritual Process: Structure and Anti-Structure. Chicago: Aldine Publishing Company.

Wallerstein, Immanuel. 1974. The Modern World System: Capitalist Agriculture and the Origin of the European World-Economy. New York: Academic Press.

4
The Boundaries of
Rural Stratification Systems[1]

Frank Cancian

INTRODUCTION

In recent years anthropology has been host to a burgeoning interest in large socioeconomic systems. The traditional focus on the village community has faded, for it has been found to be inadequate. It is widely believed that "...communities are almost never effective isolates but are articulated with larger-scale phenomena both spatially and temporally. The community cannot be understood in isolation from the larger system, nor can the characteristics of that system be extrapolated from the community" (Johnson 1981:126). This statement was made by an archaeologist, Gregory Johnson, in an explicit effort to characterize what he sees as similar shifts in archaeology and cultural anthropology. As he suggests, the ideas are commonplace today. Most of us join Johnson in the belief that the local community cannot be understood in isolation.

This shift in academic emphasis has accompanied a wide-spread popular recognition of the interconnectedness of economic process across the world. What was once a leftist vision has become the common sense of western diplomats. Multinational corporations, international labor migration and the power of OPEC countries have become part of routine consciousness.[2]

Two things have happened in the last two decades. The interconnectedness of the world has grown, and academic consciousness of that interconnectedness has grown. For my purposes, it is important to note that the change in academic consciousness has done much more than keep up with the actual changes in the world. We have seen a revolutionary shift of attention from the village to the world. Surely in Johnson's case, where the archaeological record was laid down before the modern era, the shift to analysis that emphasizes the larger system (that is, the connections of the village to the world) is a change in approach, not a change in the object of study.

For many scholars, Immanuel Wallerstein's book The Modern World-System: Capitalist Agriculture and the Origins of the European World-Economy in the Sixteenth Century (1974) has highlighted this change in orientation. Although it had many precursors, including some in anthropology, Wallerstein's statement was bold enough to capture the attention of almost a decade of research. It has swamped any reductionist tendencies left over from psychological and microeconomic approaches, and buried them in a tide of what might be called "expansionism." Explanations that used to depend on the characteristics of component parts are now cast in terms of the characteristics of encompassing systems. That is, "micro" explanations have given way to "macro" explanations.

While I generally favor holism over reductionism, and thus often find system-oriented explanations more appealing than reductionistic ones, I believe the substantive focus (as opposed to the logic) of world-system analysis is faulty. Expansionists seem to think larger systems explain local systems. I believe local systems often have their own dynamics. Thus, I want to discuss the conditions under which such systems should be seen as bounded; that is, the conditions under which smaller systems are more relevant than larger systems.3 I will begin with Wallerstein, follow with an alternative vision that is also widely held, and then propose and discuss a framework that encompasses both of them and leads to some tentative generalizations about small, bounded stratification systems.

TWO VISIONS

Wallerstein called attention to the world-wide division of labor created with the spread of capitalism. He points out that there are few if any modern social systems that encompass all the productive activities crucial to their survival. Most are per force involved in the economic, social and cultural inequality and domination associated with world capitalism. The connections across political boundaries wrought by multinational corporations and the penetration of the most distant village by transistor radios and wage-work migration are commonly known if incompletely understood. There are no isolated villages; Johnson is correct. These are the facts of the historical present. Wallerstein documents their origin in the expansion of capitalism out from sixteenth century Europe, and tries to explain the persistence of a system that extends across many national states.

Wallerstein's enthusiasm for interconnectedness has few bounds. In the final chapter of his book he says: "What characterizes a social system in my view is the fact that life within it is largely self-contained, and that the dynamics of its development are largely internal" (1974:229). He goes on to argue (provocatively) "... that the only real social systems are, on the one hand, those relatively small, highly autonomous subsistence economies that are not part of some tribute-demanding system, and, on the other hand, world-systems" (1974:230, emphasis added). (One type of world-system, politically integrated world empires have pretty much been replaced by market integrated world economies, specifically world capitalism, according to Wallerstein.) Because few of us expect rapid growth in the number of "highly autonomous subsistence economies," we are left with world-systems, that is, with multinational social systems that have no local, regional or even national bound-

aries. Expansionism reaches its limit in these ideas. According to
Wallerstein, complete analysis demands attention to the world economy in every case.

Wallerstein has, of course, been subjected to extensive criticism (see Evans 1980 and Nash 1981 for citations), much of it
avowedly friendly, and much of it more attentive to local historical detail than Wallerstein could be. Peter Evans has summed up as
follows:

> The most cogent criticisms of the world system approach
> have come from Marxists who argue that Wallerstein's emphasis
> on the effects of the overall structure of the system have lead
> him to neglect the extent to which historically given class
> structures determine local responses to the market (1980:18).

Carol Smith's work on Guatemala (1978) exemplifies this approach in
anthropology. She has emphasized the importance of local history
and local class relations, and argued that connections to the
capitalist world-system are less important. Often convincing in
their specifics, arguments like Smith's usually turn on the persistence of pre-capitalist structures. While I believe the arguments to be historically correct, they allow the unfortunate conclusion that, with time, capitalist integration will proceed further and further until a world-wide class system is the dominant
type of stratification. I believe this is historically incorrect.4

The other vision I want to describe concentrates on the continuing existence of socially-bounded local systems within modern
capitalist societies. A number of economists and sociologists have
championed the idea that most people, whether they say so or not,
and whether they are conscious of it or not, live their everyday
lives in local systems of relationships. (It is important to
emphasize that this membership is usually measured behaviorally
rather than cognitively or subjectively).

In economics the recent history of these ideas goes back to
Duesenberry's (1962) assertion that savings rates among Americans
vary with their relative position in local communities, not with
absolute income. Others had argued that, because it is known that
rich people save a larger proportion of their income than poor
people, the country as a whole would save at greater rates as mean
income went up. Duesenberry explained the failure of that predic-
tion. He showed, for example, that black residents of New York and
Columbus, Ohio, at a given income level, could be counted on to
save more of their income than their white counterparts. But the
incomes of blacks were on the average lower than those of whites,
so a given absolute income yielded a higher rank within the black
community than the same number of dollars would yield within the
white community. When Duesenberry tied savings rate to rank within
the local ethnic community he found very similar savings rates for
blacks and whites.

This positional logic has been pursued by a number of prominent
economists in their renegade moments (see Liebenstein, Scitovsky,
Thurow) and has been discussed at length by Fred Hirsch in his book
Social Limits to Growth (1976). Richard Easterlin's (1972) compar-

ison of self-reports of happiness across countries provides another straight-forward example of this orientation. He found that well-off people in poor countries tend to be happier than equally wealthy people who are living as poor people in rich countries. This is hardly surprising. I certainly know of no rich Zinacanteco who worries much about the fact that I earn almost ten times what he does. Nor do I imagine that impoverished Americans get much comfort from the notion that they have ten times the income of a poor Bolivian. It is a truism that people care about their place in comparison with their neighbors. Whatever their place in the world division of labor, people also live in local stratification systems.

But this is a paradox. The sociologist Peter Rossi phrases it nicely in explaining what he calls the local/global distinction in stratification research. He says:

> There are many issues raised by how easy it is to confuse local stratification with societal stratification. Our economy is dominated by society-wide processes. There are scarcely any local-producer-local-consumer markets anymore. The fates of our jobs, how much we pay for food, housing, and clothing, and the desirable life experiences within our grasp are all dominated by the national economy, national government, and their connections with the world market and the global power struggle. While our fates may be determined somehow by that complex that scarcely knows distance, we enjoy or suffer the consequences locally in that restricted area encompassing our homes, jobs, family and kin, and the peculiar distributional organizations that serve that area. The stratification that counts heavily is that range of difference displayed constantly (1980:41).

The paradox remains. As Rossi suggests, neither vision dominates. On the one hand, the world-wide division of labor connects urban and rural dwellers across national boundaries. On the other hand, everyday rank and domination behavior, and its corresponding subjective experience, occurs within locally defined systems.

I believe that the apparent contradiction between these two ideas is the root cause of much confusion in the analysis of stratification systems. The basic problem is the attempt to use a single rather simple framework of any kind to approach the very diverse, complex and important phenomena encompassed by the term "stratification."[5] In an effort to dispel the confusion, I will propose a somewhat more complex framework.

AN ALTERNATIVE FRAMEWORK

My vision is easy to state and hard to apply. I will argue that Max Weber's three dimensions of stratification -- class, power and status -- are characteristically operative in systems of different sizes. Class (market position or relation to the means of production) is the most extensive, as is apparent from the strong

case that can be made for an international division of labor, i.e.
for economic articulation of the world system. Power, as Richard
Adams (1970) has argued, is best studied at the national level.
Status is a community phenomenon; that is, it operates in a local
system. The bald assertion is that class is an international
phenomenon, power a national one, and status (rank) a feature of
local systems; and that these three types of stratification are
distinguishable for the purposes of analysis.

No generalization as broad as this one could possibly be true
in all cases. The lines between categories are vague and difficult
to clearly establish. Exceptions seem to abound. Even genuine ones
are no doubt numerous. Nonetheless, the assertion provides an
orientation that is useful in the study of stratification systems.
It encompasses both Wallerstein's insight (about class) and Duesenberry's (about rank). And, I will show below that it leads to some
specific guides to the analysis of rural stratification systems.

The basic contrast that concerns me is that between class and
rank, i.e., between the central elements in the two visions discussed above. Here, I will neglect power and concentrate on this
basic contrast. I will argue for attention to local systems, or
rather against exclusive attention to larger systems as explanatory
frameworks (causal theories, if you like). And, I will argue for
distinguishing social articulation of the local system from economic articulation of the larger system.[6]

Rank,[7] or more particularly competition for rank, is usually a
local, essentially social process that often has complex economic
aspects. Class, or more particularly the opposition of classes, is
an essentially economic process that usually has important ties
outside the local setting as well as complex social aspects in the
local setting. Failure to recognize the different dynamics of rank
and class has often hampered the analysis of rural stratification
systems. I will give three diverse examples that illustrate the
usefulness of making and attending to this distinction.

Norman Long and Bryan Roberts, in their discussion of internal
differentiation among peasants in the Mantaro Valley in Peru, want
to explain why differentiation "...did not lead either to the
disintegration of village organization or to a polarization of
peasants into opposing classes" (1978:316). They see among peasants
in the Mantaro Valley the typical tripartite division of strata:
those who produce a surplus with their land and/or animals, those
who produce enough for subsistence but not enough to invest, and
those who must sell their labor in order to survive.

Why do these differences fail to produce class opposition? Long
and Roberts point out that the lines between the strata are not
sharp, that there is social and economic mobility for individual
households, and that various members in combination provide households with mixed adaptations to their economic realities. In the
face of this common situation, Long and Roberts shift back and
forth from "class" language to "strata" language in a struggle to
make the existing differentiation yield to the logic of polarization. Their understanding is rich and detailed, but in the end they
are forced to develop a complex and rather awkward explanation for
the lack of polarization -- thus following the lead of Shanin

(1972) who was moved to label similarly unpolarized Russian peasants "the awkward class."[8]

The situation Long and Roberts describe has many parallels to that of the Zinacanteco peasants in southern Mexico that I have studied (Cancian 1972, n.d.). For Zinacantan it is useful to conceptualize the recent complex internal changes in the community in terms of the cross-cutting pressures of the larger economic system and the local social system. On the one hand, Zinacanteco economic relations are being buffeted by changing government support prices for maize, opportunities for non-Indian landowners to use former maize fields for milk and meat production for the national and ultimately the international market, and labor demand on construction projects fueled by the production of nearby oilfields, among other things. On the other hand, though the transformation of money into social position in the community (Cancian 1965) is being changed by many factors including some more "class-like" internal relations, Zinacanteco social life is essentially local. As Rossi put it "While [their] fates may be determined by that complex that scarcely knows distance, [they] enjoy or suffer the consequences locally in the restricted area encompassing [their] homes, jobs, family and kin, and the peculiar distributional organizations that serve that area." Even those few that migrate long distances in search of work return to enjoy the product in their own homes -- like generations of migrants who have endured great deprivation in the larger economic system for what, it seems to me, are social aspirations back home (see Piore 1979, Chapter 3).

I conclude that the local system defines the relevant social universe of many actors whose economic fate is determined by the larger system. However, in complex, multifaceted, real situations like those in Peru and Mexico discussed immediately above, it is difficult to be sure that this analytical separation of the economic and the social (of class and rank) is really useful to the analysis. An expansionist or world-system approach could refocus the interpretation to represent the dominant themes in the local social system as reflections of the larger economic system. Thus we are left with a problem that is hard to solve with studies of single cases. How can we know that the alternative framework is more than just an alternative phrasing of the situation -- that these local social systems are, in some important sense, not derivative from the larger system? In my second example I try to speak directly to this question.

This second example is of a different sort. In my study (1979a) of more than 6,000 agriculturalists in many communities in eight countries, the complex reality of the countryside was reduced to a few simple variables in order to permit comparison across various rural populations. The basic point is simple and intuitively obvious:

The theory predicts that a low-middle-rank Iowa farmer and a low-middle-rank Punjabi peasant will behave similarly relative to their respective high-middle-rank alters, but that the Iowa and Punjabi farmers will not be important reference points for each other. It is not that Iowa and Punjabi farmers have never

heard of one another, or that they are unconnected by the world
market for agricultural products; it is rather that neither is
a crucial immediate element in the other's day-to-day process
of self-definition (Cancian 1979a:35-36).

The theory tested in my study uses rank (relative position
within the "community of reference") as the predictor of patterns
of adopting agricultural innovations (Cancian 1979a, 1981). Because the theory predicts a curvilinear relationship between rank
and adoption, it is necessary to identify the boundaries of the
local system (community of reference). Figure 4.1 shows the dangers
of misidentifying the local system. The example uses a hypothetical
valley with two villages. Each village displays the predicted
relationship between rank9 and adoption. The High Middle rank
("upper middle class") is more conservative than its economic
resources constrain it to be; it is more conservative than the Low
Middle rank. But, note that if the two villages are treated as a
single system and analyzed together the pattern of upper middle
class conservatism disappears. In order to uncover the predicted
pattern, it is necessary to first correctly specify the boundaries
of the local stratification system.

In my study, the definition of the relevant community proved to
be a crucial element in analysis of the actual data from almost two
dozen studies that I was able to collect from various researchers.
I found that when the local system (community of reference) is
carefully defined, populations as diverse as Zinacanteco maize farmers, Taiwanese rice farmers and Wisconsin dairy farmers display
similar patterns of "upper middle class" conservatism. On the other
hand, broad sampling that fails to take the boundaries of the local
system into account often obscures the pattern of upper middle
class conservatism and produces a roughly linear, positive relation
that derives from the economic constraints on adoption.10

Most of the communities that display upper middle class conservatism are economically bound to the larger system. In most
places, adoption of agricultural innovations adds to the ties local
people (especially peasants) have to the larger system, because the
innovations (seeds and fertilizers in many cases) are usually
packaged, controlled and distributed by political and economic
agencies at the national and international level. There can be no
doubt that they increase the adopter's dependence on a system of
exchange in which he is at a disadvantage. Nonetheless, my findings
show that this dependence does not destroy the local rank system.
Rank, locally defined, remains crucial to the dynamics of adoption.

Finally, as the third example, I want to briefly note that
locally defined position has potential as an explanation for the
role of rural people in events in the larger society. For instance,
are the "middle peasants" that Eric Wolf makes prime movers in
Peasant Wars of the Twentieth Century (1969) responding exclusively
to the political, economic and cultural factors Wolf introduces?
Or, as the label "middle peasants" suggests, can we reorganize his
materials in terms of local positional or rank considerations as
well? I cannot answer these questions here, but I believe they are

Figure 4.1
Potential Effects of Aggregation on Curvilinear Relationships

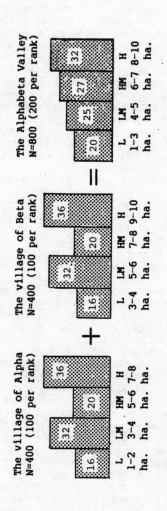

Note: The number in each bar indicates the percent of farmers of that rank to adopt in a hypothetical Stage 1. The stage is defined as the first twenty-six percent to adopt. It is assumed that, within ranks within villages, differences in hectares cultivated imply no differ-ence in innovation rate (from Cancian 1979:35).

worth asking, for a rephrasing of Wolf's argument might make local
rank the key to understanding extralocal action.

The obvious complexity of peasant-based movements of the kind
Wolf discusses is an excellent reminder that my assertion about the
most appropriate levels of analysis for class, power and rank is
not meant to cover all aspects of all situations. Nor is it meant
to deny the relevance of analyses in terms of class to many rural
situations. Rather, I hope I have shown the relevance of rank to
the analysis of many rural situations, even ones with many ties to
the world economic system, and thus have illustrated the way in
which it is useful to think of rural social systems as bounded
"communities of reference."

In general terms, I believe that class analysis is usually most
appropriate to large, economically articulated stratification systems. By class analysis I mean simply analysis of economic differentiation based on the capital that can be accumulated that fosters
polarization into owners and non-owners of the means of production.
Rank or positional analysis by contrast is most appropriate to
smaller, socially articulated systems. Rank competition involves
struggle and conflict. It is important to note, however, that these
processes need not lead to increasing polarization. This is so
because the essential resource in rank or status competition is
relative standing, not capital; and relative standing cannot be
accumulated. It is a positional good (Hirsch 1976, Cancian 1979b)
that is not subject to property relationships. The logic of polarization does not apply to it.

DISCUSSION

Having asserted the differences between class and rank, I would
like to turn briefly to other matters that will help clarify the
nature of my central assertion about systems of different sizes.
First: how does my Weberian, somewhat nomothetic, approach relate
to Marxian, historical approaches? Specifically, are there similarities between them? Second, what are the implications of taking
the rank/class distinction seriously? That is, are there any
differences between the approaches? Finally, how are the small and
the large systems considered here related to each other?

Given the long-standing incommensurabilty of historical and
nomothetic approaches, it is unlikely that any new packaging will
resolve the fundamental conflict. Each approach has strengths and
weaknesses, and each has its own way of defining reality and the
problems of knowing it. Nonetheless, they both struggle with the
same problems, and it is important to recognize their essential
complementarity so that the insights of each may advance the other.
Thus, I was pleased to find Eric Wolf's paper: "The Mills of Inequality: A Marxian Approach" (1981), for it provides another road
to a similar vision of the problems we face in analysis of the
economic, political, and status aspects of inequality.

Wolf distinguishes three fundamental modes of production. First
there is the Capitalist Mode in which monetary wealth buys labor
power, and social arrangements exclude some people from direct

access to the means of production. Second, there is the Tributary Mode, in which surplus is extracted by "other than economic processes" (quoting Marx, Wolf 1981:50), specifically by political and military means (1981:49). Finally there is the Kin-ordered Mode. The parallels are approximate but inescapable. Wolf has produced something close to class, power and status at international, national and local levels.[11]

Wolf completes the parallel to what I would like to say, when, in his closing paragraph he asserts: "In real space and time, we find particular societies embodying or combining these modes in historically or geographically distinctive forms" (1981: 55-56).[12] In my framework this means that large (economically articulated) systems may have important social aspects, and that small (socially articulated) systems may have important economic aspects, and that their combination in any given empirical situation is not routinely predictable.[13]

There are also important differences between most analyses oriented toward mode of production and those following the framework I have proposed, and these can be stated as general guides to research. I will state them without the customary qualifications.

First, there is the simple assertion that relations of production are not always superordinate. At the local level rank relations (positional considerations) have independent status and must be studied in their own terms. Expansionist approaches that seek to derive the the local system from some larger system will not adequately comprehend the local system.

Second, rank relations are characteristic of modern, urban widely-integrated societies as well as of simpler societies. Rank relations are not limited to pre-capitalist modes of production in isolated societies, nor are they fundamentally threatened by the expansion of capitalist economic articulation. While history has brought expanded and expanding worldwide economic articulation, it has not necessarily destroyed local status (rank) systems.

Third, and last, rank or positional analysis requires that we correctly identify the boundaries of the local system, for it is only relative to them that economic quantities become meaningful bits of rank behavior. The boundaries of rural stratification systems are crucial components in the study of many aspects of rank.[14]

At the same time, if the distinction between rank and class analysis that I have made is correct, then the study of small systems must attend to large systems and the study of large systems must attend to small systems. This will not be easy. When studying the nature of small systems it may help to control some of the variation in larger system influences. Thus, for example, when he set out to explain the origin of agrarian revolutions, Jeffrey Paige (1975) restricted his study to export economies, thus eliminating the complexities introduced by peasants who are principally subsistence farmers.[15] When studying large systems one must take care not to generalize across local structured heterogeneity. Thus, when he set out to explain the origin of peasant wars, Eric Wolf (1969) drew out the implications of the internal differentiation in peasant communities.

In sum, class and rank are analytically incommensurable and actually intermingled. Like so many things, they are interdependent but not responsible for each other. Thus, we cannot settle the relation of small and large systems. It requires constant attention.

NOTES

1.   An earlier version of this paper was prepared for the session on "Microlevel-Macrolevel Linkages in Anthropological Theory and Method," 80th Annual Meeting of the American Anthropological Association, Los Angeles, December 4, 1981. I am indebted to Francesca Cancian for comments on an early draft and to her, G. William Skinner, David Smith and Jonathan Turner for comments about the content.

2.   For example, on September 22, 1981, while this paper was being drafted, the Los Angeles Times reported on its first page that, in a speech to the General Assembly of the United Nations, Secretary of State Alexander Haig, "... repeated standard U.N. rhetoric, ...declaring the world's economies to be interdependent...".

3.   Barth (1978), especially the concluding essay, discusses many relevant issues from an anthropological point of view. See also DeWalt (1979) and Pelto and Pelto (1975).

4.   See the class and ethnicity literature.

5.   Here and elsewhere (Cancian 1976) I use the term "stratification" in an effort to encourage recognition of some similarities between industrial and pre-industrial societies. I have no intention to thereby prejudge the debate between those who favor "class" and those who favor "strata" in their analysis of industrial society.

6.   The term "articulation" is currently more popular than "integration" -- so I have switched to "articulation" in this paper. "Articulation" seems to contribute to the effort to avoid the functionalist implications of "integration." But the change in terminology does not solve the problems in understanding associated with the terms in recent decades. Efforts to understand the problems addressed in this paper need to take advantage of thinking about system "integration" and "levels of integration" as well as more recent work on "articulation".

7.   I am less concerned with the subjective aspects of "status honor" than is Weber.

8.   In a recent paper using data on Peruvian peasants to explicate and assess Chayanov's and Lenin's ideas on differentiation among peasants Carmen Deere and Alain de Janvry (1981) run into similar problems I think. They find clear differentiation, but it has simply not sharpened itself into anything that can usefully be called class -- see especially Table 6, page 350. As the authors point out, the data are cross-sectional, and it is thus impossible to say anything definitive about the polarization process.

Greenberg (1981) is able to make a strong case for polarization

80

and conflict in interpersonal relations.

9.   The logic of using an apparently "economic" measure like size of fields to indicate "social" rank is fully discussed in Cancian (1979a).

10.   Cancian (1981) is a detailed discussion of data on Pakistani farmers that shows how conclusions about the relation of rank and adoption vary with the definition of the boundaries of the community studied.

11.   Wallerstein's world-economies, world-empires and mini-systems (1976) offer another close parallel to Weber's three dimensions and my assertions about system size.

12.   I did not find such an emphatic statement in Wolf (1982). See, for example pages 76,77,100.

Wolf (1981) is careful to point out that, in his interpretation, the modes of production are fundamental and the relations of inequality are an accompaniment of the working out of the modes; but he finds characteristic types of inequality within each mode.

13.   At the same time I want to recall attention to an additional implication of my framework: besides implying that various aspects (modes) exist simultaneously in real situations, it implies that the appropriate level of analysis (system size) characteristically varies for each aspect (mode). Thus, the notion of a "particular society" is a problematic one in my framework, for, taking society to mean system, it is unlikely that all aspects of a situation will be bounded at the same place. Since mode of production analysis usually emphasizes the inseparability of the aspects (e.g., what I would call class, power and rank) in a situation, it should also find it difficult to handle multiple systems insofar as they are partially-overlapping. It is easy to think of actors as living simultaneously in multiple systems of different sizes. However, understanding multiple, partially-overlapping systems simultaneously remains a problem for any approach that wishes to avoid reductionist or expansionist retreats to a single level of analysis.

14.   G. William Skinner (1968) and Wolf (1960) have written (for China and Mexico respectively) excellent analyses of how and why boundaries of local systems open and close in different historical periods.

15.   For example, among the types of rural situations characterized by Stinchcombe (1961) the rank part of my rank/class distinction is clearly more appropriate to the study of family small-holding and less appropriate to the study of plantations.

I know of no sure way to predict when local situations will be dominated by class relations and when they will be dominated by rank relations. There are no doubt some clear cases somewhere, but much of the rural world is made up of people who are semiproletarians, part-time farmers, migrants and/or small holders. And, when we focus on the household rather than the individual, the mix of orientations, economic and social, of its various members often offers something for every category in even the most ambitious typology (as in the discussion of Peruvian and Mexican peasants above). At the village and regional level the real world is not apt to be pure.

BIBLIOGRAPHY

Adams, Richard Newbold. 1970. Crucifixion by Power: Essays on Guatemalan National Social Structure, 1944-1966. Austin: University of Texas Press.

Barth, Fredrik. 1978. Conclusions. In Scale and Social Organization, Fredrik Barth, ed. Oslo: Universitetsforlaget.

Cancian, Frank. 1965. Economic and Prestige in a Maya Community. Stanford, CA: Stanford University Press.

_____. 1972. Change and Uncertainty in a Peasant Economy. Stanford, CA: Stanford University Press.

_____. 1976. "Social Stratification." Annual Review of Anthropology 5:227-248.

_____. 1979a. The Innovator's Situation: Upper Middle Class Conservatism in Agricultural Communities. Stanford: Stanford University Press.

_____. 1979b. "Consuming Relationships" (a review of Fred Hirsch's Social Limits to Growth). Reviews in Anthropology 6:301-311.

_____. 1981. "Community of Reference in Rural Stratification Research." Rural Sociology 46:626-645.

_____. n.d. Proletarianization in Zinacantan. Forthcoming in Household Economies and their Transformations. Morgan Maclachlan, ed. Lanham, MD: University Press of America.

Deere, Carmen Diana and Alain de Janvry. 1981. "Demographic and Social Differentiation Among Northern Peruvian Peasants." Journal of Peasant Studies 8:335-366.

DeWalt, Billie R. 1979. Modernization in a Mexican Ejido: A Study in Economic Adaptation. New York: Cambridge University Press.

Duesenberry, James S. 1962. Income, Saving and the Theory of Consumer Behavior. Cambridge: Harvard University Press.

Easterlin, Richard A. 1972. "Does Money Buy Happiness?" The Public Interest 30:3-10.

Evans, Peter. 1980. "Beyond Center and Periphery: A Comment on the Contribution of the World System Approach to the Study of Development." Sociological Inquiry 49(4):15-20.

Greenberg, James B. 1981. Santiago's Sword: Chatino Peasant Religion and Economics. Berkeley: University of Califonia Press.

Hirsch, Fred. 1976. Social Limits to Growth. Cambridge: Harvard University Press.

Johnson, Gregory A. 1981. "Review of: Heartland of Cities by Robert Mcl. Adams." Science 213:126-7.

Long, Norman and Bryan R. Roberts. 1978. Peasant Cooperation and Capitalist Expansion in Central Peru. Austin: University of Texas Press.

Nash, June. 1981. "Ethnographic Aspects of the World Capitalist System." Annual Review of Anthropology 10:393-423.

Paige, Jeffrey M. 1975. Agrarian Revolution: Social Movements and Export Agriculture in the Underdeveloped World. New York: The Free Press.

Pelto, Pertti J. and Gretel H. Pelto. 1975. "Intra-cultural Diversity: Some Theoretical Issues." American Ethnologist 2:1-18.

Piore, Michael J. 1979. Birds of Passage: Migrant Labor and Industrial Societies. New York: Cambridge University Press.

Rossi, Peter H. 1980. "The Ups and Downs of Social Class in America." Contemporary Sociology 9:40-44.

Shanin, Teodor. 1972. The Awkward Class: Political Sociology of the Peasantry in a Developing Society: Russia 1910-1925. Oxford: Oxford University Press.

Skinner, G. William. 1968. "Chinese Peasants and the Closed Community: An Open and Shut Case." Comparative Studies in Society and History 13:270-281.

Smith, Carol A. 1978. "Beyond Dependency Theory: National and Regional Patterns of Underdevelopment in Guatemala." American Ethnologist 5:574-617.

Stincombe, Arthur L. 1961. "Agricultural Enterprise and Rural Class Relations." American Journal of Sociology 67:165-176.

Wallerstein, Immanuel. 1974. The Modern World System: Capitalist Agriculture and the Origin of the European World Economy in the Sixteenth Century. New York: Academic Press. (Citations from 1976 text edition.)

_____. 1976. "A World-system Perspective on the Social Sciences." British Journal of Sociology 27:343-352.

Wolf, Eric R. 1960. "The Indian in Mexican Society." Alpha Kappa Deltan 30:3-6.

_____. 1969. Peasant Wars of the Twentieth Century. New York: Harper and Row.

_____. 1981. The Mills of Inequality: A Marxian Approach. In Social Inequality: Comparative and Developmental Approaches, Gerald D. Berreman, ed. New York: Academic Press.

_____. 1982. Europe and the People without History. Berkeley: University of California Press.

5
Local History in Global Context: Social and Economic Transitions in Western Guatemala[1]

Carol A. Smith

INTRODUCTION

It is increasingly fashionable for anthropologists to castigate themselves (or at least to castigate other anthropologists)
for failing to take into account the larger or global processes
that affect the small communities they study. We accuse ourselves,
for example, of treating peasant communities as if they were primi-
tive isolates and of failing to consider the external forces that
created those communities and that cause them to operate the way
they do. While this accusation may be warranted for the earliest
work on peasant communities, I suggest that for quite some time now
the anthropological perspective regarding these communities has
shifted. In fact, I will argue here that many anthropologists have
been too ready to accept global views of peasant communities and
social relations without proper consideration of the interplay
between local and global processes.

When globalists assert, for example, that the present function
of peasant communities in the world economy is to supply cheap
labor to capitalist enterprises, anthropologists obligingly document how subsistence farming by peasants preserves them as a cheap
labor force (Clammer 1976). Or when a dependency theorist suggests
that the function of Latin American civil-religious <u>cargo</u> systems
(in which individuals bear the economic burden of community festivals) is to preserve relations of internal colonialism (Stavenhagen
1969), anthropologists are willing to show how celebration of
community festivals does little more than enrich oppressive merchants and priests engaged in selling liquor, candles, and masses
(Diener 1978). Those anthropologists who doggedly cling to notions
such as the "dual society," who emphasize functions of <u>cargo</u> systems that relate to local prestige, or who note the importance of
ethnic over class relations (e.g., Collier 1975) are roundly criticized for their misunderstanding of the larger dynamic in the
regions they study -- which dynamic is capitalism (see, e.g., W.
Smith 1977, Wasserstrom 1978).[2]

While I too find fault with studies of modern peasants that
ignore the interplay between international capitalism and local
adaptations, I am concerned that, in their eagerness to embrace a

global view, anthropologists will substitute a new kind of global
functionalism for the community-integration functionalism so recently discarded. In so doing, they will fail to provide an understanding of the contradictory nature of global changes, something
anthropologists are uniquely able to contribute. That is, anthropologists are usually privileged to see, and often record, how
people make their own history -- how people form local-level institutions that are often opposed to the interests of capitalism, how
these institutions are sometimes the means by which peasants or
other groups resist capitalist incorporation, and thus how they are
responsible for the particular kind of capitalism extant in peripheral social formations. Yet anthropologists remain quite one-
sided, assigning potency and causality only to the external forces.
I suspect that this one-sidedness results less from conviction than
from inability to conceptualize the other side of the process. How
does one examine and analyze a dialectical process that involves
the articulation of different layers in a multilayered system?

An obvious first step is to develop models of those structures
that mediate between the local community and the world system.
These structures include such things as regional class systems,
state and political institutions, and specific forms of production
and exchange that link the economies of small communities to the
world system. Anthropologists have generally left this task to
other social scientists. But since other social scientists rarely
understand the dynamic existing within local communities, they
describe these structures as if they came about only to meet the
needs of actors operating at the higher levels of the system --
regional elites, members of state bureaucracies, or international
capitalists. The result is an interpretation of local history in
which the masses play only a passive role. Anthropologists may not
see the masses as passive, but they do see them as responding to a
world made largely by others. They assume, in other words, that
local communities adapt to external pressures (or die out), rarely
considering the possibility that local-level processes actively
shape the larger picture.[3]

Let me use as an example of this model of adaptation a well-
known anthropological construct, relevant to the case I later
discuss, that of the closed corporate peasant community. Eric Wolf
(1957) developed this model of peasant social organization to show
how peasants reacted to the exigencies of early mercantile capitalism in Latin America and Indonesia. Wolf persuaded us that the
closed corporate community was no relic of past civilizations; it
was instead an active response to ongoing economic and political
processes. Through closure, leveling mechanisms, and corporate or
ethnic identities, peasant communities protected themselves from
the depradations of plantation or hacienda systems, the uncertain-
ties of a volatile market situation, and the dangers of internal
polarization. In so doing, peasant communities also maintained
themselves as a cheap and ready reserve of labor for the
unsteady process of capitalist expansion. Wolf's model was an
important first step toward understanding how global forces affected local-level systems.

Most of us, however, have neglected the other part of the

argument, suggested but only weakly developed by Wolf. That argument was that the organization of peasants into closed corporate communities affected in turn how the expansion of capitalism was to proceed within the social formations producing them. It cannot be accidental that wherever closed corporate peasant communities have formed, the social formations holding them have been plagued by the "agrarian problem" -- peasantries that refuse to be easily proletarianized -- as well as by countless peasant rebellions, control of the state apparatus by powerful landed oligarchies, and persistent ethnic divisions that shape the way in which regional and national political processes operate. These conditions, moreover, have produced only a weak and distorted form of capitalism, in which labor supplies must still be mobilized by force and in which the internal market is poorly developed -- at least as regards the consumption of industrial goods. Yet we tend to interpret these developments as if they were the outcomes wished by capitalism all along. This could hardly be so. Some capitalists may have wanted such an outcome, but certainly not all of them.[4]

It is much too soon to attempt a general description of how local-level processes have helped shape regional and national structures in certain types of social formation. Data are missing, especially data on the middle or regional levels of organization: how they vary and how they link to both local and higher levels. But I can attempt a first step, which is to show how various middle-level institutions, regional and national, resulted from the interplay of local and global forces in one social formation, that of Guatemala.

The sources available on Guatemala are not especially rich in the kinds of information needed to construct a history of middle-level institutions, but one is unlikely to encounter better information on any peripheral social formation.[5] One finds, on the one hand, the many standard ethnographies, contextualized as to neither time or place, that totally ignore the impact of world capitalism on the peoples under study, and, on the other, a number of world-oriented accounts which view virtually all developments within Guatemala as nothing more than aids to world-capitalist expansion. Yet, in combination, these two sources of information can be used to describe, or at least to suggest, some of the distinctive features of Guatemalan institutions, features that guided that country's particular response to global capitalism.

To orient my discussion, I have elected to use a world-system history (a generalized, composite one, in order to evaluate a position rather than an individual), for two reasons. First, it is the approach dominating anthropological discourse today, and, while no more deficient than accounts which ignore global forces as regards an understanding of peripheral formations, it is equally deficient. Second, of the two approaches available, it alone pays sufficient attention to history, and one cannot understand even local processes without some knowledge about how those processes developed through time. In the following discussion I divide modern Guatemalan history into five periods: colonial (1521-1821), early independence (1821-1871), early plantation (1871-1944), post-World War II (1944-1978), and recent (1978-1981).

What I hope to do in this brief sketch of Guatemalan history
is to capture some of the tensions and dialectic of social life in
a situation where people who had noncapitalist values and institutions confronted expanding capitalism to produce a unique historical outcome. Thus I want to show not only how capitalist expansion
affected one small local system, but also how local institutions
interacted with externally imposed forces to create a particular
dynamic that affected capitalist expansion itself. Guatemalan and
other peasants of the world were changed by the new and contradictory institutions of capitalism. So too were capitalist institutions changed by the response and resistance of Guatemalan and
other peasants to them. The revolutionary governments now in power
in many parts of the third world are only the most recent manifes-
tation of the obstacles which have arisen in the path of world
capitalism and to which capitalism has had to adapt.

THE COLONIAL PERIOD (1521-1821)

A typical global account of the colonial period in Guatemala
would make the following points:

> The Spanish conquest forcibly integrated Guatemala into an
> expanding capitalist world-system, but left the area's internal
> structures precapitalist. The region developed as a classic
> example of a dependent socioeconomic formation in which the
> various systems of production present remained dominated by and
> subordinated to the needs of an external mode, European mercan-
> tile and industrial capitalism. As a result, the local economy
> suffered an unstable alternation of subsistence farming with
> local booms incapable of sustained growth. Those of the indig-
> enous population who survived the shocks of the conquest took
> refuge in isolated highland communities structured internally
> by communal land tenure and the religio-political cargo system
> and externally by limited contact with the Ladino world. Un-
> like the Spanish of Peru, the colonizers of Guatemala made only
> limited and localized labor demands on the Indian population.[6]

Because the colonial period in Guatemala is poorly researched,
I cannot make a detailed critique of this characterization. I can,
however, raise a major problem with it. Why did the dense and
relatively productive population of western Guatemala remain as
isolated and autonomous as it did during the colonial period?
Robert Wasserstrom (1976) has shown that this was not at all the
case in neighboring Chiapas, whose indigenous population was less
dense and less productive. In Chiapas, traditional subsistence-
farming communities did not really form around cargo systems until
late in the eighteenth century. During most of the colonial period, considerable labor was taken from the Chiapas Indian communities for work on lowland plantations; because of this, communal
institutions barely survived. Ralph Woodward (1976) documents a
similar pattern to the east of Guatemala, where slavery, mining,
and indigo plantations (the latter mainly in what was to become El

Salvador) either obliterated native populations or destroyed much
of their preconquest heritage. Most scholars agree that the western highlands of Guatemala, in contrast, remained relatively neglected throughout the colonial period, even during the seventeenth
century, when Spaniards desperately sought means of finding and
holding scarce labor (MacLeod 1973:229). Most scholars also con-
cede that the economic potential of the region was as great as that
of other parts of Central America because labor was the critical
scarcity throughout the colonial period. The question is, Why was
western Guatemala neglected?

Certain preconquest features of Central America, ignored in
the global accounts, suggest an answer. We find heavy exploitation
of those Indian communities peripheral to the Quiche kingdoms, but
relative neglect of the Quiches and their immediate neighbors.
That the Quiche peoples had achieved state-level integration before
the conquest, while the more exploited groups east and west of them
had not (Carmack 1981), is not likely to be an incidental fact. In
other words, it seems plausible that the indigenous institutions of
the Quiches made possible stronger resistance to colonial labor
drafts. The Spaniards did not simply create plantation economies
where and when they wanted them, but had to adapt to local conditions, which included the variable states in which native communities organized themselves after the ravages of the conquest.

Many Spaniards left Guatemalan cities in the seventeenth century to develop small indigo farming operations. But most settled
in sparsely populated eastern Guatemala, where they had continuous
difficulties in finding sufficient labor. Most used slave labor,
raided from western Guatemala, if they had access to nonfamily
labor at all (MacLeod 1973:288-309). Why did they not settle in
western Guatemala, which was very densely populated? We cannot
assume that the lands of eastern Guatemala were more productive,
because the most successful plantation economy of Guatemala developed in western Guatemala. Nor can we assume that the colonial
authorities kept them out of western Guatemala to protect the
Indians there because the Spanish Crown, if it paid any attention
at all, frowned on the use of Indian slaves more than on any other
form of exploiting Indians. A more likely reason is that the
Indians of western Guatemala were more difficult to control unless
they were taken out of their home communities as slaves. Thus the
Spanish settlers in Guatemala, who used slavery more than any other
form of labor control, were forced by Indian resistance to contradict what has been considered a law of global capitalist expansion:
where indigenous people are abundant you use tribute extraction
methods, and only where potential labor is scarce do you use
slaves.[7]

In the western highlands the classic form of the closed corporate peasant community gradually emerged around the <u>municipio</u>. The
municipio was not an indigenous institution, nor did it closely
resemble any indigenous institution. It was a colonial administrative unit -- the lowest level political unit and the unit subject
to tribute and labor levies. The municipio was also the lowest
level unit in which the Spanish clergy operated. As many have
noted, then, this community, centered on the municipio, was a novel

structure, meeting the needs of both the colonial administratio
and the peasants subject to that administration. But this is no
to say that local institutions and local history did not play
role in the particular development of the closed corporate commu
nity in Guatemala. In fact, in Guatemala that community had sev
eral very distinctive features that were to make it more resilien
to state control than others that developed in Latin America.

In the first place, the closed corporate community develope
in western Guatemala in reaction to state taxation and authorit;
rather than as protection against hacienda encroachment or a
resistance to other kinds of land struggle. Thus it did not hav
the same functions that such communities had elsewhere. It di
not, for example, develop institutions to level differences i
internal wealth during the colonial period (MacLeod 1973; Carmacl
1979). This made it much more difficult for the state to break th
community apart later through the use of selective rewards. J
peasant community could survive without leveling mechanisms i
Guatemala during the colonial period because land was not a majo
issue then.[8] Hence there was little danger of a landless proletar
iat arising within the community if wealth (or poverty) were not
shared equally. Because the closed corporate community in wester
Guatemala did not develop as an economic entity, preserving itsel
for continuous exploitation, but rather evolved as a political
instrument wielded by, but also against, state authority, thes
Guatemalan Indians have retained greater political autonomy tha
native peoples in most parts of the world, even as they have bee
absorbed by economic systems not of their own making.

In the second place, the emergence of the municipio as a
significant unit of peasant social organization in the colonial
period did not eliminate other, more elementary, units of peasant
social organization in western Guatemala. Most municipios were
made up of several <u>parcialidades</u>, endogamous kindreds holding
rights to corporate property and usually ranked in relation to eacl
other.[9] These groups persisted as corporate units not only during
the colonial period, but up through the twentieth century, according to the documentation recently produced by Robert Carmack (1979)
and Robert Hill (1981). Thomas Veblen (1975) showed that parcialidades in several Quiche-speaking municipios continue to hold corporate property even today; Stuart Stearns and I found that these
same parcialidades also maintained important political, religious,
and marriage-regulating functions.[10]

Most anthropologists have focussed on the municipio as the
basic unit of peasant social organization in western Guatemala, to
the exclusion of other units such as the parcialidad.[11] Partly
because of this, they have been surprised regularly by the fact
that Indian ethnic identity, social traditions, and sense of community have withstood the demise of municipal institutions, such as
the cargo system. We can now help account for this anomaly with
the observation that what was perhaps the most important preconquest social institution for indigenous peasants, the parcialidad,
had a more stable existence. The parcialidad was rarely recognized
by the colonial or other Guatemalan states and thus -- unlike the
municipio -- was much less subject to direct state manipulation.

When the municipio lost its closed corporate character (because the state wished to place new demands on the peasantry), Indian communities were still able to regroup around more elementary institutions with little or no difficulty.

In summary, several institutions were important for preserving a peasant community in western Guatemala. Through the parcialidad, Indian peasants held onto much of their land, their communal institutions, and their ethnic identity. And through municipal institutions such as the cargo system, Indian peasants developed a political strategy that allowed them to struggle with some success against the more outrageous demands of the colonial authorities. None of these developments was to turn them into an especially pliable labor force for the future. On the contrary, the preservation of the indigenous community represented the greatest barrier to capitalist development throughout Guatemalan history.

THE CONSERVATIVE INTERLUDE (1821-1871)

Guatemala achieved independence from Spain in 1821 and carried out the institutional reforms necessary for establishing a major export-oriented plantation economy in 1871. The period between these two years is ignored in most global accounts of Guatemalan history, which usually slide over the chaos of the early independence period as follows:

> Political independence did not immediately alter established relations. Rather, it was the shift to large-scale coffee production which revolutionized Guatemala. Triumph of the Liberals in 1871 threw the full weight of the state behind the new export, and production rose dramatically, as did demand for peasant labor.

From this account, we would assume that 1871 was the period in which export production of plantation crops was first considered by Guatemalan capitalists; we would also assume that it was a fairly simple matter to develop that economy, given Guatemala's abundant supply of peasant labor. In fact, however, Guatemala was very slow to develop coffee plantations; Costa Rica had begun coffee production on an intensive scale as early as 1830 (Cardoso 1975). Why was Guatemala so slow?

In this little-discussed period of Guatemalan history, peasant interests were partly in the ascendancy; their interests were represented by the Conservative regimes that held power between 1837 and 1871. The Liberals, who advocated capitalist expansion in Guatemala, were the first rulers of independent Guatemala. And they attempted to do in the 1820s and 1830s precisely what Rufino Barrios was able to do in the 1870s. Their program involved (1) the establishment of a direct head tax, reminiscent of the tribute collected by the Spaniards, which had been abolished immediately following independence; (2) heavy demands on peasant labor for the development of roads and ports; (3) the suppression of the Church tithe (some of which had aided the destitute) and the abolition of

many religious holidays; and (4) a land policy that promoted private acquisition of public and communal lands as a means of
increasing production (Woodward 1971). The peasant response to
these programs was rebellion. A major popular uprising, described
by some as a race war, began in eastern Guatemala and gathered
support from peasants throughout the country.[12] The leader of this
revolution was Rafael Carrera, a former peasant who became
president-for-life of the new Guatemalan republic in 1854. Conservatives stayed in power through 1871.

Most liberal historians of Guatemala have described the
Carrera regime as one wherein traditional mercantile interests won
out over liberal capitalism. They make little mention of the fact
that it was the peasants who were largely responsible for retaining
conservative regimes in power, these peasants being considered mere
tools of the conservative Church. But recent historical work on
this period (Woodward 1971; Miceli 1974; Ingersoll 1972) has established that a peasant revolution put Carrera into power, that
Carrera represented peasant interests more than those of any other
group, and that the major consequence of Carrera's regime was the
prevention of fifty years of the capitalist development of Guatemala. There was no lack of capitalist interest during Guatemala's
conservative interlude, but there was considerable resistance to
capitalist enterprise by peasants who presumably preferred autonomy
to national integration. And for at least fifty years, the interests of international capitalism were not served in Guatemala.

It is difficult to demonstrate that the tardiness of capitalist development in Guatemala, brought about by peasant resistance,
had a major impact on the kind of development that was to ensue.
But in the following section I will show how the system of plantation agriculture adapted to the continuing problem of insufficient
labor supplies. I will also discuss the development of certain
other institutions -- marketing, urban, and political -- which must
be seen as other accommodations to local-level systems. These
institutions continue to affect capitalist development in Guatemala.

THE COFFEE PLANTATION PERIOD (1871-1944)

Ultimately, capitalist interests did triumph in Guatemala, and
coffee plantations had transformed the national and local economies
profoundly by the end of the nineteenth century. The Liberal
regime of Rufino Barrios, which began in 1871, eventually carried
out the reforms necessary for the transformation that the earlier
Liberals had tried to impose. The pattern of the reforms is described in the global accounts along the following lines:

> The new government legislated and policed systems of habilita-
> cion (debt servitude), mandamiento (forced labor), and vagracy
> laws and facilitated the transfer of communal village lands
> into private, usually Ladino, hands. Village autonomy shat-
> tered, and the Indians were forced down into the coffee fields.
> Wages could be kept depressed because of the absence of a free

market for labor and because wage income did not have to pay
the full cost of labor maintenance/production. Coffee's seasonal demand for large amounts of labor released the Indians
for much of the year to support themselves as best they could
on their shrinking highland plots.

What made possible in the 1870s that which was impossible in
the 1830s? No anthropologist or historian has tried to answer this
question because all have taken it for granted that global rather
than local factors were responsible for the transformations. But I
suggest that only by considering what were the internal dynamics of
peasant communities during the Carrera period can we understand why
Barrios's liberal program did not evoke the widespread, violent,
and effective opposition of Indian communities that had occurred
earlier. While I have no direct evidence as to changes that took
place in Guatemala's peasant communities in the nineteenth century,
I am willing to hazard some guesses based on contemporary travellers' accounts[13] and on what we know about peasant communities from
anthropological studies undertaken in the early part of the twentieth century.

Anthropologists who worked in Guatemala in the 1930s, e.g.,
Ruth Bunzel (1952), Sol Tax (1953), and Charles Wagley (1941), as
well as their associates Raymond Stadelman (1940) and Felix McBryde
(1947), describe the maintenance of certain traditional features of
the closed corporate community during this period, especially of
the civil-religious cargo system. But they also note the considerable involvement of the peasantry in markets and a cash economy
(travellers' accounts indicate that this began in the nineteenth
century), the importance of wage income for peasant subsistence,
and the impact of the replacement of communal land tenure systems
by holdings under private title. Two transformations of the peasant community stand out in particular: the development of significant differentiations according to wealth, wherein poorer individuals came to work for wages from richer individuals within the
community, and the development of a vigorous regional marketing
system manned primarily by indigenous merchants, who traded international imports as well as local commodities and who helped ease
peasants out of their exclusive preoccupation with agriculture. It
is not entirely clear when these changes occurred.[14] But these two
developments, which shook the foundations of the closed corporate
community, may well have begun before the implementation of forced
labor drafts for plantation needs and have resulted instead from
the increased commercial opportunities for some of the peasants in
the region during the Carrera years.

At the same time, the anthropologists of the 1930s did not
ignore the impact of plantation labor on peasant communities. All
of them describe the abuses of the labor enganche system, through
which poor Indians were given advance payment of wages, often
during festivals and while drunk, that had to be worked off on the
plantations. Most observe that whereas poorer peasants had to seek
wage labor on plantations, richer peasants were absolved from this
necessity. Most also discuss chicanery on the part of plantation
agents, who were often assisted by wealthy or powerful local peas-

ants, but they describe little forcible implementation of the labor draft laws. We can take the position that these anthropologists simply refused to see the larger dynamic. Or we can use their accounts to construct a pattern whereby local changes in the native communities assisted plantation expansion, as follows.

It seems likely that the conservative Carrera regime allowed a period of economic expansion among peasants the like of which they had never experienced before. Local production specialization and commerce were expanding during a period when tribute and labor drafts on native people were lighter than ever. Under these circumstances, the peasant communities of the western highlands opened up to an unprecedented degree, and this opening was accompanied by a great deal of economic differentiation within the communities. Some peasants became much wealthier than others and these were the people who were most likely to exercise local political power, rather than the traditional elders. Such leaders had their own instead of their community's interests in mind, and they were much less likely to be revolutionary leaders than were their more traditional predecessors.

Among other important developments during the expansive Carrera years were (1) a high rate of population increase in the native communities, brought about by improved material conditions (Veblen 1975); (2) breakup of the extended patriarchal family, brought about by, and exacerbating, economic differentiation (cf. Collier 1975); (3) decentralization of the corporate community through the movement of many peasant families to remote rural areas and to other communities (cf. Davis 1970), and (4) the loss of some urban monopolies held by Spaniards and urban Ladinos, which led to greater economic opportunities for some Indians and to greater spatial mobility for many Ladinos.[15] All of these developments undermined the corporate nature of the peasant community. The private titling of lands, a process begun with independence and reaching a fever pitch by the end of the nineteenth century, dealt only the final blow. By the first decade of the twentieth century, Indian communities had lost about half of the lands they traditionally claimed during the colonial period. But not all Indians were passive victims of this onslaught. Most Indian communities managed to survive, holding on to some land (though much less than was rightfully theirs) by obtaining both individual and group titles.[16] Thus while the titling of land destroyed the material base of the corporate peasant community, it did not destroy a land-based peasantry.

The Barrios reforms were successful, then, because of certain changes that had already taken place within the indigenous communities. That is, Barrios was able to move this vigorously against the peasantry because by the time he did so, these acts would have been differentially perceived within the local communities. Only the poorest members of Indian communities were forced into plantation labor, not all of them. Only Indian traditionalists lost political power, not all Indians. Only native customs that stood in the way of migratory labor movement needed to be suppressed, not all native customs. Needless to remark, the changes that ensued in native communities ultimately disadvantaged the entire community.

But once opened and differentiated, the indigenous communities simply could not put up the resistance they did when closed and corporate.

There is another and equally important reason why the Barrios reforms were successful. Barrios, unlike his predecessors, used great caution in acting against the native communities and did not assault them all at once. According to David McCreery, who documents the Liberals' successes and failures of the nineteenth century,

> Barrios, who understood Indian attitudes better than many of his supporters, rejected [certain] request[s] for levies of forced labor, fearing both the disruption of the coffee labor supply and the real possibility of an Indian revolt. Quick to quash isolated opposition to his authority, he consistently avoided antagonizing the indigenous majority unnecessarily (1976:450).

As McCreery argues the case, it was more efficient to attack communal land tenure and to assault the individual (and poorer) peasant than to impose a general head tax or massive labor conscription. Playing on the internal differentiation that had taken place within native communities was the key to Barrios's success. While the accommodation to potential peasant resistance assisted in the transformation of many indigenous institutions, it also helped maintain certain other features of native communities, and of native resistance, that were later to work against the aims of capitalist development in Guatemala. McCreery puts it this way:

> The spread of coffee cultivation in Guatemala generated fundamental structural change not because it represented a transition to a new capitalist mode of production; reliance upon extra-economic coercion continues today to characterize Guatemalan owner-laborer relations. Rather, the expansion of coffee production was the first instance in Guatemala of the penetration of commercial agriculture into the fiber of indigenous society (1976:459).

The main failure of the Liberal program, then, was its inability to create a free wage-laboring class, the necessary ingredient for capitalist agriculture. This was not a premeditated failure, designed to keep labor cheap, for as McCreery's documentation makes clear, the Guatemalan elites wished to create a full-fledged proletariat. They even tried unsuccessfully to import such a class from Europe and the United States by offering comparatively high wages in the international labor market. Meeting little interest abroad and strong resistance at home, these nineteenth-century Liberals were unable, not unwilling, to make a successful transition to a capitalist mode of production. It remains to delineate some of the social and political consequences of this failure.

McCreery mentions one of the consequences, the development of large <u>latifundia</u> for export production, a system which supported a very small oligarchy. Large holdings were not the only or even the most efficient way to grow coffee for export; Costa Rican producers grew coffee for export on much smaller holdings and have always produced coffee more efficiently in terms of both land and labor. Nor were latifundia remnants of the colonial past; before coffee production, few large properties existed in Guatemala. Large holdings developed in Guatemala because of the labor problem: only large producers had enough political power to obtain forced labor, which was supplied by the state, and enough economic power to afford the production inefficiencies that use of forced labor entails.

Large operations required large amounts of initial capital, a scarce resource in nineteenth-century Guatemala. Much of the capital came from the outside, mainly from German merchants, which tied Guatemalan coffee production to one particular market and which allowed the Germans to control a good deal of Guatemalan production (Jones 1940:206-8). As it turned out, the German presence was not to have longstanding repercussions because the events of World War II allowed Guatemalans to expropriate most of the German holdings. Thus the development of large export-oriented plantations did not lead to foreign domination of production, a national problem that has a readily apparent solution. The development of large plantations, which relied on cheap forced labor and imported capital, led to certain other consequences, much more difficult to eradicate and holding much longer-term consequences for Guatemala's social and political history. The consequences were these: first, Guatemalan plantation agriculture remained undercapitalized, inefficient, and tied to relatively few crops from 1871 on; second, a small oligarchy, the latifundists, came to dominate Guatemalan politics from 1871 on; and, third, a highly centralized state apparatus developed in order to assist in the acquisition of both capital and labor, and this apparatus was to grow only stronger and more rigid after 1871.

Some of the political consequences of oligarchic control over a highly centralized state are fairly obvious. One need only point to the political histories of Guatemala and El Salvador, where this pattern emerged, as opposed to that of Costa Rica, where it did not. All three countries became dependent on export coffee production in response to global forces in the latter half of the nineteenth century. But Costa Rica became a showcase for democratic political institutions within Latin America, while Guatemala and El Salvador have had strongly centralized, repressive regimes from the beginning of the export era to the present. The oligarchies developed where peasant labor had to be coerced; the democratic regime developed where small holders produced coffee with a free labor force.[17]

Other political consequences are less obvious, partly because they depend upon what happened to the other classes in society. In El Salvador, for example, the coffee economy gradually absorbed most of the peasantry (though not without bloodshed), because plantations could be established only where peasants already lived (Cardoso 1975). Because most peasant holdings were expropriated, proletarianization of the Salvadorean peasantry was advanced considerably over that evolving in Guatemala. From the 1930s, which saw the great _matanza_ or slaughter of El Salvador's peasants, Salvadorean politics have reflected an ongoing struggle between a full-fledged working class (whose members retain few traces of their Mayan heritage) and a small but highly unified oligarchy.[18]

The situation was different in Guatemala. Peasants remained a distinct class in Guatemala and retained an ethnic identity separate from that of nonpeasants, at least in western Guatemala. And in the region where peasants resided, another distinctive class remained as well, an urban Ladino class.[19] Urban Ladinos never had the political clout of the plantation oligarchy, but they did hold considerable sway over or within many Indian communities and they helped shape the direction that economic structures took outside the plantation economy. The combination of a small, but entrenched, urban Ladino class (which controlled certain aspects of internal commerce and local-level political administration) and an even smaller and much more powerful plantation oligarchy (which directed the state apparatus) with a very large and ethnically distinct rural population (which held onto a community-centered way of life) produced in Guatemala three regional structures unique in Central America.

First, Guatemala was the only republic to develop (in the western region only) a dense, competitive, rural marketing system whose traders were almost entirely rural peasants. Elsewhere in Central America, small towns, which were also administrative centers, remained the centers for trade between rural and urban producers. The small-town pattern helped link rural producers to the national economy and to regional elites more than to each other; it also preserved a very heavy reliance on agricultural activities among the rural people. The Guatemalan pattern, however, allowed many peasants to lessen their dependence upon agriculture without requiring them to move to towns and cities where they would have been more fully integrated into national culture. This fostered the retention of ethnic divisions in western Guatemala. The rural marketing system developed in western Guatemala at the same time the plantation system was imposed. I surmise that a rural marketing system arose because the urban commercial classes could not make their marketing practices, based on monopoly, serve the consumption needs of plantations as efficiently as could peasant traders in competition with one another. Thus when the Liberals, who represented plantation interests, ousted the Conservatives, who represented urban Ladinos among other groups, they allowed rural marketplaces to flourish. In so doing, they divided and weakened their political opposition, for on most other issues urban Ladinos and rural peasants were united in opposition to the Liberals.

The second difference from the typical Central American pattern concerns the political position of Guatemala's urban-based regional elites. In most of Central America, regional elites had some commerical monopolies, but they also owned most of the land on which peasants worked. Through patron-client ties and direct economic coercion, regional elites were able to mobilize local support to gain national power. Thus Central American politics usually revolved around plural interest groups, aligned in vertical segments; moreover, the potential power of regional elites always

conditioned the power of the state. In Guatemala, however, regional elites had no local-level power base.[20] The enormous social and
cultural gulf between Indians and Ladinos prevented patron-client
ties from linking rural groups to regional interest groups, and
Guatemala's regional elites rarely had the degree of economic
control over peasants that was typical of the elites in the rest of
Central America. On the other hand, Guatemala's regional elites
were of great importance to the state in controlling the masses
through political means. Nor did the state prevent these elites
from intimidating, exploiting, or expropriating from peasants in
any way they could -- as long as they did not instigate serious
rebellion or threats to state power. This treatment, of course,
exacerbated the polarization between Indians (most of the rural
people) and Ladinos (most of the urban people and the only people
holding state offices); it also prevented the development of plural
interest groups aligned in vertical segments, and created instead a
nationwide horizontal segmentation between the peasants and the
state; and it allowed all political power to concentrate in a
highly centralized state. Regional elites were merely granted
state power through appointment to political office; they could not
challenge state power by mobilizing local support -- state-granted
power was the only power they had.[21]

Because of the limited strength of regional elites, then, the
plantation oligarchy in Guatemala became the national elite and the
power of this small group was rarely contested by any other group.
El Salvador also developed a powerful plantation-based oligarchy,
but its oligarchy was less removed from the masses because El
Salvador's plantation system, unlike Guatemala's, encompassed the
entire country. In fact, El Salvador's plantation oligarchy carried out the same political functions as Guatemala's urban Ladinos
and at the same time tied the peasants to them in relations of
personal dependency.

The third distinctive feature of Guatemala, which follows from
the other two, was its urban system. All urban population growth
and most economic infrastructure became concentrated into a single
city, the national capital, while provincial towns that had previously mediated between the national and local levels, both economically and politically, languished. Only Costa Rica developed
an equally top-heavy urban system. But in Costa Rica, a much
smaller country, most of the rural population lived within easy
reach of the capital city, even by foot. In Guatemala, dense rural
populations were far outside the sphere of the national capital.
The direction taken by Guatemala's urban system not only fostered a
greater disparity in income distribution than that of any other
Central American republic, but also led to increasing problems of
political control.[22]

Guatemala's three distinctive sociopolitical patterns, derivative of the plantation economy established in 1871, were not fully
realized until after World War II. I therefore delay elaboration
on their consequences until the following section. For now, I sum
up the consequences of plantation agriculture apparent to the
observer in the early 1940s, the end of the period under discussion
here.

An accommodation had been reached between plantation development and native-community development, which must be seen as a real
accommodation rather than the result of the will of capitalist
expansion. Plantations obtained labor from native communities for
meager wages by tapping the labor of poorer families on a seasonal
basis; native communities held on to diminished community land, now
mostly privately titled, and made up in wage labor, artisanry, and
commerce what they had lost in agricultural self-sufficiency. The
Ladino plantation-owner class gained peasant labor, but the Ladino
urban merchants lost many of their commercial monopolies. Rural
peasants over-all lost autonomy and self-sufficiency, but some of
them gained new possibilities for obtaining an income. Large-scale
export agriculture was established in the lowlands, but it was not
capitalist agriculture; force was still required to obtain labor.
What was irretrievably lost was the old colonial system of tribute
extraction, along with its complement, the closed corporate peasant
community. Yet the basis for peasant resistance was not destroyed.
It only changed.

THE FREE WAGE PERIOD (1944-1978)

The global, and most widely accepted, view of Guatemala during
the period following World War II is that peasants became significantly more impoverished and that the short-lived reform government
that initiated the era had little impact on the continuing sway of
external forces over Guatemala's internal pattern of development:

> Partial integration of the indigenous population into the ex-
> port economy through wage labor acted to preserve the peasant
> community. The community persists not because of isolation or
> cultural resistance, but because the contradictory effects of
> expanding world capitalism are such as to reproduce as well as
> erode precapitalist formations. Precapitalist modes of produc-
> tion serve capitalism in a number of ways. Indigenous peasant
> communities reproduce labor power cheaply and can be coerced
> into making it available as needed by the more advanced sectors
> of the economy. These communities also supply cheap goods and
> services through a market not dependent on industrial wages.
> And while the village functions to pump cheap labor into the
> migratory circle, the money the laborers earn there also plays
> an important role in sustaining and reproducing the community
> itself by permitting an ecological balance and population den-
> sity much above that which could be sustained with available
> land. When Guatemala's reform government (1944-1954) chal-
> lenged the material base of the economy by threatening to
> institute land reform, it had to go.

The reform government did accomplish one thing; it abolished
in 1945 all forced labor laws in Guatemala. Plantation owners
shrieked that their enterprises would be jeopardized, that they
would be unable to obtain necessary labor; but labor materialized
on plantations without much of a hitch in response to the mere

offering of a very low minimum wage. Nor did the basic pattern of
seasonal labor dependence of both the peasant and plantation economies undergo any major change. If anything, plantation owners
were able to utilize more seasonal labor (as opposed to permanent
wage labor) than ever before -- at least through the 1960s (Schmid
1967). Thus the "free wage" era involved minimal disruption of the
symbiosis existing between plantations and peasant communities. In
fact, the short period of sociopolitical reform in Guatemala merely
brought about a deepening of capitalist relations of production in
agriculture by allowing the market rather than the government to
deliver labor to plantations. It did not, however, eradicate the
increasing contradiction between the peasant economy and plantation
agriculture.

I shall not attempt to explain what brought on Guatemala's
abortive reforms of 1944-1954 because it is not necessary for my
discussion and others have thoroughly covered it (see especially
Jonas 1974; Wasserstrom 1975). Suffice it to say that most ana-
lysts did not believe it represented an entirely new direction for
Guatemala's economic system or its political system; it represented, instead, a power struggle within Guatemala's national bourgeoisie. The reformers, who represented the petite bourgeoisie,
wanted a share of the wealth and power held by the plantation
oligarchy. The established bourgeoisie, who were mainly plantation
owners, did not want to share. The struggle between these two
groups did allow a third power, the United States, to enter the
scene more actively, and from 1954 on, the United States was to
play an increasingly important role in Guatemala's internal affairs. But the struggle between the principal groups did not have
a significant impact on the peasantry.[23]

Anthropological opinions differ about the nature of the reform
govenment but not about the negligible impact of the reforms it
instituted on local peasant communities. Richard Adams (1957) and
Robert Ebel (1957) document for several indigenous communities the
process whereby Indians contested local Ladino municipal control.
Most of these anthropologists conclude that the local Indian leadership squandered in factional rivalry the opportunity to take
greater charge of their local affairs. Wasserstrom (1975), who has
recently reviewed the materials produced by Adams (1957) and Ebel
(1957), suggests otherwise. He argues that the goals of the reform
government never converged with those imagined to exist in native
communities, that it hoped only to develop a strong and independent
form of capitalism based on peasant labor (not a new social order
freeing peasants of capitalism's thrall). He also argues that the
condition of the Indian communities was long past what could be
seen as representing a single unified interest. Wasserstrom summarizes his thesis as follows:

Ethnic stratification in rural Guatemala was not a particularly
tenacious and long-lived form of European feudalism, as most
Guatemalans believed. Having emerged during the early
twentieth century as a consequence of economic development, in
the highlands it had fragmented Indian society into a series of
incipient social classes. One signal effect of fragmentation

was apparent in the revolution: prosperous Indians made common cause with those conservative politicians in Guatemala City who shared their desire to contain, not expand, the process of agrarian reform (1975:178).

But while anthropologists differ about the potential of the reform government for effecting reform at the local-community level, they are of one voice on the new character of the local communities. They agree that with few exceptions the last institutional remnants of the closed corporate community had now disappeared, most notably the civil-religious cargo system. They also agree that wealth and social differentiation were significant factors in local-level politics and that market dependence (whether for wages or for the sale of commodities) was well developed everywhere. As for the level of peasant welfare, anthropologists document two contradictory trends; one of increasing poverty and one of increasing wealth.

Waldemar Smith's (1977) study of three communities in the western department of San Marcos describes both patterns. Smith found that differentiation <u>within</u> communities was not nearly so marked as differentiation <u>among</u> communities: one community he describes was almost totally impoverished, sending more than eighty percent of its adult male labor force to the plantations seasonally in order to make ends meet; another community was doing very well on the whole, relatively few of its people needing to seek plantation wages in order to maintain a satisfactory level of living. What distinguished these communities was not so much the amount or quality of land retained, but rather access to commercial and artisanal occupational alternatives.

My 1968-1970 work on the regional marketing system (1976, 1978) showed this division of Indian peasant communities to be general. Those Indian communities in the western highlands that were located near major urban centers of the region (especially in the departments of Totonicapan and Quezaltenango) had more diverse occupations, more access to capital, and better standards of living than communities located in the northwestern periphery of the region (especially San Marcos, Huehuetenango, and northern Quiche). Dependence on income from seasonal labor on plantations followed the same division: communities in the northwestern periphery exported upwards of fifty percent of their adult labor force to the plantations seasonally, whereas communities in the core of the regional marketing system exported less than ten percent. Obviously, then, it is incorrect to describe as general a pattern of increasing impoverishment of peasant communities in this period, though one could point to increasing penetration of market relations into the fiber of indigenous society.

An apparent effect of the division of the region into poorer and richer communities was the slowing down of the process of internal differentiation within the communities. Thus John Watanabe (1981) observes that the pattern of land distribution in Santiago Chimaltenango (a peripheral community), documented earlier by Wagley, was less uneven in the 1970s than in the 1930s, even though all indications at the time of Wagley's study (1941:81-83) pointed in the opposite direction. I have found the same to be true of Totonicapan (a core community), even though the research I carried out there in 1977-1978 was motivated by the hypothesis that peasant differentiation in that community would be on the increase. What accounts for this anomaly?

One of the unanticipated effects of the plantation economy for peasants is that many of the poorer peasants either became completely proletarianized and remained in the plantation area, thus relieving population pressure on the peasant community, or they returned with enough savings to begin small businesses, take up trade, or otherwise find new outlets and sources of income for themselves (See Wagley [1941:51,78-79] for a description of this latter phenomenon even in the earlier period when plantation wages were much lower). Nearly half of the present petty commodity producers I interviewed in Totonicapan in 1977-1978 had obtained part or all of their initial capital from plantation work or from trade in the plantation area. And the percentage of people who took up specialized (nonagricultural) occupations in Totonicapan had more than doubled in the period between 1945 and 1978. Thus a fairly significant number of peasants in Guatemala found in the plantation economy the means by which they could hold onto a peasant way of life. Plantation work was never a preferred occupation anywhere. But the plantation economy, both directly and indirectly, helped many peasants retain their peasant holdings and invest in measures that made their lands produce more than twice as much as they did before.[24]

So far, the argument presented here does not contradict that of the global account, which suggests that peasant communities were better maintained by dependence on plantation labor than they would have been without the economic outlet. The global account, however, suggests that economic dependence on plantation labor should be on the increase and should be associated with both increasing internal differentiation of communities and increasing poverty of Indian communities in general. And here my data contradict the global view. In my 1977-1978 survey of 131 communities (rural hamlets) in the western highlands of Guatemala,[25] I found that fewer and fewer people were able to make a living from subsistence farming, as one would expect. But the slack was not taken up by increased participation in plantation labor; it was taken up by increased participation in occupations outside of agriculture altogether.

Table 5.1 presents data on male primary occupations (most individuals had more than a single occupation) from my survey of 1,341 males in peripheral communities, 1,556 males in core communities, and 1,263 males from communities in the intermediate zone. My survey shows that only 32.5 percent of all males reported their major occupation to be in any form of agriculture -- whether subsistence farming (thirteen percent), local wage-labor in agriculture (11.4 percent), or in plantation wage-labor (8.1 percent). (Most male respondents, however, reported a secondary or tertiary occupation in agriculture). Nearly ten percent reported some plantation work in association with another primary occupation, and eight percent claimed it as their primary occupation, which yields

Table 5.1
Primary Occupations of Indian Males in Rural Guatemala, Percentage
Distribution by Type of Community

	Core Communities (n=1,341)		Peripheral Communities (n=1,556)		All Communities (n=4,160)	
Agriculture		18.5%		37.9%		32.5%
Subsistence	9.4%		10.7%		13.0%	
Local-wage	7.8		13.0		11.4	
Plantation-wage	1.3		14.2		8.1	
Commerce		20.7		14.1		16.8
Manufacture		53.8		35.6		41.1
Crafts	5.4		7.9		7.0	
Artisanry	25.1		15.7		18.8	
Crafts-wage	0.7		0.9		0.9	
Artisanry-wage	22.6		11.1		14.4	
Construction		5.6		12.3		8.9
Building	4.1		8.8		6.1	
Building-wage	1.5		3.5		2.8	
Other		1.2		0.1		0.8
Services	0.5		0.1		0.5	
Government	0.7		–		0.3	

Note: This table is based on a stratified random sample from my
1977-1978 survey of rural occupations in the western highlands of
Guatemala which covered a representative 131 rural hamlets. Procedures for obtaining this information are described in note 24. I
do not give a breakdown of the 1,263 individuals from intrmediate
communities here.

a total of eighteen percent of males ever employed on plantations
These figures were much lower than I had expected from my earlier
survey (1969-1970),[26] in which thirty to forty percent of adult
males worked seasonally on plantations and more than fifty percent
were also employed in local peasant agriculture.

The difference between the core and peripheral zones remained
marked, with only 1.3 percent of the core males dedicated primarily
to plantation work (less than five percent working on plantations
at all during the year) and only 18.5 percent primarily engaged in
any form of agriculture, while 14.2 percent of peripheral males
made most of their income from plantation work (twenty-four percent
working on plantations at some point in the year) and nearly
thirty-eight percent were primarily engaged in some form of
agriculture.

The more recent survey year, 1977-1978, can be considered a
"good" year for peasants. Reconstruction after the major 1976
earthquake provided more local employment than was normally available. But the difference between a good year and a bad one would,
according to local estimates, affect only about ten percent of the
population. Both individuals and communities generally reported a
much lower dependence on plantation income than was formerly the
case. Communities that in the 1960s had exported upwards of sixty
percent of their adult male population to work on plantations were
now sending as few as ten to fifteen percent.

What were the new income sources for these peasants? They
were derivative of the new kind of commercial distribution system
in the peasant highlands, described earlier. This system emerged
during the early years of independence, it expanded alongside the
plantation economy in order to keep it supplied, and it boomed
throughout the period under discussion here, fueled by modern
transportation, urbanization, and the increased cash incomes of
peasants and workers in the region. By the beginning of the free
wage era in the mid-1940s, the new commercial distribution system
had eroded all the Ladino commercial monopolies to the point that
rural market centers rather than Ladino-controlled urban centers
accounted for most of the commerce. The initial impetus for this
development came from the plantation economy, but by the end of the
period under discussion, a fair amount of the peasant production
was intended for urban as well as rural demand. The fastest-
growing cottage industry was tailoring, the market for which was
not only peasant Guatemala but also the working and middle classes
of Guatemala City.

Because peasants had developed a variety of ways to cope with
the increasing penetration of market relations into their communities, there can be no single characterization of their stratagems. One can argue, however, that certain expectations for this
period were not realized: there was no general trend toward increasing dependence on plantation wages, no general impoverishment,
relatively little internal class polarization, and much less destruction of indigenous community organization than would be expected from the usual accounts of the period. The closed corporate
community no longer existed, but in any event it had expired much
earlier. Yet, contrary to anthropological expectation, social

relations within indigenous communities remained coherent -- organized by the traditional values of formal courtesy, reciprocity, and respect for age, hard work, and properly accumulated wealth -- even without the cargo system and the other institutional devices of the closed corporate community. Indians in both poorer and richer zones maintained a steadfast stance of preserving cultural if not economic or political autonomy, and the assimilation process that had produced the Ladino culture elsewhere made little progress in the highlands.[27]

Let me turn to two other developments in the region that furthered the economic and political independence of indigenous communities, but which also hid them from view. As noted in the previous section, Guatemala's regional elites, the urban-based Ladinos, held a peculiar political and economic position. On the one hand, they were important to the state in controlling the peasant areas and held virtually all state-granted political offices. On the other hand, they had no local-level political base by which they could gain state power and through which they could influence state policy. The plantation oligarchy, domiciled in Guatemala City, was virtually the only group guiding state policy. Holding political office in a peasant area was lucrative only insofar as it could provide an official with the means to maintain commercial monopolies or otherwise obtain income from peasants. But as the Ladinos' commercial monopolies, such as control of transportation, were gradually eroded by intense competition from rural Indian commerciantes, and as some wealthy peasants gained the education to enter traditional Ladino occupations (law, medicine, education), the economic position of the Ladinos began to deteriorate seriously. And urban Ladinos began migrating in large numbers to Guatemala City, the only place where alternative sources of income were available.[28]

Normally, one would expect successful or wealthy peasants simply to replace the urban Ladino group as their new lifestyles diverged from that of a typical peasant. But because most peasants were Indians, and because the social and political gulf separating Indians and Ladinos remained constant, relatively few Indians became Ladinos or abandoned their native communities.[29] Thus the number of people remaining in peasant areas upon whom the state could depend to help carry out its political objectives dwindled. Nor did members of the state bureaucracy recognize the significant transformations taking place among the Indians. When Indians began successfully to operate within the Ladino world, the national census, for example, simply counted them as Ladinos (Early 1974). Thus it appeared to the bureaucracy that the ethnic majority was shrinking rather fast. But these "new Ladinos" were hardly the trustworthy political operatives that the old Ladinos had been. And they were too new, even in Guatemala where "passing" was widely recognized and approved by the national powerholders, to be granted much political force. Thus the system of political control in peasant areas gradually deteriorated without anyone recognizing the extent of the problem.

Guatemala City grew between 1950 and 1973 at an unprecedented rate, accounting for almost all of the urbanization responsible for moving Guatemala's population from thirty percent to 36.4 percent urban. Most other cities grew no faster than the rural population. The people who moved into the national capital were largely Ladino, many from smaller urban centers, mostly well educated and fairly young (Roberts 1973). Guatemala City also grew in number of industrial establishments, as the plantation oligarchy diversified its investments and as foreign investors (mainly from the United States) found Guatemala City a good source of cheap labor (Adams 1970). Plantation agriculture also diversified, with cotton, sugar, and cattle becoming significant exports. Coffee production remained strong, however, for the new exports were grown in different areas of the country. Some plantations attempted to mechanize, but relatively few actually succeeded. Thus demand for labor throughout the 1950s and 1960s remained strong (Williams 1978), and the major source of labor continued to be the peasant communities of the western highlands.

Guatemala's national economy boomed throughout the 1960s and early 1970s, both in export agriculture and in urban industrialization (CSUCA 1978a). The local economies in the Indian highlands also grew and diversified but without any greater incorporation into the national economy than had been achieved at the beginning of the era. Few Indians migrated to urban centers, ethnic artisanal production was not replaced by world-system imports, and imported capital goods (fertilizer, sewing machines, and the like) only furthered the self-sufficiency of indigenous communities vis-à-vis national capitalist development. Most important, a relatively smaller amount of labor was available from the highlands for agricultural or industrial expansion than ever before.[30]

Plantations responded to dwindling labor supplies from the highlands in two ways. First, they moved against their resident work force, the <u>colonos</u>, who had in the past been retained as a labor reserve by the plantations through grants of land for use in subsistence farming. Making these partially proletarianized workers fully proletarianized by taking away their subsistence plots released more labor for expanded coffee, cotton, and cattle production throughout most of the 1970s (Winson 1978). Plantations also sought labor in urban centers, a rather new development in Guatemala (CSUCA 1978b), and in addition came to rely on labor from El Salvador, where similar movements against colonos had already taken place (Durham 1979). These new sources of labor, however, made for a much more volatile political situation in Guatemala, as recent developments in the region attest.

A crisis point was reached by the late 1970s as Guatemala's industrial expansion, based on the Central American Common Market, was cut short by war and revolution in other Central American republics and as growing labor unrest on Guatemalan plantations led to work stoppages and strikes. By 1978 peasant and capitalist interests were once again in direct conflict in Guatemala, and the result of that conflict is the full-scale war now being waged against peasants by the state. Recent events show more clearly than anything else that the preservation of the indigenous community was not brought about by, nor was it in the interest of, capitalist development in the region. When the free wage era ended

in 1978, Guatemala's economy was still dominated by a large peasantry whose labor potential was far from being fully tapped and
whose intransigence as a labor force for Guatemalan development
remained a continuing problem for capital. Force was still needed
as an implement to draw these peasants into capitalist relations of
production.

THE PREREVOLUTIONARY CRISIS (1978-1981)

With news that more than one hundred Guatemalan Indian peasants had been massacred at Panzos in May 1978[31] and with the documentation by Amnesty International (1981) of the following three
years of murderous repression undertaken by the government of Romeo
Lucas Garcia, the world has become aware that another revolution is
brewing in Central America. The global explanation for the new
crisis in Guatemala presents the following picture:

Changing needs of the export sector indicate a falling relative, if not absolute, demand for seasonal labor. This is
forcing growing numbers of the highland population permanently
out of the village community. Faced with the extinction of
their communities and the loss of means to sustain themselves,
increasing numbers of Guatemalan peasants have achieved some
measure of revolutionary consciousness.

My recent work on local-level processes in Guatemala leads me
to a very different reading of the economic processes bringing
about the present revolutionary situation. I argue that in recent
years increasing numbers of peasants have been able to build up
their local economies to the point that fewer and fewer of them
have needed to seek work on plantations. Some have achieved greater economic independence by joining colonization projects. Some
have used plantation earnings to develop their own farming systems
to the point that wages are no longer needed to supplement farming.
More have become traders and petty commodity producers feeding not
only other specialized peasants and plantation workers, but workers
in the growing urban centers as well. In any event, local developments within peasant communities have created a labor shortage on
the plantations, and the recent actions of the state are at least
in part a response to the resulting economic crisis.
Little information exists on the current political situation
in western Guatemala because of the absence of reports from sociological investigators and the virtual blockade on regular news
sources. Thus I have had to base the following analysis of this
early period in the Guatemalan revolution on a systematic review of
the available news accounts,[32] limited information as to how locals
interpreted the political situation, and virtually no knowledge of
how their interpretations may have changed since 1979. Yet I think
it is important to record the unfolding of the peasant revolution
before the myths inevitably created by the victors of such struggles become the accepted view of the matter. Because I have tried
to understand how Guatemalans have made their own history, even if

they have made it not exactly as they have pleased, I think I can
make better sense of the present situation in Guatemala than many
others. It is certainly clear that events there were only influenced, but not directed, by global forces.

In 1978-1979 highland Indians listened spellbound to radio
reports of the Nicaraguan revolution, but remained convinced until
the end that the revolutionary forces would lose.[33] Not only did
the Guatemalan press make it appear that the Somoza regime would
ultimately prevail, but Guatemalan Indians had had enough experience with insurgent movements, local rebellions, and even peaceful
reforms (1944-1954) in their own country to know that such efforts
rarely succeed. Even after the Sandinista victory in July of 1979,
Guatemalan Indians gave little thought to revolutionary change of
their own situation. The only ones interested in the possibility
of a Nicaraguan-style revolution were the offspring of the most
successful people in the richer communities, Indian children now
attending secondary school in significant numbers for the first
time in Guatemalan history.[34] Even these radical students, however, were more interested in their personal futures as teachers or
other petty professionals than they were in guerilla movements. It
took a full-scale declaration of war against peasants, unions,
teachers, students, journalists, and political opposition by the
Lucas Garcia regime to change Indian consciousness on armed warfare. Indian awareness of the source and nature of their oppres-
sion had always existed. But the struggles they undertook before
-- and these were real struggles -- mostly took a nonviolent form,
of the kind described above.

No one who has followed events in Guatemala since the Panzos
massacre questions that the state is waging a war against its
peasants and agrarian workers. There has been a clear pattern of
repression directed against potential popular leadership in rural
areas,[35] utilizing government forces in a countrywide reign of
terror. The object has been to intimidate the entire Guatemalan
population, especially the Indians, through the use of torture and
brutal attacks on defenseless communities. Children, women, and
elderly men have been targetted as often as potential recruits for
guerrilla groups. People are frightened, but many have now begun
to resist.

It is difficult to know exactly what the Lucas Garcia regime
had in mind -- how it selected the areas in which it terrorized
peasant villages, or what it hoped to gain from bloody and ruthless
attacks whose effect was to mobilize peasant resistance far more
successfully than could any leaflets distributed by leftists. After the state's military moves against the Indians, guerilla
groups, especially the Poor Peoples' Guerrilla Army (EGP) and the
Organization of People in Arms (ORPA),[36] recruited more Indian
peasants than they ever had earlier, finding support and protection
in Indian areas that had formerly reported guerrilla activities to
the authorities. Few Indians now volunteered for service in the
Guatemalan military; in reaction, military recruitment began to
concentrate on Ladino communities in the east rather than Indian
communities in the west. Most Guatemalan civilians and even some
members of the military forces became convinced that the repression

created more resistance than it destroyed. The pattern of repression, however, suggests that the particular course chosen by Guatemala's military regime was governed by certain considerations, as outlined below.[37]

Repressive moves against the peasants of western Guatemala began in 1975 in the northern transversal area or "zone of the generals," so named because most of the land in the region had been recently claimed by people of high military rank -- including Guatemalan presidents. Considerable development potential was thought to lie in the area, which promised both mineral and petroleum wealth. But in order for that wealth to be claimed and exploited, three changes were necessary. The land had to come under the control of people willing to promote capitalist development; the Indians who had farmed that land for centuries, had to be removed from it; and more labor had to be released from Indian communities in order to help exploit the potential resources. In 1978 the Panzos massacre occurred as a result of these peasants' resistance to expropriation. This opened the period of outright war in the region.

When Guatemala's political leaders made their move against the peasants in the northern transversal, they must also have been aware that even more had to be done to increase the potential labor supply for capitalist development everywhere. Labor was needed on the plantations, in the cities, and in the transversal, where a major road and other infrastructure for exploiting the area had long been planned but never built because of the labor shortage.[38] Guatemala's political leaders already had a model of how to meet their various goals from what they had accomplished in eastern Guatemala in the recent past. Between 1965 and 1966 government troops had brought a similar reign of terror to eastern Guatemala, ostensibly to eliminate a few hundred guerrillas active at that time. They not only destroyed more than 20,000 peasant lives and all active political resistance in that region, but also helped eradicate the base of much peasant livelihood there.[39] Ever since the late 1960s, eastern Guatemala has been an unending source of proletarianized labor -- for the cities, for plantations, and for the army. Indian communities in that part of Guatemala have nearly vanished. It must have seemed plausible to Guatemala's political and military leaders in 1978 (allegedly still directed by Carlos Arana Osorio, who masterminded the CIA-assisted military campaign in eastern Guatemala) that the same methods would bring about the same effects in western Guatemala, where there was both more potential labor and more potential use for it.

Beginning with the rule of Rufino Barrios, who took office in 1871, political regimes in Guatemala have done the bidding of those wishing to promote the capitalist development of the country. The reform government of 1944-1954 was no exception, different only in trying novel means to the same end. Many stratagems have been used over the years to try to incorporate peasant (especially Indian) communities within these development plans. Among the less violent were the encouragement of foreign missionary work and tourism in the Indian areas, the promotion of colonization projects that promised to make yeoman farmers out of Indians, and the various

self-help and cooperative projects of aid programs directed by the
United States. It must have seemed to the government in 1978 that
many of these programs had backfired, locking peasant labor into
community projects and encouraging peasant political ambitions at a
time when peasant labor was needed for grander schemes and when
peasant political leadership could only mobilize resistance. In
any event, the areas where these projects had been most successful
were the ones pinpointed for assault by the regime-directed death
squads.

From published accounts I have tried to analyze the distribution of communities against which the government's attacks have
been most persistent and brutal.[40] My survey shows that they are
not located where guerrilla activities have been most successful,
the southern plantation area, or guerrilla supporters most numerous, the urban centers. Instead, they have been those communities
where Indian political organization has been most fully developed
(Chimaltenango, Solola); where self-help projects sponsored by
missions have been most successful and peasant cooperative organizations most numerous (northern Huehuetenango, Quiche, Solola,
Chimaltenango); where colonization projects have taken root (the
Ixcan, Peten, and Panzos areas); where considerable tourist-based
development has taken place (Solola, southern Quiche, and
Sacatepequez); and areas of potential capitalist expansion now
occupied by peasants (the transversal area of northern Quiche,
northern Huehuetenango). Guerrilla groups, to be sure, now gain
considerable support and some recruits from these areas, but support has come from these areas mainly as peasants have reacted to
attacks on their communities, rather than because peasant revolutionary consciousness was already strong there.

This particular pattern of attack suggests to me that the
Guatemalan government has been blind to the basic source of peasant
resistance to the needs of Guatemalan capitalism -- the internal
economic growth of the peasant economy -- and has assumed, like
most social scientists who have worked in the region, that only
where outside help and influence have been strong (through missions, tourism, AID-sponsored cooperative projects, and the like)
will peasants find the means to resist the full proletarianization
always sought by Guatemalan capitalists. (Indians in the more
commercialized and politically autonomous areas of Quezaltenango
and Totonicapan, regions where Indian peasant resistance to the
state has historically been strongest, have been relatively immune
from government attack; yet these are the very areas of greatest
peasant economic autonomy.) But though misguided as to the underlying bases by which Guatemala's peasants have resisted the goals
of Guatemala's capitalists, the military actions undertaken by the
current government may nonetheless undermine these bases through
its wanton destruction of peasant life. At the same time, however,
the savagery of the present attack on peasants may lead to an
ultimate defeat for Guatemalan capitalism. The government now
encounters resistance to its program of repression and murder
everywhere, and many Guatemalans, rich and poor alike, are now
willing to risk everything to attempt the overthrow not only of the
present regime but of capitalism.[41]

I close this account of the latest and most savage period in Guatemalan history not knowing how it will end or who will ultimately prevail. Whatever the outcome, however, no one group will have willed it. I have emphasized the role of the Guatemalan govenrment during the early period of violence because they began and directed the concerted attack against what they perceived to be the bases of peasant resistance. I also recognize the fact that those in power have been aided and directed in their aims by global capitalist interests in Guatemalan resources. But pursuit of these interests has not produced the intended consequences. Even if the present Guatemalan government ultimately wins the present struggle, which is by no means assured, they will have produced enormous losses for international and Guatemalan capital, will have destroyed rather than released much of Guatemala's potential labor force, and will not necessarily have eliminated the basic sources of peasant resistance. Surely this was not the desired end.

At the same time, I do not think it reasonable to assert that Guatemala's peasants, if victorious, will achieve their intended objectives either. While peasant resistance to the state and to capitalism lies at the heart of the present struggle and goes much deeper than reaction to the recent political attack on them, that resistance was not initially directed toward the overthrow of the state or the elimination of capitalism in Guatemala, aims embraced by the political groups siding with the peasants. If peasants are victorious in their present struggle, they will be caught up in a new struggle that will as surely threaten their goals of cultural autonomy and economic independence as the present political economy of Guatemala. I assume, however, that a new regime will have to accommodate itself to elements of peasant resistance, as have all previous regimes.

CONCLUSIONS

In this essay I have tried to suggest ways in which the expansion of capitalism within a particular peripheral region was strongly influenced by local response and cultural resistance. Given the slow, incomplete, and peculiar development of capitalism in Guatemala, I argue that it is difficult to sustain the position that Guatemala turned out the way it did because global capitalism needed that particular pattern of development. To understand any particular local system, such as that in Guatemala, one must look instead at the interaction of global and local forces. Indeed, the dialectic of global and local forces must be considered to understand the nature and progress of world capitalism itself.

Today, most anthropologists recognize that global forces help shape the environments in which local systems operate, and they actively seek information to document that process. But rarely do they look at the way in which local systems affect the regional structures, economic and political, on which global forces play, which prevents them from describing the way in which global forces have adapted to local conditions. Thus anthropological versions of social history remain far too parochial. The work of other social

110

scientists, who are even more likely to view local systems as the passive recipients of global process, has not been of great help in this regard. They have given us, essentially, only two models of the modern world. The older of these, whether in the guise of modernization theory or in the guise of classic Marxist thought, is that of capitalist diffusion. In this model, capitalism is seen as expanding on a world scale, inexorably developing new markets, inevitably proletarianizing the masses, and constantly homogenizing culturally and making dependent economically the working classes. The process may be slow but it is thought to be continuous. Local events are read through the lens of this model, by many anthropologists as well as others. Dependency or world-system theorists, recognizing that the global expansion of capitalism has not been so constant or inexorable, have provided a revised view of the modern world, the second model.[42] This model acknowledges that there have been highly resistant pockets of noncapitalist producers, that there has been continuous segmentation of the working classes and even of the bourgeoisie, and that there have been successful, but "premature," revolutions in peasant social formations, led by neither the bourgeoisie nor the proletariat. In this model, the anomalies with respect to capitalist development have been explained as being "functionally" necessary to the capitalism of the time. A preserved peasantry and segmented labor markets keep the costs of capitalist production low, premature revolutions change the status of places within the world-system zones in order that accumulation can continue, struggles among factions of national bourgeoisies allow greater penetration by world-scale capitalism. Local events are also read through this model, even by anthropologists.

The two global models are highly economistic, tending to view the international expansion of capitalism as a purely economic phenomenon. Although many anthropologists reject such economistic models, they do so not in order to reinterpret the pattern of development in the modern world; they simply eschew any attempt to deal with the relations between economy, social relations, and culture, dealing instead with culture as a process sui generis. I want to plead for a different approach. It seems to me that one way we can account for the distorted, uneven, and unanticipated events resulting from the global expansion of capitalism is to view capitalism as a social and cultural phenomenon as much as an economic one, as a process that can be and is affected by class struggle and human agency all along. And to understand the nature of social classes, not to mention the aims or objectives of social groups, we need to take social relations and cultural phenomena into account. Classes form and struggle long before the ultimate polarization takes place between wage labor and capital, and in their formations and struggle they affect whether and how capitalism is instituted in their social formations. In the approach I advocate, then, we cannot assume a universal logic to the unfolding of capitalism; instead, we must examine the social processes that produce a varied rather than a single response.

NOTES

1.   This study was prepared for the meeting of the American Anthropological Association held in Los Angeles in December 1981. The last section, on the current revolution in Guatemala, reflects the situation at that time; no attempt has been made to bring it up to date.   I would like to thank the following people for helpful comments on the first draft of this article: Richard Adams, Jeffrey Boyer, Shelton Davis, Les Field, David McCreery, Sidney Mintz, Joseph Pansini, Benjamin Paul, Edelberto Torres Rivas, Katherine Verdery, John Watanabe, Robert Williams, and Margery Wolf.   I would also like to acknowledge the help I received from Ronald W. Smith and from several Guatemalan research assistants, who must remain anonymous for obvious reasons; they assisted in the fieldwork on which part of my analysis is based.   Alice Saltzman, Ruth Nix, Robert Jackson, and David Jackson helped with later data analysis. The National Science Foundation supported the fieldwork through Grant No. BNS 77-08179 and also provided partial support during the write-up period.   The Center for Advanced Study in the Behavioral Sciences, Stanford, California, provided the facilities and additional support for the preparation of these materials.   This article was originally published in Comparative Studies in Society and History (Volume 26, No. 2, pp. 193-228, 1984).

2.   Both Waldemar Smith and Robert Wasserstrom have made some useful points about the external forces affecting peasant communities in Mesoamerica.   My critique is not directed at them in particular but at a whole school of thought that has been of increasing influence in anthropology.

3. I should note in this context that social historians have also faced this interpretive problem but have solved it differently.   At least the "new social historians," of which the most widely known is E.P. Thompson (1966), are now trying to develop historical interpretations that credit the masses with considerable influence on the course of human events -- whether or not their struggles erupt so visibly that no one could mistake them.   I acknowledge the influence of these historians on my attempt to provide a social history of Guatemala.

4. It has been pointed out that I am guilty in this study of assuming a single, uncontradictory logic to capitalism.   Because this is the position taken by the scholars I am trying to critique, I do not attempt to correct for this.   To deal with all the contradictory elements within Guatemalan capitalism would take me far beyond the bounds of this article -- indeed it would call for several volumes.   The primary task here is to introduce Guatemalan peasants as active agents of the historical development of Guatemala.

5. See, however, Richard N. Adams (1970).   Adams must be credited for trying to look at larger systems, regional and national, long before it became fashionable in anthropology.   His analysis of Guatemalan politics (1970) has become an anthropological classic of macro-level studies.   Yet, like most social scientists who look at the larger picture, Adams tends to interpret much of Guatemalan history as if it were determined almost entirely by

struggles among elites. In Adam's account, the Guatemalan peasant, especially the Indian peasant, is merely a long-lived anachronism.

6. My global account can be ascribed to no particular individual, but elements of it can be found in the summaries of Guatemalan history by Adams (1970), Jonas (1974), W. Smith (1977), Stavenhagen (1969), Torres Rivas (1971), Winson (1978), and Woodward (1976).

7. This law of global development is clearly stated by Immanuel Wallerstein (1974), though many others have discussed it.

8. Land, of course, is always an issue to peasants, and considerable litigation clogged the colonial courts in Guatemala. But most of the land disputes in this period were between rival Indian municipios (or parcialidades), and those who lost these battles did not become landless, but had to go much farther afield for water, firewood, or pastureage. Landlessness became a serious problem only in the latter part of the nineteenth century (see, e.g., Davis 1970). Because of the absence of mining in Guatemala, the classic land-hungry hacienda never developed there.

9. In the Quiche-Cakchiquel area of western Guatemala, the parcialidad was known as chinamital, while in the Mam area it was known as molab. Both groups were simultaneously neighborhoods and kinship units. Hill's work (1981) on the chinamital in Sacapulas shows that Spanish authorities occasionally recognized the parcialidad landholding tradition, but preferred to impose their own categories of social organization and landholding through the municipal organization, their own creation.

10. Veblen worked primarily in Totonicapan, but he discussed parcialidad landholding in neighboring municipios as well. Stuart Stearns (personal communication) found that the parcialidad in Totonicapan had a variety of social functions. Stimulated by Stearns (and indirectly by Robert Carmack) I pursued this line and found that most hamlets in Totonicapan were identified with a particular parcialidad and that the hamlet, rather than the municipio, was the significant endogamous unit.

11. The smaller municipios in Guatemala were less likely to retain several functioning parcialidades in them than were the larger municipios. Since most anthropologists have preferred to work in the smaller municipios, it is understandable that the importance of the parcialidad might be overlooked.

12. A rash of serious peasant rebellions accompanied independence, many of them in western Guatemala (see Contreras 1951, Carmack 1979, Falla 1971). Some rebellions were occasioned by the Bourbon reforms undertaken by the last colonial governors; others were brought on by programs attempted by the early Liberal government. The pattern of uprisings suggests that whenever the state attempted a general reform program and tried to implement it through state officials, peasants were likely to rebel, regardless of the details of the particular reform. But when the state allowed municipal authorities to interpret and carry out the reform in accordance with established practice, rebellion was much less likely -- even if the reform was damaging to many peasants.

13. Many nineteenth-century travellers describe aspects of Guatemalan society and most describe considerable commercial activ-

ity among Indians (see Baily 1850, Boddam Wetham 1877, Dunlop 1847, Dunn 1828, Morelet 1871, Tempsky 1858, and Thompson 1829). Unfortunately, however, none of these accounts is systematic enough to establish if or how peasant commercial activity was restricted.

14. It is clear, however, that during the colonial period marketplaces were allowed only in urban centers where they could be taxed and controlled by the colonial authorities. It is also clear that by the beginning of the twentieth century there were many rural marketplaces throughout the western highlands that were not subject to state or Ladino control. I have been unable to establish, however, whether the transformation occurred during the Conservative interlude (before the plantation economy) or with the Barrios reforms (as part of the whole effort by the Liberals to establish a freely functioning economy).

15. Population increase was pronounced throughout the nineteenth century. The other developments I mention may have taken place only with the Barrios reforms and the plantation economy. But population dispersion was well under way by 1880, when Guatemala undertook its first national census (never completed because of peasant resistance in the western highlands). Ladinos were also well established in many Indian communities by 1880. This leads me to surmise that these processes were begun much earlier than 1871.

16. Shelton Davis (1970) describes the process of land titling in northwestern Huehuetenango in the latter decades of the nineteenth century. He shows that, while most Indians gained access to some land in this period, the distribution of titled land was extremely uneven and many people never gained clear legal title. Thus the Barrios reforms were to have bitter, even tragic, consequences for many Indians. Yet we should not overlook the fact that most peasant victims did what they could to minimize the damage and that the lands of most peasants were not fully expropriated.

17. C. F. S. Cardoso (1975) contrasts the development of coffee export production in Guatemala, El Salvador, and Costa Rica. He shows that the three export systems differed from one another in important ways because of significant differences in the class structures of the three republics; he also shows that the consequences of coffee export production for class structures were necessarily different in each case. See also Torres Rivas (1971).

18. White (1973) observes that the ethnic traditions of El Salvador's Indians (as numerous, proportionately, as Guatemala's Indians) disappeared with their land base. Cardoso (1975) suggests that the political histories of Guatemala and El Salvador differed primarily because El Salvador successfully proletarianized its peasants whereas Guatemala did not.

19. Joseph Pansini (1977) must be credited for making the distinction between the national Ladino class, or Guatemaltecos, who own plantations and major industrial enterprises in Guatemala City, and urban Ladinos, who live in provincial towns and hold bureaucratic offices, engage in professional occupations, or run local commercial establishments.

20. The position of regional elites in eastern Guatemala was slightly different from the usual pattern (see Adams 1970:217-237), conforming more closely to the position of elites in the other

Central American republics. But their potential power in dealings with the state was small because of their relative poverty.

21. Adams (1970) describes the same centralization of power that I do, but he proffers a different explanation for it. Whereas I argue that regional elites in Guatemala never had a local-level power base from which they could gain access to, and influence over, national-level politics, Adams argues that local and regional elites never realized their potential power because they never exercised it collectively.

22. I have described some of the causes and consequences of the different urban patterns in Central America in greater detail elsewhere (Smith 1980). The urban system in all five republics are immature even today, and urban primacy seems to be developing in most of them. But only in Guatemala is there such extreme disparity between the national capital and provincial towns, reflecting and exacerbating the class polarization in Guatemala.

23. Some people accord the 1944 revolution much greater significance than I do. Robert Williams (1978), for example, suggests that the struggle taking place in that period was between the old-fashioned coffee bourgeoisie and a potential industrialist class. Williams goes on to argue that the reforms enacted by the revolutionary government allowed much greater industrial development to take place than would otherwise have been the case. Adams (1970), however, shows that most supporters of the 1944 revolution were professionals, small storekeepers, or potential bureaucrats rather than potential industrialists; he also shows that considerable industrial investment was made by the traditional coffee oligarchy.

24. Watanabe (1981), for example, shows that while individual peasant holdings in Santiago Chimaltenango have dwindled to approximately one third of what they were in the 1920s (mainly because of population increase), these lands produce at least three times as much as they did in the 1930s because of fertilizer and later native crop mixes.

25. Because my earlier Guatemalan fieldwork had indicated that there were twelve regional subsystems within western Guatemala, each having a distinctive pattern of occupation and market dependence (see Smith 1976), I designed the present survey so as to include three municipalities from each subsystem. The particular municipalities were selected so as to cover places in which other anthropologists had worked and so as to cover a certain amount of municipal variation (in size, language, accessability, and so forth). For each municipality I selected randomly three or four hamlets. Within each hamlet I did a full household survey for primary occupation of household heads; from the occupational survey I then randomly selected between 20 and 35 percent of all households for further questioning. Guatemalan assistants (all Indians, most of them multilingual) carried out the household interviews; Table 5.1 is based on information from these interviews.

26. The earlier survey was done on a municipal basis rather than a household basis. I questioned municipal authorities (almost always Indian officials) in 152 municipios as to the general occupations within the municipio and as to the number of households dependent on seasonal plantation work. This survey is likely to be

dependent on seasonal plantation work. This survey is likely to be much less accurate than my later one (see note 24).

26. Most anthropologists working in Guatemala before 1970 had predicted that extreme wealth or poverty would lead individual Indians to leave their communities and to take on the cultural attributes of Ladinos. In recent years, however, it has become clear that the process of becoming a Ladino is more complex than had been thought. Most wealthy Indians stay on in their communities (as do many very poor Indians) and though they take on some "cultural" aspects of Ladinos, most of which simply reflect greater wealth, they continue to identify themselves as Indians. The people most likely to become Ladinos are young men who marry outside of their community and never return. These individuals are rather few in the western highlands. Thus the trend toward increasing Ladinoization in Guatemala documented since the turn of the century reflects census definitions of ethnicity more than the actual rate of change in people's self-identification (see W. Smith 1977, Early 1974, Dow 1981).

27. See Adams (1970:124-137) on the migration pattern in Guatemala during the 1960s. Adams observes that most migrants to Guatemala City are Ladinos from provincial centers, but he does not attempt to explain why this is so. My guess is that the commercial and administrative incomes of these Ladinos have been declining because of increased competition from newly prosperous and educated Indians.

28. See W. Smith (1977), Dow (1981) and Pansini (1977) on the retention by successful Indians of their ethnic identity.

29. Many Guatemalan scholars would dispute this point, given their agrarian bias in understanding peasant livelihood. Assuming that peasants farm, for someone else if not themselves, these scholars believe that dwindling peasant land (minifundia) translates into excess supplies of labor for plantations (latifundia). Since my data come from the peasant rather than the plantation side of Guatemala's economy, I cannot be sure of my interpretation. But Joseph Pansini, one of the few scholars to know something about Guatemala's plantations in recent years on a regional scale, finds evidence from the plantation side to support my interpretation (personal communication).

30. For a detailed report on the Panzos massacre that includes several perspectives on the events leading up to it, see IWGIA (1978).

31. For news on Guatemala since 1978, I have relied primarily on two periodicals, News from Guatemala (Toronto, Canada) and Guatemala! (Berkeley, California). Both periodicals reprint articles from a variety of sources, including Guatemalan newspapers.

32. I was doing fieldwork in the highlands at the time, and this report is of my own observations.

33. Various scholars have remarked on the increased number of Indians attending secondary and higher level schools, among them W. Smith (1977), William Demarest and Benjamin Paul (1981) and Leslie Dow (1981).

34. The pattern whereby rural leaders or potential leaders are selected for attack was pointed out in the Amnesty International

116

selected from grassroots organizations outside official control" (1981:6).

36.   At present there are three major guerrilla organizations operating in Guatemala. The oldest of these is the Rebel Armed Forces (FAR), the organization active in eastern Guatemala during the 1960s and composed largely of middle-class students and long-time leftists. ORPA was founded in 1975, as a FAR splinter group, and operates mainly in the western highlands among Indians. The EGP was founded in an Indian municipio in 1973 and includes many peasants and Indians. All of these organizations have grown considerably since 1978. A recent article in Time (January 15, 1982) suggests that more than 3,000 people are actively engaged in guerrilla warfare against the government and another 30,000 people are providing economic and other support to the guerrilla groups.

37.   There is no documentation concerning the present goals of the military regime in Guatemala and the following analysis is based only on my own reading of events. For a similar view, however, see the report of Frederico Gil, Eurique Baloyra, and Lars Schoultz.

38.   For background information on the transversal development program, see Cultural Survival, 5:(1981),15-16.

39.   For documentation on the government program of repression and its consequences in eastern Guatemala, see Jonas (1974) and Diener (1978).

40.   The analysis is based on department figures on casualties assumed related to the present civil war as reported in News from Guatemala (September 1979 through December 1981).

41.   According to both Time (January 15, 1982) and News from Guatemala, the level of Indian participation in guerrilla resistance is at an all-time high.

42.   This literature needs little introduction today, but for the dependency approach, see Andre Gunder Frank (1966), and for the world-system viewpoint, Immanuel Wallerstein (1974).

BIBLIOGRAPHY

Adams, Richard N. 1957. "Political Change in Guatemalan Indian
    Communities," in Community, Culture, and National Change, R.N.
    Adams, ed. New Orleans: The MiddleAmerican Research Institute
    at Tulane University, Publication No. 24, pp. 1-54.
_____. 1970. Crucifixion by Power: Essays on Guatemalan Na-
    tional Social Structure, 1944-1966. Austin: University of
    Texas Press.
Amnesty International. 1981. Guatemala: A Government Program of
    Political Murder. London: Amnesty International Reports.
Baily, John. 1850. Central America: Describing Each of the States
    of Guatemala, Honduras, Salvador, Nicaragua, and Costa Ri-
    ca.... London: Trelawney Saunders.
Boddam Whetham, J.W. 1877. Across Central America. London: Hurst
    and Blackett.
Bunzel, Ruth. 1952. Chichicastenango: A Guatemalan Village. Seat-
    tle: University of Washington Press.
Cardoso, C. F. S. 1975. "Historia Economica del Café en Cen-
    troamèrica." Estudios Sociales Centroamericanos (San Josè,
    Costa Rica),4:10,9-55.
Carmack, Robert. 1979. Historia social de los Quichès. Seminario de
    Integbacitn No. 38. Guatemala City.
_____. 1981. The Quiche Mayas of Utalan. Norman: University of
    Oklahoma Press.
Clammer, John. 1976. "Economic Anthropology and the Sociology of
    Development: 'Liberal' Anthropology and Its French Critics,"
    in Beyond the Sociology of Development, I. Oxall, T. Barnett,
    and D. Booth, eds. London: Travistock.
Collier, George. 1975. Fields of the Tzotzil: The Ecological Bases
    of Tradition in highland Chiapas. Austin: University of Texas
    Press.
Contreras, J. Daniel. 1951. Una Rebelitn Indìgena en el Partido de
    Totonicaptn en 1820. Guatemala City: Imprenta Universitaria.
CSUCA (Consejo Superior Universitario Centroamericano). 1978a.
    Estructura Agraria, Dinàmica de Poblacitn y Desarrollo Capi-
    talista en Centroamèrica. San Jose, Costa Rica: Editorial
    Universitaria Centroamericana.

_____. 1978b. Estructura Demografica y Migraciones Internas en Centroamérica. San Jose, Costa Rica: Editorial Universitaria Centroamericana.

Davis, Shelton. 1970. Lands of Our Ancestors. Ph.D. dissertation, Harvard University.

Demarest, William and Benjamin D. Paul. 1981. "Mayan Migrants in Guatemala City." Anthropology UCLA 11:43-73.

Diener, Paul. 1978. "The Tears of St. Anthony: Ritual and Revolution in Eastern Guatemala." Latin American Perspectives 5(2):92-116.

Dow, Leslie. 1981. Ethnicity and Modernity in the Central Highlands of Guatemala. Ph.D. diss., University of Michigan.

Dunlop, R. G. 1847. Travels in Central America. London: Longman, Brown, Green, and Longman.

Dunn, Henry. 1828. Guatemala [sic], or the United Provinces of Central America in 1827-1828. New York: G. and C. Carvill.

Durham, William. 1979. Scarcity and Survival in Central America. Stanford: Stanford University Press.

Early, John D. 1974. "Revision of Ladino and Maya Census Populations of Guatemala, 1950 and 1964." Demography 11(1):105-17.

Ebel, Robert Ewald. 1957. Political Modernization in Three Guatemalan Indian Communities. In Community, Culture, and National Change, R. N. Adams, ed. New Orleans: The Middle American Research Institute at Tulane University, Publication No. 24, pp. 82-152.

Falla, Ricardo. 1971. "Actitud de los Indígenas de Guatemala en la Epoca de la Independencia, 1800-1850." Estudios Sociales Centroamericanos 2(4):701-18.

Frank, Andre Gunder. 1966. Capitalism and Underdevelopment in Latin America. New York: Monthly Review Press.

Gil, Frederico G., Enrique A. Baloyra and Lars Schoultz. 1981. "The Deterioration and Breakdown of Reactionary Despotism in Central America." Report prepared for the United States Department of State. Manuscript.

Hill, Robert M. 1981. "Continuity of Highland Maya Principles of Social Organization: The Chinamitales of Sacapulas." Manuscript.

Ingersoll, Hazel. 1972. The War of the Mountain: A Study of Reactionary Peasant Insurgency in Guatemala, 1837-1873. Ph.D. dissertation, University of Maryland.

IWGIA (International Work Group for Indigenous Affairs). 1978. The Massacre at Panzos. IWGIA Document No. 33. Copenhagen.

Jonas, Suzanne. 1974. "Guatemala: Land of Eternal Struggle," in Latin America: The Struggle with Dependency and Beyond, R. Chilcote and J. Edenstein, eds. New York: John Wiley and Sons.

Jones, Chester L. 1940. Guatemala, Past and Present. Minneapolis: University of Minnesota Press.

McBryde, Felix W. 1947. Cultural and Historical Geography of Southwest Guatemala. Smithsonian Institution, Institute of Social Anthropology Publication No. 4 Washington D.C.

McCreery, David. 1976. "Coffee and Class: The Structure of Development in Liberal Guatemala." Hispanic Anerican Historical Review 56(3):438-60.

MacLeod, Murdo J. 1973. Spanish Central America: A Socioeconomic History, 1520-1720. Berkeley: University of California Press.

Miceli, Keith. 1974. "Rafael Carrera: Defender and Promoter of Peasant Interests in Guatemala, 1837-1848." The Americas 31(1):72-95.

Morelet, Arthur. 1871. Travels in Central America.... M. F. Squier, trans. New York: Leopold, Holt, and Williams.

Pansini, Joseph J. 1977. "'El Pilar,' a Plantation Macrocosm of Guatemalan Ethnicity." Ph.D. dissertation, University of Rochester.

Roberts, Bryan. 1973. Organizing Strangers: Poor Families in Guatemala City. Austin: University of Texas Press.

Schmid, Lester. 1967. The Role of Migratory Labor in the Economic Development of Guatemala. Ph.D. dissertation, University of Wisconsin.

Smith, Carol A. 1976. "Causes and Consequences of Central-place Types in Western Guatemala," in Economic Systems, Vol. I of Regional Analysis, Carol A. Smith, ed. New York: Academic Press.

_____. 1978. "Beyond Dependency Theory: National and Regional Patterns of Underdevelopment in Guatemala." American Ethnologist 5(2):574-617.

_____. 1980. "On Urban Primacy, Export Dependency, and Class Struggle in Peripheral Regions of World Capitalism." Manuscript.

Smith, Waldemar. 1977. The Fiesta System and Economic Change. New York: Columbia University Press.

Stadelman, Raymond. 1940. Maize Cultivation in Northwestern Guatemala. Carnegie Institution Publication No. 523. Washington D.C.

Stavenhagen, Rodolfo. 1969. Social Classes in Agrarian Societies. Garden City, New York: Doubleday.

Tax, Sol. 1953. Penny Capitalism: A Guatemalan Indian Economy. Smithsonian Institution, Institute of Social Anthropology Publication No. 16. Washington D.C.

Tempsky, Gustav F. 1858. Mitla, a Narrative of Incidents and Personal Adventure.... London: Longman, Brown, Green, and Longman.

Thompson, Edward P. 1966. The Making of the English Working Class. New York: Random House, Vintage Publications.

Thompson, Goerge A. 1829. Narrative of an Official Visit to Guatemala from Mexico. London: John Murray.

Torres Rivas, Edelberto. 1971. Interpretación del Desarrollo Social Centroamericano. San José, Costa Rica: Editorial Universitaria Centroamericana.

Veblen, Thomas. 1975. The Ecological, Cultural, and Historical Bases of Forest Preservation in Totonicapan, Guatemala. Ph.D. dissertation. University of California, Berkeley.

Wagley, Charles. 1941. The Economics of a Guatemalan Village. Menasha, Wisconsin: American Anthropological Association.

Wallerstein, Immanuel. 1974. The Modern World-System: Capitalist Agriculture and the Origins of the European World-Economy in the Sixteenth Century. New York: Academic Press.

120

Wasserstrom, Robert. 1975. "Revolution in Guatemala: Peasants an Politics under the Arbenz Government." Comparative Studies i Society and History 17(4):433-78.

_____. 1976. "White Fathers, Red Souls: Ethnic Relations i Central Chiapas, 1528-1975." Ph.D. dissertation, Harvard University.

_____. 1978. "Population Growth and Economic Development i Chiapas, 1524-1975." Human Ecology 6(2):127-43.

Watanabe, John. 1981. "Cambios Economicos en Santiago Chimaltenango, Guatemala." Mesoamerica 2(1):20-41.

White, Alistair. 1973. El Salvador. New York: Praeger.

Williams, Robert. 1978. The Central American Common Market: Unequal Benefits and Uneven Development. Ph.D. dissertation Stanford University.

Winson, Anthony. 1978. "Class Structure and Agrarian Transition i Central America." Latin American Perspectives 5(4):27-48.

Wolf, Eric. 1957. "Closed Corporate Peasant Communities in Mesoamerica and Central Java." Southwestern Journal of Anthropology 13(1):1-18.

Woodward, Ralph L. 1971. "Social Revolution in Guatemala: The Carrera Revolt," in Applied Enlightenment: Nineteenth Century Liberalism. Middle America Research Publications No. 23. New Orleans: Tulane University.

_____. 1976. Central America: A Nation Divided. New York Oxford University Press.

6
Bringing the Period Down: Government and Squatter Settlement Confront Induced Abortion in Ecuador

Susan C. M. Scrimshaw

INTRODUCTION

Induced abortion to terminate an unwanted pregnancy is illegal in Ecuador. Technically, induced abortion is permitted only if the woman's life is in danger, if she has been the victim of rape, or if fetal deformity is established. In any instance, the abortion must be performed by an M.D. (Issacs 1975, Liskin 1980). Despite this, women terminate unwanted pregnancies, a fact largely denied in official government circles in the early 1970s. This paper addresses the question of macro and micro levels of analysis in at least two dimensions: one is methodological, the other deals with levels of perception of induced abortion ranging from the individual woman, the aggregate group of low income urban families in Guayaquil, and the national government.

I was invited to Ecuador by the government and by the local University in Guayaquil, many of whose officials felt that induced abortion was rare in Ecuador. The Minister of Health had conducted the only existing research on the topic, and was confronted with the medical, legal and social complexities of abortion and contraception. As a health program evaluator, I examined government health clinics that offered little in the way of contraceptive services. I visited private clinics such as those run by the local IPPF (International Planned Parenthood Federation) Affiliates, which were providing contraceptive and infertility services in a few communities. I studied an urban squatter settlement where abortion was something to be concealed, but which was permissible under extenuating circumstances. I also spent six months living among the women of one barrio who, when they feared they were pregnant and didn't want to be, tried to "bring their periods down."

The discussions following begin with methodological approaches, and then move from data on individual women in a barrio (neighborhood) of Guayaquil to aggregate data on the city. Finally, I refer back to the macrolevel of national policy.

METHODOLOGY: FROM MINISTERIO TO SUBURBIO

Micro and Macro Level Research

Few foreign researchers coming to the U.S. would meet with th
Secretary of Health and Human Services before proceeding to conduc
research in Watts or Harlem. Yet this is precisely the situatic
that U.S. researchers often encounter in work overseas. From 197
to 1976, I served as part of an evaluation unit attached to th
Ecuadorian Ministry of Health staffed by a team of internationa
scientists and their Ecuadorian Ministry of Health counterparts
Throughout the six years that I worked in Ecuador (not all i
residence in Ecuador), I had the opportunity to observe people an
offices responsible for the entire health system in the country a
well as the crowded clinics and the homes of people for whom th
Ministry of Health was a mysterious and fairly distant entity
Much of this paper is based on participant observation at all thes
levels. However, my earlier research on human fertility in Barbado
had convinced me that strategies beyond those then commonly em
ployed by anthropologists were necessary.

In the late 1960s Moni Nag pointed out that anthropologist
have tended to "lack sophistication in the techniques of populatio
studies and...lack interest in collecting and presenting data i
quantitative terms, even on those topics that are amenable t
quantitative analysis" (1968:8). Fertility and family size are no
only amenable to quantitative analysis; they require a relativel
large sample in order to draw many conclusions. An anthropologica
explanation of a demographic process like fertility change will b
strengthened by data based on relatively large random samples
Such data have another advantage: they can help the anthropologist
cope with some of the problems of studying a large city, whicl
cannot be approached in the same way as a small village where every
individual can become an acquaintance of the researcher.

Although the nature of some of the data needed in fertility
research is inconsistent with the small (and not random) sample of
people usually studied by anthropologists, the advantages of the
ethnographic method should not be discounted. These include the
long-term in-depth contact with people, the opportunity to observe
behavior, the close friendships during which many aspects of individual behavior are revealed, the participant experience and the
observation of dynamic interrelationships among different aspects
of culture. Most of all, the ethnographic method permits the
inclusion of data that had previously seemed irrelevant, and yet
provides keys to understanding difficult questions. All the same,
I was aware of the accusations that anthropological studies cannot
be generalized beyond the small group of people studied, and that
findings may be based on "cases" that cannot justifiably be subjected to standard statistical analyses. The advantages of combining the ethnographic approach with more quantitative data gathering seems clear.

As early as 1935, Hellman wrote that urban studies should
involve both survey and observation, but that statistical data are
more important in urban research. A similar approach was proposed

in 1950 by Steward, who argued that the qualitative nature of the ethnographic method treats the local groups as though the larger society did not exist. He suggested the use of preliminary qualitative research followed by quantitative data collection. Communities studied ethnographically should also be related to a larger context, through the inclusion of data from other disciplines (1950:22). Similarly, in an article entitled "Field and Case Studies" de Laune commented that: "Direct observation of groups and individuals...allows a more complete picture to be presented in the life of men in their social setting and is the only way of interpreting some of the data from the often more superficial extensive surveys" (1964:55). He suggested that urban studies require an interdisciplinary approach incorporating ethnography, sociology, and social psychology. Like Steward, de Laune recommended a period of observation and participation, followed by quantitative studies (1964:56).

In more recent discussions, Pelto described the use of a "quantitative-qualitative mix," a "weaving back and forth between quantitative and qualitative research operations" (1972:16). He suggested multiperson-multidiscipline research using such a mix as an important research strategy for the study of complex societies (1972:16), but cautioned against "reducing anthropological research to the level of 'count 'em' mechanics" (Pelto and Pelto 1978:37).

Another area of complementarity between survey and ethnographic levels of data collection lies in the distinction between ideal and actual behavior. The survey researcher is more likely to record ideal behavior. Surveys tend to elicit the responses people believe are <u>appropriate</u> responses, or perhaps statements about what people think they do with rationalization about why they think they do it. In Guayaquil, the former is exemplified by women's reluctance to admit to the interviewer that their male partner has another <u>wife</u>, even when they know all about her. Also, in Guayaquil, people told survey interviewers they had latrines in their homes in areas where the ethnographer had been in the homes and knew there were no latrines. The problem of peoples' lack of awareness of their own behavior is illustrated by the inaccuracy of the Guayaquil survey data in questions concerning how much people spent on food. Comparison between ethnographic (observational) and survey data on the <u>same families</u> revealed that people erred significantly both over and under in their estimates of expenditures on food.

A summary of the advantages and disadvantages of the two methods is found in Table 6.1. Clearly, a combination of these two approaches would overcome some of the weakness inherent in each methodology. Survey data would make it possible to relate the indepth studies to the wider population, whereas ethnographic research would support and, if necessary, correct the survey results. In fertility studies, some data, such as age, parity, retrospective breastfeeding and contraceptive histories can be obtained fairly easily by the survey method. Other data, such as number of sexual unions, present union, attitudes, use of contraceptives, induced abortion, frequency of intercourse, and other observed behavior patterns are often best studied or at least

TABLE 6.1
A Summation of the Advantages and Disadvantages of Two Methods

Ethnographic	Large Scale Survey
-Random sampling not usually possible	-Random sampling usually possible
-Few significant statistical data	-Statistical analysis
-Cross-checking used	-Little cross-checking
-Possible to identify ideal vs. real	-Tend to get ideal behavior
-Sensitive topics can be explored due to more time, greater rapport,etc.	-Difficulty in dealing with sensitive topics
-Attitudes revealed	-Attitudes may be revealed with careful research design
-Observation possible	-No time or rapport for much observation
-Problems in relating data to large populations	-Large populations can be surveyed
-Requires much time per household or case	-Relatively rapid ("per household")
-Problem of data collector bias	-Fewer problems with data collector bias as more structure, but problem of structural bias
-Patterning and inter-relationships observable. Discovery of new variables and interrelationships occurs during the research process	-Interrelationships among variables must be specifically designed in advance
-Open ended -- i.e., any factors affecting a problem can be observed	-Closed: information often limited to pre-selected and precoded questions

confirmed through ethnographic studies. Fortunately, in the research reported here, funding was available for using such a combined approach.

Guayaquil

The tropical port city of Guayaquil draws hundreds of thousands of migrants from the Ecuadorian countryside each year, all of them searching for jobs, schools, and other urban advantages. People from coast and mountains meet and mingle in the city, joining their predecessors in the squatter settlements and central city slums, where housing is rented or shared with relatives until some land for building can be claimed from the swamp and built upon. These areas were the focus of my research, which concentrated on the adaptation of migrants to the city, and particularly on changes in their fertility behavior.

The population of Guayaquil, roughly one million people in 1970, reflects the diversity of Ecuador itself, including Indians from the Andean region, people of predominantly Spanish descent from both the mountains and the coast and Blacks from the northern coast. Despite this cultural diversity, both the migrants and long-term urban dwellers studied were relatively homogeneous in terms of education, economic status, housing, and many other factors. This homogeneity reflects both the rapid adaptation and positive selection of migrants (Scrimshaw 1974:192).

Data Collection Procedures

Sixty-five families in one small area of the squatter settlement were studied for six months in 1971 using the traditional anthropological methods of participant observation, conversation, informal interviewing, and observation. After a brief analysis of those data, interview schedules were designed in order to interview men and women about migration and fertility, including induced abortion.

In the Fall of 1971, approximately two thousand households were surveyed in the squatter settlement and the central city slum using probability cluster sampling. The sample included all women between the ages of fifteen and forty-five and their current partners. Because many women were not in unions at the time of the survey, and men were less likely to be home, we interviewed fewer men (1,157) than women (slightly over 3,000).

The question of "how representative is your village (or your city neighborhood?)" was addressed in the research described here both by the random sample survey and by having survey interviewers interview the families studied during the ethnographic phase. The ethnographic field site was picked in a way common to most anthropological research. Time was spent visiting many parts of the city, studying data on population trends and income levels, talking with people in leadership roles both at the city level (the Mayor and other officials) and at the neighborhood level, talking with people in different neighborhoods, and finally, selecting a neighborhood that appeared "typical." The fact that this method produced families that do not differ significantly in most respects from two thousand families selected at random from the two zones of the city is very gratifying to anthropologists who have long insisted that, just because their selection of community is not "statistically random," it does not mean it is not representative (Scrimshaw 1974).

Comparisons of Survey and Ethnographic Data

The families studied ethnographically fit statistically as intermediate between the samples from the older and newer areas of the squatter settlement, corresponding exactly with the principal location of the ethnographic study site. Some of the differences between the data collected in the macrolevel and microlevel studies have already been mentioned. Not surprisingly, some of the differences revolve around reproduction and contraception. For example, more men and women in the ethnographic sample report using coitus interruptus (thirty-seven percent ever use for men and nineteen percent ever use for women in the ethnographic sample) as compared to twenty-one percent and thirteen percent respectively, in the survey sample. I believe people were more willing to talk about a subject they admittedly found embarrassing with someone they knew well (in the ethnographic study).[1]

On the topic of induced abortion, the proportions reporting induced abortions are similar for both methods. In part, this may reflect the application of detailed questioning techniques developed during the ethnographic phase. In particular, this involved questioning all long intervals between pregnancies during the taking of the fertility history. Interestingly, the reported attitudes towards induced abortion differ for the ethnographic and survey samples. In general, more approval of abortion is noted at the ethnographic level (see Table 6.2). For example, nineteen percent of the men in the survey said they would approve of abortion if the family could not afford another child, as compared to thirty-three percent of the men in the ethnography. Very few men and women (six percent and five percent respectively) in the survey approved of abortion if a woman simply wanted no more children, while eighteen percent of the women and twenty-six percent of the men in the ethnography approved of abortion under those same conditions. Trends, however, were consistent between the two samples. In general, people were less approving of abortions because people simply wanted them and more approving under difficult circumstances. In both samples, more men than women thought a woman should have an abortion if her life were threatened by the pregnancy.

Since the two samples were comparable in so many other ways, it is likely that these differences are because the ethnographic methodology elicited a different kind of attitudinal information about abortion. It is probable, but not certain, that this information is more accurate (see Footnote 1).

TABLE 6.2
Opinions on Induced Abortion (Ethnographic Sample)

Would you accept (agree to) a woman's having an abortion	WOMEN (N=68)			MEN (N=46)		
	no	yes	nr	no	yes	nr
1. If she became pregnant and already had children that she couldn't feed or dress?	71%	29%		67%	33%	
2. If the mother may die in childbirth?	31%	67%	2%	19%	81%	
3. If the woman knows that the child may be born deformed?	46%	52%	2%	43%	57%	
4. If the woman doesn't want any more children and become pregnant?	81%	19%		74%	26%	
5. If the baby isn't the husband's or companion's?	62%	34%	4%	55%	33%	12%
6. If the husband left (abandoned) her?	86%	14%		74%	24%	2%
7. If the mother was raped?	59%	41%		48%	52%	
8. If she became pregnant and the man didn't want to marry her?	95%	5%		79%	21%	

128

The detail and depth that ethnographic studies can provide are extremely complementary to survey data, as will be evident later on in this paper. The validation the survey data provide are also important. For example, we know that the proportion of induced abortions in the ethnographic sample is not an accident of chance in a small sample, because the data are approximately the same in a sample of 3,000 women. The similarity between the ethnographic and survey samples is particularly important for anthropologists, because their findings are often criticized on the basis of sample size and bias in sample selection.

WOMEN AND UNWANTED PREGNANCY

Cases

One day, as several barrio women were gossiping about the possible (and unwanted) pregnancy of an absent neighbor, they suddenly realized that at age twenty-six she wanted no more children but could become pregnant "until after forty." They were horrified when they began applying the idea to themselves. Then someone else mentioned the woman down the street who had had fifteen pregnancies and was only thirty-five. They called that "the house where children die" because every year at least one child in that extended family died. Such high fertility and mortality were discussed as frightening prospects.

Maria[2] had five children. She said the doctor in her health center told her she should not have any more children, nor did she want any more. Before becoming pregnant with her last child, she had taken the pill for eight months but said it gave her terrible headaches, so she couldn't stand it any longer. She stopped taking it and immediately became pregnant. She had an induced abortion, then took another brand of pill. Once more she felt the headaches and stopped. When she found herself pregnant again, she had the child. The doctor at her health center has tried to persuade her to use the IUD, but "people say the IUD makes you bleed too much. Besides, it isn't natural, it will bring me cancer." At the time of the research, she and her husband were trying to avoid pregnancy by not "finishing" at the same time. "But it only works if the women turns face downward immediately after intercourse."

This woman's contraceptive history summarizes the prevalent pattern: the desire to avoid pregnancy, occasionally an abortion, the real and imagined complications of "modern" contraceptive methods, and finally the lack of adequate protection.

When an unwanted pregnancy occurs, women usually try home remedies (herbal teas) and self-prescribed injections (usually of calcium) in order to induce menstruation. For anywhere from a few days to as long as two months after a menstrual period is expected, women speak of "bringing the period down" rather than of "taking out a child," a common way to refer to abortion. As long as a woman can speak of her problem as a recalcitrant menstrual period, she does not have to face the emotional or social anguish of admitting she is trying to induce an abortion. Carole Browner described

similar attitudes in Colombia (1969, 1980), as did Shedlin and
Hollarbach for Mexico (1981). In at least some Latin American
countries, it is possible to be "a little bit pregnant."

The process of facing up to a late period, seeking discreet
and easy solutions, and (if these don't work), trying to find a
safe and affordable abortion is often a tortured one. The following case is typical. Julia had three children. She felt three
were enough, and added that her "husband" (who was married to
another woman and visited Julia) was so unreliable she couldn't be
sure he wouldn't take off with another woman some day and leave her
alone with the children. "I don't want any more of that man's
children." When she found herself pregnant in July of 1970 (after
stopping the contraceptive pills she had been getting at a drugstore because people say "they eat the red blood cells"), she had
an induced abortion. She was only two months pregnant at the time,
so the abortion was not too expensive (300 sucres or U.S. $15.00).
She borrowed some money from her sister to add to a little she had
saved, and managed to pay for the operation without her husband's
ever knowing she was pregnant ("He would have been furious"). The
abortion was done by an MD, under general anesthesia, and she
described it as "completely painless."

I met her in December of that year. In January of 1971 she
told me of her abortion and mentioned her fear that she was again
pregnant. Her period had been due November 10 and now she was
nauseous. She had already had four calcium injections to "bring
her period down" but none had worked. She mentioned that one of
the neighbors had made a snide remark about the size of her abdo-
men, which she had attempted to laugh off. "What do I do? I don't
want another child, but I don't have any money this time."

In early February she told me she was determined to have the
abortion. She had borrowed money from various friends and told her
husband she needed more money for the boys' school. The day before
she had called [3] the doctor who had performed the first abortion,
but he had said she was too far along in her pregnancy. He only
did abortions up to eight weeks. She called two more doctors, but
neither would see her. But one of her friends (to my knowledge the
only person besides myself with whom she discussed her predicament)
knew a nurse-midwife who did abortions up to three months. Julia
was by then slightly over three months pregnant, but was determined
to give the midwife false dates.

I accompanied Julia to the nurse-midwife's. The fee was
stiff, 500 sucres ($25), but the nurse-midwife tried to get 700 and
only backed down when she realized Julia simply didn't have more.
The nurse-midwife's "office" (a tiny room in her home) was crowded
and filthy. There was barely room for an examining table, a sink,
and a couch. A small desk in one corner was littered with papers,
bottles of medicine, instruments, children's toys and dust. She
rinsed a speculum (she apparently had only one) under running
water, and after examining Julia, put a plastic tube up through the
cervix into her uterus and then packed the vagina with gauze. She
told Julia to return the next day.

Early the next morning Julia told me she was bleeding. We
hurried to the nurse-midwife, who was annoyed because we came

earlier in the day than she had told us to. After an hour's wait, during which she could be heard playing with her children, the nurse-midwife put on the same stained white coat of the day before and proceeded to do a fast and apparently skillful curettage. She had given Julia no anesthetic, and Julia screamed during much of the procedure. Meanwhile, the nurse-midwife whistled a cheerful tune. When it was over, she gave Julia a shot of penicillin and a prescription to "contract the uterus." Julia did not get the prescription, arguing that she had no time and no money. It was important for her to get back, reclaim her children from a neighbor who thought we were shopping, and to go about her normal chores. No one was to suspect what she had done.

My field notes for March 18, 1971 provide another example of repeated induced abortions:

> We talked for a while of this (children) and she said she had had three induced abortions. She said that only she, God and myself knew, but I am sure she told her friends. I assured her that this was confidential and I showed her the number I had on the file, nothing about names. The woman mentioned a few times that it had been a sin and that perhaps God would forgive her because of how hard her life has been. I asked her how she "took them out." She told me that the first time she went to a doctor's house (a woman, probably a nurse-midwife) and there they put her to sleep with a mask over her face. It cost 200 sucres. The second time she went with the same "doctor" and the same price. The third time it was in another "doctor's" office and she charged her 250 sucres. She said that then they took the fetus out with a "tallo"[4] (fetus was the word the woman used). She also told me that her husband knew nothing about these incidents. I asked her where the money had come from and she said that at that time she worked and that she could take the money from her job.

Attitudes

The field notes and case studies just presented reflect some womens' attitudes towards induced abortion: they would rather not do it, but sometimes it is necessary. The men and women contacted in the ethnographic work were also asked a series of more formally worded questions about induced abortion. These were discussed briefly in the section on methodology. The results are also summarized in Table 6.2. Seventy-nine percent of the women and eighty-nine percent of the men approved of abortion under at least one circumstance. Nineteen percent of the women said they would have an abortion if they became pregnant again and wanted no more children. Twenty-six percent of the men said they would approve of their wife having an abortion under the same circumstances. Both men and women were most approving of abortion if the mother's life was endangered by the pregnancy, and least approving if the woman was pregnant by a man who didn't want to marry her. As mentioned previously, I do not believe that the ethnographic population is so

different from the survey sample, but rather that questions asked
by an ethnographer who has spent time in the community received
more accurate answers.

In both cases, the approval rates are high for a Catholic
country where abortion is illegal. In fact, when the 109 respondents were asked about any Church opinion on induced abortion only
fifty-two percent of the ninety-one Catholics said it was forbid-
den. Surprisingly, thirteen percent said the Church is not against
induced abortion, twenty-two percent said the Church doesn't say
anything about abortion, and thirteen percent didn't know. Sixty-
one percent of the eighteen Protestants said their church was
against abortion while eleven percent said it was not against it,
seventeen percent said the Church says nothing about it and eleven
percent didn't know. More people may have known their church was
against induced abortion, but not admitting it is a way of denying
church involvement in the matter.

INDUCED ABORTIONS IN GUAYAQUIL (A POPULATION PERSPECTIVE)

Incidence

When I described Maria, Julia and others to my colleagues in
the Ministry of Health, the descriptions were greeted with interest
and concern, but also indignation. "So you ran into a few women
who had abortions. They should be jailed, and so should whoever
did the abortion." These reactions made the collection of data on
induced abortion using a larger, randomly selected sample important, but controversial.

Incidence

Data on induced abortion are extremely difficult to obtain,
particularly where it is illegal, as in Ecuador (Browner 1979).
The survey interviewers were carefully instructed on how to probe
for data on induced abortions during the taking of the pregnancy
history. Despite this, the proportion of admitted induced abortions was relatively low. Table 6.3 shows the outcome of pregnancies by year of termination for over 2,000 urban women (regardless
of migration status). The proportion of pregnancies that ended in
live births decreases from ninety-five percent to eighty-one percent in the years from 1967 to 1971. The proportion of stillbirths
was relatively constant over time, but the drop in live births was
balanced by a rise in admitted induced abortions and spontaneous
abortions. Because spontaneous abortions were likely to decrease
with improved health and hygiene in the years since 1942, the
increase was probably due to concealed induced abortions. Thus,
induced abortions probably occurred in at least seven percent of
all pregnancies. In all, 125 women admitted to one or more induced
abortions. This is five percent of the total number of women in
unions. Their abortions constituted two percent of the total

TABLE 6.3
Pregnancy Outcome by Age of Mother, Pregnancy Order and Date of Delivery

Age	Live births per cent	Stillbirths per cent	Spontaneous abortions per cent	Induced abortions per cent	No.
Less than 15	89·9	5·0	5·0	—	138
15–19	87·8	1·7	9·8	0·6	1,919
20–24	87·0	1·1	9·8	2·0	3,428
25–29	84·8	1·6	11·4	2·2	2,613
30–34	81·1	1·2	13·5	3·9	1,532
35–39	79·7	1·9	15·3	2·9	620
40–45	80·0	1·1	17·9	1·1	95
Order					
1	91·1	1·8	6·9	0·2	1,934
2	87·0	1·7	10·2	1·1	1,933
3–4	85·9	1·2	11·3	1·6	2,901
5–6	84·7	0·9	11·3	3·1	1,800
7–8	79·0	2·0	14·6	4·2	1,004
9–10	74·7	1·9	17·2	5·9	477
11+	71·6	1·7	19·9	6·4	296
Year					
Before 1942	100	—	—	—	20
1942–46	88·7	1·6	9·7	—	186
1947–51	87·3	3·0	8·7	1·1	644
1952–56	87·8	1·8	8·9	1·4	1,382
1957–61	86·4	1·8	9·9	1·9	2,104
1962–66	86·5	0·8	10·7	1·9	2,924
1967–71	81·5	1·4	14·0	3·0	3,085

Source: Wolfers and Scrimshaw 1975:487.

number of pregnancies, or twenty-three abortions per 1,000 live births.

A look at "spontaneous" abortions will also provide clues to the rate of induced abortions. In the case of the women studied, the "spontaneous" abortions equal about 12.8 percent of the live births, or 128 "spontaneous abortions." While surprisingly low,[5] this rate is high in proportion to admitted induced abortions. There is a strong possibility that a number of induced abortions were reported as spontaneous.

Table 6.3 also reveals some potential macrolevel effects on individual behavior. Admitted and probable induced abortions increased from 1942 to 1971. Why should this occur? At the societal level, general improvements in health correlated with lowered infant mortality over the same period, thus resulting in more surviving children. Increases in induced abortion could be attempts to maintain previous family sizes in the light of this mortality drop. Another explanation (not mutually exclusive) is that as awareness of contraceptive methods increased beginning in the

1960s, women gained a sense of control over their fertility, although they did not always have "modern" methods. This increase in induced abortions during the early phases of the introduction of contraceptive methods has been reported in other countries as well (Liskin 1980).

Another view of behavior related to abortions is provided by Table 6.4, that shows the frequency and outcome of first and subsequent pregnancies. This reveals that the highest probability of a pregnancy ending in a live birth is with the first pregnancy, which on strictly biological terms should be a riskier pregnancy than the next few. Nonetheless, the proportion of pregnancies terminating in a live birth is highest for the first birth (91.1 percent), and still high for the second birth (87.5 percent). After that the proportion of pregnancies ending in a live birth goes down to as low as seventy-five percent (at eleventh pregnancies) before the numbers become too small for meaningful analysis. The key difference beyond the third pregnancy is not the proportion of stillbirths, which reflect medical problems in pregnancies carried to or near term, but in the proportions of admitted induced abortions and "spontaneous" abortions. This indicates that while few actions are taken to terminate first and second pregnancies, women are less desirous of bearing children from the third pregnancy on, and act to terminate such pregnancies more readily. While the greater chances of spontaneous abortion as women advance in age and parity must be considered, the admitted induced abortions and the increase in "spontaneous" abortions support the idea that the decrease in the proportion of live births after two children is often due to deliberate intervention.

Abortion rates for Guayaquil appear low in comparison to a country like Chile, where in 1970 it was estimated there were at least 500 abortions per 1,000 live births (Armijo and Monreal 1965). Many of the Chilean estimates are based on incomplete or completed abortion cases that reach hospitals, and on maternal deaths.

A pilot study by Drs. Cesar Serrano Gomez and Mario Jaramillo Gomez on 100 admissions to Guayaquil's largest maternity hospital for complicated or incomplete abortions found that fifty-nine percent of the abortions were "probably induced" according to the physician in charge of the case (1971:3). In addition, four percent of the abortions were admittedly induced. Although hospital admissions for septic abortions are a likely place to look for induced abortions, the identification of induced abortions that reach the hospital is an indicator of the much higher proportion of induced abortions that are concealed and never come to the attention of medical personnel.

Another study was conducted in 1969 using a sample of 1,400 patients seeking family planning in Planned Parenthood Affiliate (APROFE) clinics. Seventeen percent of these women had had at least one induced abortion at some time (Parra Gil and Marangoni, n.d.). Most were reportedly done by a doctor, but because the women studied ethnographically referred to both MDs and nurse-midwives as "doctor," it is doubtful that all ninety-five percent of the abortions were done by MDs. It is likely that the seventeen

TABLE 6.4
Frequency and Outcome of First and Subsequent Pregnancies for Urban
Women

PREGNANCY NUMBER	TOTAL (n=10925) *	INDUCED ABORTION (n=209) **	SPONTANEOUS ABORTION (n=1198) **	STILL BIRTH (n=141) **	LIVE BIRTH (n=9377) **	CHILDREN DEAD AFTER BIRTH (n=1008) ***
1	20.7	0.3	7.4	1.1	91.1	10.9
2	18.1	0.9	9.9	1.5	87.5	11.2
3	15.0	1.5	10.9	1.2	86.2	11.8
4	12.1	1.4	11.0	0.9	86.6	10.9
5	9.4	2.6	11.3	0.9	85.1	9.4
6	7.2	2.6	10.4	1.2	85.6	8.9
7	5.4	3.8	15.8	1.8	78.5	10.3
8	3.9	3.9	13.5	1.1	81.4	9.5
9	2.7	6.2	17.2	1.3	75.2	12.3
10	1.8	5.7	16.9	2.4	74.9	15.4
11	1.2	4.4	17.6	2.2	75.7	10.7
12	0.7	4.6	13.9	0.0	81.4	14.3
13	0.5	5.3	21.4	1.7	71.4	20.0
14	0.2	6.2	12.5	3.1	78.1	12.0
15	0.1	10.5	36.8	0.0	52.6	10.0
16	<0.1	12.5	37.5	12.5	37.5	0.0
17	<0.1	0.0	40.0	0.0	60.0	0.0
18	<0.1	33.3	66.6	0.0	0.0	0.0
19	<0.1	33.3	33.3	0.0	33.3	0.0
PERCENTAGE OF TOTAL PREG-NANCIES	99.8	1.9	10.9	1.2	85.8	10.7

 * Percentage of Total Pregnancies
 ** Percentage of First Pregnancy. etc.
*** Percentage of Live Births

Source: Scrimshaw (1976:123). Used by permission of The Carolina
Population Center, University of North Carolina at Chapel Hill.

percent of the women reporting abortions is a higher rate than in
the population of women of reproductive age as a whole, because the
sample is based on women who are seeking contraception.

It is possible that the relatively low incidence of admitted
induced abortions and even of spontaneous abortions may be representative of reality. While there are undoubtedly more induced
abortions than this survey shows, it is unlikely that the ratio of
induced abortions to live births in Ecuador is as high as in Chile.
The five percent figure for women admitting to induced abortions is
only slightly lower than that obtained during the ethnographic
research, where I knew most of the women well over a period of six
months. During this time, I knew women trying to decide whether or
not to have an induced abortion, and two women did so while I was
living in the barrio. One of the obstacles they faced was the
difficulty of finding someone they believed competent to perform
the abortion, a difficulty stemming from the illegality of the
operation. Another serious obstacle was the expense, which ranged
from 200 sucres ($10) for a midwife to as high as 800 sucres ($40)
for a good doctor. One of the two women who got an abortion while
I was there borrowed the money from several friends, the other
pawned a ring for part of the fee and was allowed to owe the
remainder. Another problem was the opposition of husbands, which
often meant the women had to raise the money and go through with
the operation secretly, not an easy thing in a society where men
watch their women fairly closely. Given factors such as these it
is likely that many women who might have wished to have an induced
abortion could not obtain one.

Methods of Inducing Abortions

The women who had admitted to induced abortions were asked a
series of questions about their experience. Table 6.5 shows who
reportedly performed the abortions: surprisingly, the overwhelming
majority of abortions were performed by trained professionals such
as doctors and nurses (actually nurse-midwives, called obstetrices
in Ecuador). Only in a few cases did women rely on matronas (non-
professionally trained midwives), friends or their own efforts.

If the women themselves or a friend performed the abortion,
they reported using "potions," a stick, tallo or douches. Tallo is
a piece of root that is inserted in the cervix and swells with the
moisture there, thus dilating the cervix and (theoretically) producing an abortion.

The women who had abortions performed by doctors, nurse-
midwives, or midwives were also asked about procedures (for the
most recent abortion only if they had had more than one). Most,
(eighty-nine percent) of these women said they had been given
something for the pain. Most often this was "injection," but pills
and "a mask" were also reported. Seventy-eight percent of the
women said they were asleep during the procedure. Those who were
not sedated reported feeling pain. The majority (seventy-eight
percent) said they were given other medicines to take later such as
"injections" (forty-two percent) or "pills" (forty-six percent). A

TABLE 6.5
People Performing Induced Abortions for Urban Women

Abortion Number	M.D.* (n=92)	Nurse-Midwives (n=100)	Midwife (n=5)	Friend (n=4)	Herself (n=12)	Don't Answer (n=3)	TOTAL N	% age**
1	39	50	1	3	6	1	125	57.9
2	38	53	2	0	5	2	40	18.5
3	59	27	5	0	9	0	22	10.2
4	40	50	10	0	0	0	10	4.6
5	43	29	14	0	0	14	7	3.2
6	60	40	0	0	0	0	5	2.3
7	67	33	0	0	0	0	3	1.4
8	75	25	0	0	0	0	4	1.9
Percentage of Total Abortions	42.6	46.3	2.3	1.9	5.6	1.4		100.0

* Percentage of first abortion,etc.   ** Percentage of total abortions

few women reported receiving vitamins, plasma, and other medications.

All the women were asked if they felt pain after the procedure. Over half (fifty-five percent) said they felt none, but thirteen percent remembered feeling one day of pain, five percent two days, six percent three days, five percent four to six days, and nine percent seven or more days. Over half the women bled for one to three days, another eighteen percent bled for three to six days, and twenty-five percent reportedly bled for seven or more days. One-fifth (twenty-one percent) still reported problems at the time of the interview. These included "pain in their ovaries," inflammation, vaginal discharge, and other complications.

Attitudes

As discussed earlier, men and women were asked during the ethnographic phase whether they would approve of induced abortion under a series of circumstances that ranged from simply not wanting another child to the pregnancy threatening the life of the mother. Three questions that appeared to distinguish attitudes most clearly were asked during the survey. Only five percent of the women and six percent of the men said they approved of induced abortion if a woman simply wanted no more children. However, twenty-five percent of the women, and nineteen percent of the men said they approved of induced abortion if a woman or a family did not have enough money to "care for" her children. The approval rates rose to eighty-one percent for the women and eighty-nine percent for the men if the woman's life was threatened by the pregnancy. Respondents were also asked if they would have an abortion (women) or allow their wives to have one (men) if the woman became pregnant and they wished no more children. Twelve percent of the women and eight percent of the men answered affirmatively, thus contradicting their answers to the first question in some cases. All of the differences discussed above were statistically significant at the .01 level (for details see Scrimshaw 1978:50).

Family Size Desires and Actual Family Size

Most people, (sixty-eight percent of the men and seventy-seven percent of the women) did not want more children at the time of the interview.[6] They were then asked if they wished they had fewer children. Fifty-two percent of the women and forty-seven percent of the men replied affirmatively. Finally, they were asked how many children they felt comprised a "good" family. The results are presented in Table 6.6. The great majority (sixty-seven to seventy-five percent) thought from one-three children was an ideal family size. Less than one percent wanted no children, about two percent wanted seven or more, and the remainder wanted four-six children. Men appear to want slightly more children than women do (p < .05). The mean numbers desired for both groups are 2.96 children (men) and 2.83 children (women). Despite these desires,

TABLE 6.6
The Number of Children Thought to Comprise an Ideal Family According to Men and Women

# of Children in an "Ideal" Family	Women		Men	
	N	%	N	%
0	14	1	11	1
1-3	2156	73	791	70
4-6	692	23	295	26
7+	74	2	22	1
Total	2936	100	1119	100

completed fertility was about seven pregnancies, with five children
still alive.

These discrepancies between ideal family size and the reality
of too many pregnancies, and between the attempts at contraception
and the failures, contributed to the motivation for induced abortion.

THE GOVERNMENT AND THE HEALTH SYSTEM

Attitudes within the Government

When the research discussed here was initiated, the attitudes
of government officials, including the President, were extremely
negative toward abortion, primarily on religious and moral grounds.
Among the individuals I encountered and with whom I worked, abortion was not regarded as an option in the area of fertility control. In fact, the idea of contraceptives was still controversial,
with officials divided on whether or not they should be available
to the "people," and particularly, whether they should be offered
through government clinics. The objections were religious, moral
(contraceptives were seen encouraging promiscuity) and political
(contraceptives were seen as an instrument to help the U.S. control
Latin America by keeping the population down). Those who favored
contraception did so primarily for health reasons, arguing that
spacing pregnancies contributed to healthier mothers and children.
A few also argued that women and men have a right to plan their
family size and spacing.

Despite the political climate against abortion as a back-up
method of fertility regulation, some health officials were deeply
concerned about the existing levels of induced abortion. The
Minister of Health at the time I initiated the research described
here had conducted (along with the head of the local IPPF affiliate) the only existing study of abortion (Parra and Maragoni,

n.d.). For them the health effects of illegal induced abortions were a major concern.

These attitudes contrast greatly with those at the level of the squatter settlement where approval rates for induced abortion rose to over eighty percent if a woman's life was threatened by a pregnancy. The poor of Guayaquil also saw the church as relatively uninvolved in issues of contraception, and even abortion in nearly half the responses. In addition, a majority of the people already had more children than they wanted, and were anxious to prevent additional pregnancies.

The gap between government and people was even wider when it came to perception of actual behavior. When I arrived in Ecuador I was told repeatedly that there was little induced abortion. True, the rates I encountered were much lower than those reported for some other Latin American countries such as Chile, but abortion existed. What is interesting is that fewer pregnancies ended in abortion before improvements in health care lowered infant mortality rates. That is, the rise in induced abortion accompanied an increase in child survival, thus necessitating fewer pregnancies to achieve a desired family size. The first response to these changes for some women appears to have been the drastic measure of abortion. This may have been in part because of the relative unavailability of reliable contraception.

When the survey results reported here became available, government officials and the press reacted with shock and incredulity. Not only were women inducing abortions, but the majority of these abortions, at least in Guayaquil, were being done by nurse-midwives and doctors, members of the medical establishment. How could nurses and doctors be doing this if it was illegal? Who was doing it? I was pressured to name names, which was obviously out of the question. Colleagues in the Ministry of Health took some comfort, but not a lot, in the idea that at least a greater proportion of abortions were being done under safer conditions than in many Latin American countries, even allowing for poor practices by individuals such as the nurse-midwife I had observed.

Attitudes Within the Health System

At both national levels and the levels of the individual health center, many staff felt that "the people" were not ready for contraception, that they would not know how to use contraceptives properly and that attitudes toward them were negative.

In fact, the population studied in Guayaquil demonstrated high levels of knowledge of modern contraceptives, and of interest in their uses (see Scrimshaw 1978). Some methods, such as the pill, were mentioned by as many as eighty-three percent of the women when they were asked how to avoid pregnancy.

During the survey, attitudes towards each contraceptive method were recorded verbatim. To facilitate analysis, each response was given a negative, a positive, or a neutral rating. Over half of each sex expressed negative opinions on the pill, the IUD, the condom, and coitus interuptus. Over half of the men were also negative about jelly or cream, injections, and the diaphragm. Over fifty percent of each sex was positive about foam tablets, foam, and rhythm.

Approximately half of the women were positive about douching. The other methods received relatively neutral reactions. Interestingly, the women gave more neutral reactions (such as "it's good for some women, bad for others") than men. In fact, injections, the diaphragm, and female sterilization received many more neutral and positive reactions from women than negative ones.

Even the most disliked method, the condom, received positive reactions from at least one quarter of both the men and the women. Such varied attitudes toward each method would indicate that family planning programs should offer the widest possible choice of methods. Few people find all methods unacceptable.

In the early 1970s, clinics that offered contraception tended to offer two methods, the pill and the IUD. These were said to be the only methods women could understand, as well as being the most effective methods. The women studied expressed high levels of dissatisfaction with both methods (sixty-two percent and seventy percent respectively) and greater interest in other methods (Scrimshaw 1978:54).

When both folk and modern methods are combined, the practice of some form of contraception was quite generalized. About twenty-two percent of all women were currently using one form or another of contraception. Forty-four percent of the women have at one time used one or more methods (13.5 percent have only used one method, thirty-one percent have used more than one). While not all the methods used were the most effective, nearly half the women had actually tried to prevent pregnancy (Scrimshaw 1978:55).

After the knowledge, attitudes and practice section of the interview, women were asked where they could obtain "things" to avoid becoming pregnant. Their first four answers were recorded. Over half the women's first answer was "the drugstore." An additional nineteen percent replied "a doctor," and twenty-one percent said they did not know. Only two percent mentioned a government health clinic, and only two percent mentioned a "family planning clinic." Another two percent mentioned the Maternity Hospital, where family planning services were not available during this study. It is apparently a logical place for such services for some women. After mentioning clinics as a source, relatively few gave reasons for not going back. "No money" (cited by nineteen percent) and wanting another child (twenty-eight percent) were clearly important factors, but other reasons such as "They didn't take good care of me" (five percent), "afraid" (five percent), and "doesn't want to" (thirty-one percent) all appear to be related to feelings of discomfort with the clinics (Scrimshaw 1976).

In another part of the questionnaire all the women were asked if they would seek out family planning if they didn't want any more children. Eighty-two percent said "yes." However, because seventy-seven percent of the ever "married" said they want no more children and only twenty-two percent actually sought family planning (most through private MD's), we know that a large majority were not going to do what they said in response to that survey question. However, when it is remembered that seventy-seven percent of the women said they wanted no more children, it is clear that there remains a large unmet need for family planning.

There is evidence that clinics could meet more of the current need, but that visiting a clinic for family planning services is a difficult step for many women to take. Women were discouraged by factors such as actual cost, lack of accurate knowledge about cost and procedures, clinic hours, and embarrassment at the questions of the gynecological examination (Scrimshaw 1976). Efforts to motivate women by sending around "motivators" to individual homes had apparently not been successful. Women mentioned the motivadoras' visit, but had an exaggerated impression of the cost of a clinic visit and said they had been told to come only when they had their periods. This deterred some women, who had trouble finding time to go to a clinic at all, much less on a few specific days. While obviously convenient for the clinic staff who would be assured the women weren't pregnant, this recommendation had the effect of delaying the visit so that the idea could be more easily put off or forgotten. There was also the woman who wailed: "But I'll be pregnant again if I try to wait that long!"

Women who did get to a clinic reacted to the experience with mixed feelings. Many (seventy-eight percent) started out by saying it was fine, but after probing for details, forty-four percent of the women who attended clinics appeared to reflect some degree of reticence (Scrimshaw 1976).

During six years of visiting clinics, it was clear that clinic staff had a great deal of ambivalence toward family planning. In a brief informal survey conducted by Mario Jaramillo, many staff were against contraception, even for their own use (personal communication 1972). These varying attitudes mean that even if the government declared contraceptives as part of its health care delivery system, access to them would be very uneven. In some clinics, staff refused even to discuss contraception, in others they were helpful and supportive. In many instances, even when staff were amenable, deliveries of contraceptive supplies were irregular. In general, access to contraception, with the exception of some private sources such as the local IPPF affiliate,[7] was very poor. In my opinion, this contributed to the proportion of unwanted pregnancies and thus to the number of induced abortions.

CONCLUSIONS

In this study I have examined two main aspects of the relationships between microlevel and macrolevel phenomena. The first is simply the statistical resemblance between the ethnographically studied small community (in this case, less than 100 families), and the larger unit, the thousands of families that comprise the urban poor of Guayaquil. The data indicate quite clearly that this barrio can be regarded as a credible representation of the generality of urban poor of the city. Statistical similarities with regard to fertility attitudes and behaviors (including abortion) give me confidence that the complex processes of coping with

pregnancies and repeated childbirths that I observed in the barri
are widespread in the low-income settlements of the city. Thus, i
is a strong assumption that the patterns observed in one cluster o
sixty-five families reflect general, macrolevel economic, cultura
and social realities of urban Ecuador in the early 1970s. Many o
the cases and correlates of peoples' behaviors at the microleve
were not "localizable" or "containable" within the bounds of th
local neighborhood. The very act of seeking contraceptive serv
ices, or seeking an abortion, required that a woman explore th
wider social system to find the medical professionals or parapro
fessionals who might supply these services. On the other hand, th
dynamics of decision-making about contraception and abortion tak
place in the context of families and individuals plus their imme
diate frameworks of economic/social aspirations and resources.

The second major aspect of microlevel-macrolevel relations i
that complex linkage between national level governance and th
people affected by these political/administrative structures. Th
Ecuadorian government maintains certain policies and services witl
regard to health care, including contraception and abortion.
found that the policies were based on certain moral/religiou
principles, as well as on perceptions (and misperceptions) abou
"the people." One of the most interesting aspects of the macro
level view of a complex sociocultural system is the administrators
and policy makers' theories concerning the knowledge, attitudes
and behaviors "out there" in the multitudes of microlevels -- the
grassroots communities and families. My ethnographic research at
the macrolevel (national administrative offices) demonstrated that
there is considerable error and misunderstanding in the macrolevel
"theories" concerning microlevel behavior patterns.

"Theory" about the people "out there" is one aspect; the
actual implementation of national policies raises many additional
issues. Nationally prescribed (as well as the proscribed) health
services in general, and contraceptive services in particular,
reach down to various microlevels (the "consumers") through facilities such as clinics and other locations established and maintained
by governmental actions. As found in this research, governmental
policies -- especially in controversial areas such as contraception
and abortion -- take various forms depending on factors operating
at the intermediate levels. Lack of supplies, attitudes of personnel, physical location, and other features strongly affected the
ways in which contraceptives services reached, or did not reach,
women such as those I encountered in the barrio.

From the perspective of the national policy levels in Ecuador,
abortion is illegal and reprehensible. Abortion services are certainly not provided by governmental facilities, according to national policy. Nothing in national policy is supposed to be encouraging abortion in any way. However, another part of the macrolevel system of Guayaquil -- the sector of practicing medical
professionals and paraprofessionals -- does provide the supposedly
proscribed abortion services. Clearly, these services have developed in response to general increases in "felt needs" for induced
abortions among urban women. Ironically, the increased "demand"
for these services appears to have resulted in part from the ef-

fects, including the successes, of national health policy. Declining infant mortality rates, reflecting improved health services and other public health measures, contribute to increased family sizes, which in turn seriously strain the economic and social resources of urban families. Induced abortions are one mode of dealing with the strains of unwanted increases in family size.

These data from research in Ecuador show that anthropologists can, and must, use combinations of methodologies in the study of complex systems. Ethnographic research -- at both the microlevel and macrolevel -- continues to play a central role, especially when articulated with carefully constructed survey data. Other methodologies, including archival research, analyses of census data, and mapping of various population features, also aid in delineating the linkages and interactions between local level (family and neighborhood) processes and the macrolevels of national and international governance. Research in population and fertility behavior is one sector in which such eclectic methodology appears to be especially valuable.[8]

NOTES

1. My colleague Patricia Engle points out that the ethnographer in this case was from the U.S., while the interviewers for the survey were Ecuadorian. It is possible people felt a U.S. researcher would be more understanding of their contraceptive attitudes and gave me more information for that reason.

2. Pseudonyms are used throughout this paper.

3. Making a phone call involved walking several blocks to a store which had a phone, then hoping no one would be around to overhear.

4. _Tallo_ is reportedly a root which swells up after contact with moisture. It is placed in the cervix and dilates the cervix as it swells.

5. This rate may be low in part because pregnancy is not diagnosed early and so many spontaneous abortions in the first month or two go unrecognized.

6. Over three-fourths of both men and women who wanted more children only wanted one or two more.

7. The private sector was an important factor in increasing the availability of family planning to women in Guayaquil in the early 1970s. At that time, APROFE, the Ecuadorian IPPF affiliate, operated two clinics in Guayaquil, one in the center of town and one in the suburbs. Clinic staff were supportive both of contraceptive use and attempts to overcome infertility. The choice of methods was fairly limited, with most of the emphasis on the pill and the IUD.

8. This paper is based on a study supported by USAID from 1970-1972 (Contract Number 0113-26332-11, AID csd-2479 task force order number 3B) and by the Ford Foundation. The original invitation to work in Ecuador was extended by Dr. Francisco Parra Gil, then Minister of Health of Ecuador and by Dr. Pablo Marangoni of the University of Guayaquil and head of the Associaciôn Pro-Bienestar

144

de la Familia Ecuadoriana (APROFE). I deeply appreciate both the
invitation to carry out this study and their support throughout :
duration. Dr. Felipe Aroca, then director of Health Services i
the Ministry of Health, also greatly facilitated the fieldwork,
did many others. Their help is gratefully acknowledged, but th
should not be held responsible for the interpretations and opinic
expressed by me in this paper. The original research and da
analysis were carried out while I was a Research Associate with t
Center for Population and Family Health, Columbia University Scho
of Public Health.

Drs. Solomon Katz, Patricia Engle, Pertti Pelto and Bill
DeWalt provided useful comments on earlier drafts of this pap
Their help is gratefully acknowledged.

BIBLIOGRAPHY

Armijo, R. and T. Monreal. 1965. "The Problem of Induced Abortion in Chile." Milbank Quarterly 43(4):263-280.

Browner, Carole. 1979. "Abortion Decision Making: Some Finds from Colombia." Studies in Family Planning 10(3).

_____. 1980. "The Management of Early Pregnancy: Colombia Fold Concepts of Fertility Control." Social Science and Medicine 14B:25-32.

Cambell, Moore-Cavar, Emily. 1974. International Inventory of Information on Induced Abortion. Division of Social and Administrative Sciences, International Institute for the Study of Human Reproduction. New York: Columbia University.

de Laune, P.H. Chombart. 1974. Field and Case Studies, Handbook of Social Research in Urban Areas. Philip Houser, ed. Belgium: UNESCO, pp.55-72.

_____. 1964a. Social Organization in an Urban Mileau, Handbook of Social Research in Urban Areas. Philip Houser, ed. Belgium: UNESCO, pp.140-158.

Hellman, Ellen. 1935. "Methods of Urban Field Work." Bantu Studies 9:185-202.

Isaccs, Stephen I. and Hernan Sanhueza. 1975. "Induced Abortion in Latin America: The Legal Perspective." Epidemiology of Abortion and Practices of Fertility Regulation in Latin America: Selected Problems. Pan American Health Organization, Scientific Publication No. 306:39-49.

Jaramillo Gomez, Mario. 1972. Personal Communication.

Liskin, Laurie S. 1980. "Complications of Abortion in Developing Countries." Population Reports, Population Program, The Johns Hopkins University, Series F, VIII (7):F-105-F-156.

Nag, Moni. 1968. Factors Affecting Human Fertility in Non-Industrial Societies: Cross-Cultural Study. Yale University Publications in Anthropology No. 66.

Parra Gil, Francisco and Pablo Marangoni. 1968. "Encuesta de Fecundidad Levantada en Guayaquil". Revista Ecuatoriana de Higiene y Medicina Tropical 25(1):115-126.

146

Pelto, Pertti J. 1972. Research Strategies in the Study of Complex
    Societies: The "Ciudad Industrial" Project, Anthropology of
    Urban Environments. Thomas Weaver and Douglas White, eds. The
    Society for Applied Anthropology Monograph Series, Monograph
    11.
Pelto, Pertti J. and G.H. Pelto. 1978. Anthropological Research:
    The Structure of Inquiry. New York: Cambridge University
    Press.
Scrimshaw, S.C.M. 1974. Culture, Environment and Family Size: A
    Study of Urban In-Migrants in Guayaquil, Ecuador. Department
    of Anthropology, Columbia University, New York. Doctoral Dis-
    sertation.
_____. 1976. Women's Modesty: One Barrier to the Use of Family
    Planning Clinics. In Culture, Natality and Family Planning.
    John Marshall and Steven Polgar, eds. University of North
    Carolina Population Center, Monograph No. 22.
_____. 1978. "Stages in Women's Lives and Reproductive Deci-
    sion Making in Latin America." Medical Anthropology 2(3).
Serrano Gomez, Cesar and Mario Jaramillo Gomez. 1971. "Aborto
    Provocado en Guayaquil." Estudios de Evaluacion.
Shedlin, Michelle and Paula E. Hollerbach. 1981. "Modern and Tradi-
    tional Fertility Regulation in a Mexican Community: The Proc-
    ess of Decision-Making." Studies in Family Planning 12(12):6-
    7.
Steward, Julian. 1950. Area Research: Theory and Practice. New
    York: Social Science Research Council.
Wolfers, D. and S. Scrimshaw. 1975. "The Epidemiological Signifi-
    cance of Spacing Pregnancies in Guayaquil, Ecuador. Population
    Studies 29(3):479-496.

7
The Political Economy
of Rural Transformation:
A Mexican Case[1]

Scott Whiteford and Laura Montgomery

INTRODUCTION

The last two decades of anthropological research and theory
building have witnessed a significant paradigmatic shift. The
focus has moved away from examining social relationships as isolates, toward understanding them as part of a broader regional, national, and international matrix. The shift occurred partially as
anthropologists recognized the profound impact that two related
processes -- the growth of state power and the expansion of capitalism -- were having on communities, households, and individuals.
The shift has raised a series of methodological and theoretical
issues about units of analysis, the nature of articulation, systemic integration, and socio-cultural change in general.

The political economy approach is one of the major perspectives that anthropologists are using to analyze forces that generate and condition social change.[2] Although this approach is an
attempt to integrate the economic and political domains, scholars
have tended to emphasize one domain over the other (Ortner 1984).
Nevertheless, the focus of the studies has been on how economic and
political forces over time have changed the social environment in
which people make decisions. At the same time researchers have
tended to treat "local systems as passive recipients of global
process" (Smith 1984:225). Yet as Carol Smith and others have
demonstrated, local struggles and alliances can affect regional
structures, subsequently shaping the ways that macro processes are
played out in a specific context.

THE TRANSFORMATION OF A REGIONAL SOCIETY AND ECONOMY

In this chapter we examine the transformation of a regional
society and economy -- the Mexicali Valley located in Northern
Mexico. In less than thirty years, control of the regional economy
has shifted from foreign companies unencumbered by government constraints to a highly regulated system of state capitalism. Taking
a political economy perspective, we examine macro and microlevel
processes that generated and conditioned the expansion of state

148

power and the nature of its impact on the social and economic
organization of the region. In contrast to the generally held
notion that social change is generated almost exclusively at the
macrolevel, we show in this chapter that microlevel factors can and
do influence some macrolevel processes while not affecting others.

In our analysis, we trace the processes that led to increased
state control of agricultural production through structural penetration -- the creation of new state organizations and institutional transformation -- and the takeover of previously independent
organizations by the state (Corbett and Whiteford 1983). In this
chapter, we focus on the state as it takes control of agricultural
production and marketing. The process is more than economic; it is
one of increased political and social control. Increased state
penetration was, in part, a response to mobilization at the local
level. We map out not only the patterns of control over means of
production but also we examine the processes occurring at different
levels that led to changes in control over means of production and
systems of exchange. From the perspective of the individual agri-
culturalist, shifts in control of critical resources create important changes in power relationships. By contrasting, at different
periods of time, who controls agriculturalists' access to land,
water, credit, marketing and production, we are able to show differing degrees of state penetration of the agrarian economy. This
model of access-making could also be used in the comparison of
regions.

A second dimension of our analysis is the focus on linkages or
intermediary structures as structural components of the political
economy. The linkages are points of interface between the
processes operating at a different level. Intermediary structures
created by the state play a major role in managing systems of
distribution, accumulation and control. Yet as Wells and Climo
point out, "intermediaries, be they bureaucratic agencies or
strategically well-situated individuals" can independently generate
change (Wells and Climo 1984:152).

The expansion of state power and programs in a region may
result from processes occurring in the national or international
arena. In the case examined in this chapter, a series of changes
at different points in time contributed to the expansion of state
power in a traditionally peripheral region. These processes included the expansion of foreign capital into the region, shifts in
international capitalist commodity markets, and the destruction of
the productive bases of the region by salinization occurring outside national borders. The state may also respond to pressure from
local actors for support or services. Although state systems are
constantly changing, they continue to serve elites by maintaining
political control and "enforcing appropriation of value" (Wallerstein 1984:4). State programs are implemented and translated on
the local level through intermediary structures. States develop
bureaucracies to manage the production, accumulation and distribution of resources.

In Mexico, the state has taken increasing control over the
basic means of production in the agricultural sector; however,
state penetration of agriculture has been uneven (Carlos 1981). In

large irrigation districts, such as the Mexicali Valley where commercial crops are grown for export or for domestic urban markets, the state has played a very active role. From the allocation of credit to the formation of state enterprises, the state intervenes in the production, processing, and marketing of agricultural products. Through its control of irrigation water, _ejido_ land, credit and marketing systems, and the production and sale of inputs such as fertilizer and pesticides, the state has emerged as a dominant force in the productive process. As a result, "access to resources essential for production is obtained directly through politics as well as through conditions imposed by the state" (Warmen 1976:9). The expansion of state control through the creation of new organizations to regulate and support agriculture has been an important feature of the Mexican countryside since the Revolution of 1910.

The bureaucratic structures created by the Mexican state to manage the system of resource distribution has played an important role in the maintenance of the stability of the regime (Grindle 1977:8). As these organizations expand, they become increasingly formalized. Although the formal structures link levels, the more important set of relationships are informal networks that compete for control over the formal positions. The consequences of these power struggles has a direct impact on how state penetration affects the social organization of the region.

We draw on the history of people living in one agricultural community in the Mexicali Valley, El Tiburón, to document the shifts and to trace factors that influenced the transformation. For analytical purposes we have divided the history of the region into three periods: (1) the preagrarian reform period, (2) the post-agrarian reform period, and (3) the agrarian crisis and rehabilitation period. Each period is characterized by a distinctly different structure of control over land, water, credit, processing, and marketing. For the agriculturalists, the shifts had a profound impact on their lives, requiring different household economic strategies.

The Mexicali Valley is one of the major agricultural regions of Mexico. Irrigated by water from the Colorado River that flows into the Valley from the United States and ground water from aquifers that Mexico shares with the United States, the region is susceptible to the resource policies of its northern neighbor. The city of Mexicali, located on the border, has historically been a service center for the agricultural hinterland. The rich alluvial soil of the Valley was deposited by the Colorado River over thousands of years. Water is the critical resource in the Valley. Because of water scarcity, only 297,294 hectares of the district's 308,400 hectares are under cultivation.

The water is shared by 13,126 users, of which 7,471 are ejidatarios.[3] Fifty percent of the land is held by ejidatarios, whose holdings average twenty hectares. The Valley economy was built upon cotton until the salinization crisis in the mid-1960s, after which agriculture became diversified. Wheat is the second most important crop in the district that now produces alfalfa, safflower, barley, vegetables, citrus, grapes, and rye grass and sorghum for cattle feed. Cotton, vegetables, and raisins are the major exports while the rest of the production is for the domestic market.

PRE-AGRARIAN REFORM PERIOD

The agricultural development of the Mexicali Valley was forged by foreign entrepreneurs intent upon exporting produce to the expanding American markets. With concessions from Porfirio Diaz, a group of California capitalists headed by Henry Chandler gained control of land and the irrigation water necessary to convert the sparsely settled lower Colorado River delta into a center of commercial agriculture. The Chandler group formed the Colorado River Land Company (CRLC), an affiliate of their California-Mexico Land Cattle Company. By the end of the nineteenth century, these American capitalists owned 321,721.4 hectares of the Mexicali Valley and 400 hectares in the Imperial Valley; they clearly controlled the region.

Given the region's aridity, irrigation water was crucial to agricultural development on both sides of the border. Claiming the Colorado River to be a navigable stream, the U.S. government had denied several requests to build a canal diverting water from the river into the Imperial Valley. A firm named the Colorado River Irrigation Company decided to bypass the problem by constructing a fifty-mile-long canal, the Alamo Canal, on the Mexican side of the border through an old river bed that curved into the Imperial Valley. (Building on the Mexican side also avoided the engineering problem of building a canal through the shifting sand dunes on the U.S. side). The Colorado River Irrigation Company, now the California Development Company, started building the canal in 1893, without formal permission from the Mexican government, although the company did own the water rights to the land owned by the Colorado River Land Company. The canal was completed in 1901. The California Development Company then formed a Mexican counterpart, the Sociedad de Irrigación y Terrenos de Baja California, with Guillermo Andrade, Mexican counsel in San Francisco, as the Mexican partner. The Mexican government finally granted the company formal approval for the canal with the provision that Mexico would have rights to one-half of the water that flowed through the canal. Even though water in Mexico was property of the state, the government gave the company a concession to build a canal system and to regulate and manage water distribution in the Mexicali Valley. In turn the company could charge a user fee for the water, a setup quite consonant with Porfirian policies. Until 1904 when Andrade sold his share of the company to the California Development Company, the CRLC did not have access to water for its land on either side of the border (Grijalva Larranaga 1983:176). But after the sale it was able to negotiate a long-term water agreement to develop its lands. Once the irrigation structure was in place, the company reaped tremendous profits from cotton and cattle production (Grijalva Larranaga 1983:353).

By the early 1900s, American companies controlled agriculture in the Mexicali Valley. The Mexican government participated only as a benign governing state. In 1917, the government instituted the Comisión Irrigadora del Río Colorado in Mexicali as an agency of the Secretaría de Agricultura y Fomento. It was the first official bureaucracy to govern water distribution in the nation. In reality, however, the commission's purpose was to make sure that the California Development Company was fulfilling its obligations of the concession; it did not take an active role in the distribution and management of water resources (Villarreal 1971). The area had a small Mexican population, and in the early days of the Colorado River Land Company, Mexican labor was not important in the company's operations. Because of the lack of Mexican labor, the company imported Chinese laborers to clear and cultivate the land. It also rented out much of its agricultural land to other American firms, who in turn subcontracted to sharecroppers.

Understandably, the company -- known as "La Colorada" -- dominated the political and economic life in the valley. In response to world demand and high prices, the company exclusively cropped cotton -- "El Oro Blanco" -- and ran cattle on its Mexicali Valley lands. Cotton grown on the company's land had to be sold at La Colorada, which provided credit to growers. The success of the company spawned a complex of other companies owned by the same group of investors. These included a cotton ginning plant, a cotton seed plant, a bank, and a railroad to transport products to the West Coast. At the peak of its power, La Colorada directly employed 4,000 to 8,000 laborers, owned 8,000 mules, and managed 3,000 miles of canals (Oden 1984:1).

The next thirty years saw an increase in investment of foreign capital in the Valley. In 1926, another major American-owned company, the Compañía Industrial Jabonera del Pacifico, moved into the Mexicali Valley from the La Laguna region. The company had an oil mill, a soap factory, a cotton gin, and a shortening factory. Working with the Banco del Pacifico and Banco Mercantil, the Jabonera gave agricultural credit to farmers growing cotton. Anderson Clayton bought the Jabonera in 1931, and by 1950 the Mexicali operation represented over half of Anderson Clayton's operations in Mexico. In Mexicali, it was a major processor of cotton by-products.

As we have discussed, the pre-reform period was one in which the resources necessary for agricultural production as well as the production process itself essentially were controlled by foreign companies producing for export. During the 1930s, however, the Mexican government, in response to national and international events, began to exert greater control over land, water, credit, marketing and production. This initiated great changes in the Valley's political economy.

AGRARIAN REFORM AND THE NEW COMMUNITIES

The end of the 1930s brought the beginning of the end of foreign capital hegemony in the Mexicali region. The Mexican population in the Valley had been increasing as people fled north-

152

ward to escape the increasing violence of the Mexican Revolution. Many of these migrants went to work for the Colorado River Land Company. Additional Mexicans had migrated to the region as colonists and held 21,000 hectares in small private holdings. Most depended on the CLRC and other foreign companies for credit and a market for their cotton. The increasing population created pressures for land reform, but local authorities quickly stamped out attempts to organize such reforms. Demand for land further increased when many Mexicans who had been working in the U.S. migrated to the border area after the U.S. deported them during the Great Depression in order to increase jobs for American citizens. The local population petitioned the national government for help.

In 1936, President Lázaro Cárdenas, who was sensitive to the region's problems and seriously wanted to implement the Revolution's promises of land reform, announced plans for a massive transformation of the Valley. His program included the colonization of the region by Mexican farmers, both as small private holders and ejidatarios, based on a redistribution of land and water rights. The government would establish new credit sources -- The Banco Ejidal -- to break the dependence on foreign companies, and would build a railroad to link the Valley with central Mexico. On January 27, 1937, Mexicans wanting land staged a major land invasion that forced the national government to pursue land reform aggressively. In that year, a large portion of the Colorado River Land Company's lands were expropriated and over eighty ejidos and eighty colonias with twenty hectares for each family were granted land titles and water rights. In 1946, foreign ownership of Valley land ended when the Mexican government purchased the last holdings of La Colorada.

Even though the land was now out of foreign hands, the U.S.-owned Sociedad de Irrigación y Terrenos still managed the irrigation infrastructure and distribution of water. However, the government was beginning to expand and institute bureaucracies to oversee water resources in the region. In 1938, Cardenas created the Distrito de Riego del Rio Colorado as a federal agency in the Valley. In the beginning, the power of the Irrigation District administration was minimal. In 1941, however, by presidential decree the Irrigation District managers were given the responsibility of approving all future construction of irrigation works.

Throughout this period, cotton was the dominant crop raised in the Valley. The international cotton ginning companies, dominated by La Jabonera and later Anderson Clayton linked the region to the world capitalist commodity system. The companies exerted tremendous control over agriculturalists who needed credit from the companies and the markets for their produce. The companies extracted high profits from both the cotton seed and the cotton fiber.

The 1937 land reform was the first aggressive assertion of government power in the Valley's agricultural sector. The government was able to promote the revolutionary ideology of egalitarianism by distributing land and water rights to as many individuals as possible. Two historical factors unique to the Mexicali Valley have permitted and pressured the government to maintain this equity

up to the present, although this has not been the case in many
other regions of Mexico. First, the landed elite were foreigners,
so issues of nationalism made it impossible for the Colorado River
Land Company to regain their landholdings. Second, because no such
national landed elite had traditionally controlled the region, no
group could manipulate government policies to reconcentrate landholdings and monopolize the benefits of government services as has
occurred in other areas. Land distribution thus represented the
beginning of powerful peasant organizations. Though later co-opted
at times by the national government, this peasant power base both
propelled and uniquely shaped the growth of state capitalism in the
region. The latter is an important point that we will discuss
later in the paper.

Ejido Tiburón was one of eighty-seven ejidos created by the
land reform. Presidential decree established the ejido in 1937,
granting sixty-seven ejidatarios twenty hectares each of land with
water rights, plus eighty hectares for a school and urban zone.
Many of the original ejidatarios had been laborers for the Colorado
River Land Company. Most were migrants from the states of Guana-
juato, Jalisco, and the Baja California territories. While some
had been agriculturalists before coming to Mexicali, many were
miners who had worked for French-owned copper companies in the
lower Baja Peninsula. When the world price for copper dropped,
many migrated to the Valley attracted by the plentiful agricultural
jobs.

In accordance with Cárdenas's policies, the ejido was formed
as a collective credit society and given machinery by the government's Banco Ejidal to begin crop production. At first, sharecroppers from La Colorada continued to crop the ejido's newly
acquired land, and the ejidatarios had to petition the government
to intervene. The government did intervene on the behalf of the
ejidatarios, forcing the sharecroppers off the land.

Agricultural production in Tiburón centered around wheat and
cotton. Most ejidatarios cropped cotton, contracting with and
acquiring credit from private gins. Those who cropped wheat did so
with federal credit. According to ejidatarios who had worked with
the bank, during this early period the Banco Ejidal was very cor-
rupt in its lending practices. In spite of the fact that two
ejidatarios were thrown in jail for not paying their debts to
Anderson Clayton, many preferred to crop with the private companies
because they could work with less outside interference. Also,
since the government controlled the pricing and marketing of wheat,
growing cotton was more lucrative and thus preferred.

Ejido Tiburón underwent many changes during its early history.
By 1940, forty-three percent of the original ejidatarios had left
and thirteen new members replaced them, making a total of forty-
eight ejidatarios. Several factors may explain the major out-
migration. First, many of the original ejidatarios were not agriculturalists and decided to return to the city. Second, ejido
records show a lot of friction within the ejido because of the
original collective farming arrangement. In 1940, the ejido asked
for permission to replace collective farming with the individual
operation of farm units. Third, the beginning of World War II

created many jobs in the United States, which may have lured away those dissatisfied with ejido life.

During the next two decades, the Mexican government slowly took a larger role in the legal control of water resources in the Valley, largely because of their increasing recognition that political interests in the U.S. wanted to curtail, or even cut off, Mexico's use of Colorado River water. Still, the Sociedad de Irrigación y Terrenos continued to manage the day-to-day operations of the Valley's irrigation system. In 1944, the United States and Mexico finally signed a treaty allocating Mexico a restricted and fixed amount of water -- 1,850,234,000 m^3 (1.5 million acre-feet) annually. Although it would have liked a larger allocation, Mexico was in no position to refuse the offer. The All-American Canal had been built to supply water to the Imperial Valley, eliminating the need for the Alamo Canal. The All-American Canal would allow the U.S. to cut off all water to Mexico, and during this period the southwestern U.S. was suffering from a drought. Mexico realized the benefits of a guaranteed flow, although the negotiators were unhappy with the amount of water Mexico was to receive. The restriction in the amount of water available for irrigation set the limits to future development and expansion of the valley's agriculture. However, because the United States during the 1950's was not using its full allotment of water guaranteed by the treaty, Mexico received more water than it was officially allocated. As a result, land under irrigation in the Mexicali Valley expanded above what would have been possible had the water been restricted to the treaty allotment.

In an attempt to bring agricultural production under national jurisdiction, President Aldolfo Ruíz Cortinez in 1953 created agricultural Comités Directivos in the irrigation districts. These were to coordinate and program agricultural production to meet the agricultural goals and priorities set by the Secretaría de Agricultura for the nation as a whole. The committees are composed of ten voting members: seven represent government agencies and three represent the major agricultural unions. Every year the committee plans how much land, water, and credit will be allocated to which crops. In the planning, there is an attempt to coordinate regional and national needs. While the recommendations of the committee are supposed to be strictly followed, in practice they are not. While officially agriculturalists have little voting power on the committee, the unions unofficially lobby the various government agencies and the state governor. They also protest in the newspapers if the recommendations do not coincide with the needs and wants of agriculturalists. Currently, the influence of the unions is such that they can achieve major modifications in the committee's recommendations.

In 1955, following protests from farmers over insufficient and unequally distributed water, the Mexican government froze all water rights in the valley. Farmers of all tenure categories were restricted to water rights sufficient for twenty hectares and only one agricultural cycle. This shift profoundly affected both ejidos and the private farming sector. Its positive benefit was that all farmers now received some water. But the restriction to a twenty-

hectare allocation seriously constrained the private cotton companies, some of whose clients had been cropping over 100 hectares.
These companies formed the Asociación Algodonera, which petitioned
the government for permission to drill 100 wells at their own
expense to augment their water quotas. The government agreed,
allowing the high profits of the cotton companies to continue. The
government did not at this time, however, provide assistance to
ejidatarios who lacked the capital to sink wells and thereby augment their water supplies.

The restriction of water by the treaty, drought, and the 1955
government action affected Ejido Tiburón in several ways. The now
restricted water supply, combined with poor drainage, contributed
to a growing salinity problem. By 1944, this had rendered portions
of fields unproductive for fifty-nine percent of the ejido's members. By 1950, seventeen of those with affected parcels had abandoned their fields and migrated out of the ejido, some to become
agricultural workers in the Bracero Program. The Confederación
Nacional Campesino (CNC) was not a major political force at this
time in the valley and the politics of the dominant Partido Revolu-
cionario Institucional (PRI) prevented ejidatarios in the valley
from demanding government assistance with the problem until it
became a serious international issue in 1961. The 1955 freeze on
water rights meant that ejidatarios could crop during only one
agricultural cycle instead of two, further reducing farm income.
Those with salt problems sought additional income from off-farm
employment in both agricultural and non-agricultural activities, as
well as self-employment. A few ejidatarios built political ties in
the local, state, and national governments, as well as the CNC;
these networks later became critical in obtaining government financial assistance and other benefits for the ejido. The ejidatarios
also began a shift away from private to public credit as cotton
companies began to refuse credit for production on salinized land.

The agrarian reform period brought about a major transformation in the agricultural sector of the Mexicali Valley. During
this time patterns of control over resources shifted greatly. Land
switched from exclusive foreign control to an exclusive domestic
control with half of the land in the ejidos, the public sector.
The ejido program gave hundreds of families access to land and
water. Although the government's active role in determining water
rights brought about greater equity in distribution, it reduced
some individuals' productive capacity. The government began to
provide credit through public institutions. For those with salinized land, the government banks were their only source of credit.
Except for the case of wheat, marketing remained in private control.

The implications for the local level were multiple. The increased government participation created farming communities and
gave families access to water and land that they previously had not
had. While many ejidatarios are aware that government control of
resources has in fact made their way of life possible, they also
acknowledge that the government now has the ability to deny the
access to the very resources they need to carry out that life.

156

AGRARIAN CRISIS AND REHABILITATION

A series of changes that had their origins outside of the
Valley brought about a profound crisis for people of the Mexicali
Valley. On the international level, a sharp decline in world
cotton prices created severe problems for cotton growers and international cotton firms located in the Valley. A second process,
linked to the development of the western United States, had a
direct impact on the Mexicali Valley: the increased salinization
of Colorado River water, water critical for agriculture in the
Mexicali Valley. Because no international agreement was established to control quality of the water going from the United States
to Mexico, the salinization of the Colorado was allowed to increase
until it forced an international crisis after destroying agriculture throughout much of the Valley.

The local level responses to these changes drew the Mexican
national government into the process of resolving the salinity
crisis and rehabilitating the region. This process in turn
restructured not only local level economic, social, and political
organization but also created a whole new set of intermediary
institutions linking the different levels. New resources were
brought into the Valley from the national and international levels,
leading to a transformation of regional economic and political
structure. In the process, the state and the dominant political
party, PRI, expanded their control over the agrarian sector.

The turning point in the history of the Valley occurred in
1961 when the Wellton-Mohawk project in Arizona was completed. The
project was an elaborate irrigation drainage system of a very
saline area. It transferred the saline water to the Colorado just
above the channel that carried water to Mexico. The salt level of
the river jumped to 2,700 parts per million, three and one half
times the amount the river normally carries. The impact on the
Mexicali Valley was rapid and devastating. Crops were destroyed
throughout the Valley, drastically reducing farmers' incomes
(Oyarzabal- Tamargo 1976:114).

In El Tiburón, salinity had been a problem even before the
Wellton-Mohawk project, but the increased salinity finally forced
people to abandon fields that had once been productive. All families were not affected equally by the salinity in El Tiburón because of micro-ecological variations in the land. Those who had
land with poor drainage had their crops completely destroyed and
could not continue to farm. Many of them rented their water rights
to other members of the community who had better land. The additional water was used to double crop good land. Many families with
unproductive land were forced to migrate from the ejido in search
of employment. Many eventually relinquished their rights to ejido
land.

Like agriculturalists throughout the Valley, people in El
Tiburón pressed the Confederación Nacional de Campesinos (CNC) to
get the federal government's help in resolving the problem. This
was a period of bitter conflicts within the local CNC over the
nature of the problem and how it should be handled. Initially the
CNC seemed incapable of getting any support from the government.

In 1962 the <u>Liga</u> <u>de</u> <u>Communidades</u> <u>Agrarias</u>, previously a division
within the CNC, split from the CNC taking with it more than half of
the CNC membership to affiliate with the <u>Central</u> <u>Campesina</u> <u>Indepen-</u>
<u>diente</u> (CCI). The split was led by Alfonso Garzôn Santibañez who
wanted the union to take a stronger anti-U.S. position. Both the
CNC and CCI held massive demonstrations in Mexicali and Mexico City
but the CCI was the dominant force during the early stages of the
crisis. Yet, the CCI was perceived by the Mexican government as a
challenge to the status quo. As the government became more involved in the region, it systematically channeled resources to the
CNC-based communities and leaders and excluded those of the CCI.
The role of the CCI in the protest movement was further reduced by
periodic jailing of its leaders (Mumme 1980).[4] Throughout this
period the people of El Tiburôn remained in the CNC. Their loyalty
was based on a patron-client network of relationships that included
union leadership positions for several members of the ejido.

The mobilization of the agrarian sector did pressure the
national government, which had previously ignored the salinity
problem, into becoming involved. Through their national organizations the unions linked the rural sector to the state apparatus,
but they could not deal directly with the United States nor could
they get farmers in the United States to abandon the farms that
were creating the salinity. An international level of articulation
(Adams 1970) had to be established by Mexico with the United States
if the problem was to be effectively addressed.

Early Mexican negotiations with the United States were unproductive. Mexican President Lopez Mateos called salinity the single
greatest problem confronting the two countries and threatened to
take the case to the World Court if a binational agreement could
not be negotiated. Mexico claimed that the United States had
violated the treaty of 1944 by providing Mexico with water that
could not be used for agriculture. The United States responded
that the Treaty of 1944 had no stipulation about the quality of
water. Mexico's reply was that it would not have signed a treaty
for water that could not be used. Fearing that Mexico would cut
off Río Bravo water to the Texas Río Grande Valley and that the
World Court would rule against the U.S. if the Mexicans brought the
case before it, the U.S. agreed to negotiate.

In the spring of 1965, Mexico and the United States agreed
upon the first steps in resolving the salinity problem. The agreement known as Minute 218 was to last 15 years until a final solution could be found. The agreement was extended two additional
years. In Minute 218 the United States agreed to build a canal to
divert the drainage water from the Wellton-Mohawk district, which
had been going into the Colorado River above the point where Mexico
was receiving its water, directly to the Gulf of California. In
exchange for the diverted water, the United States substituted
water of higher quality from the Imperial Dam. As a result the
salinity was lowered to approximately 1,300 ppm by 1970.

President Echeverría made a strong effort to negotiate a
"final solution" to the problem. He made a series of trips to the
region, accompanied by national PRI and government leaders. They
toured the devastated agricultural lands, and met with agricultural

union and state leaders. As a result of the crisis these leader
gained unique access to major national political figures and head
of major ministries. As a result, Mexicali leaders have had excel
lent ties to national leaders and have been very effective i
gaining national resources for the region. In 1972, Presiden
Echeverría and President Nixon agreed upon a four point program t
resolve the problem. In 1974, Mexico and the United States agree
upon Minute 242 of the International Water and Boundary Commissior
The United States acknowledged that it had the obligation to pro
vide Mexico with water with an average salinity not to exceed 11
ppm more than the salt content of the water going to the Imperia
Valley on the American side of the border.

In the meantime, the regional economy suffered another blow --
the spread of the pink bollworm into the region in 1967. Th
Mexicali Valley had previously been relatively plague-free. Th
bollworm reduced the cotton yields by fifty percent or more an
raised the cost of production at a time when world prices fo
cotton were falling, in part due to the systematic dumping o
cotton on the world market by the United States. The impact o
cotton growers in the Valley was a sudden and mounting debt to th
cotton processing companies, particularly Anderson Clayton.

The regional economy, already badly depressed by the salinit
crisis, was on the verge of being destroyed by the new problems
People in El Tiburón participated with thousands of other CN
members to pressure the national government to play a more activ
role. The international cotton companies practically stopped loan-
ing money for cotton production. Considering that these companie
provided ninety-five percent of credit for cotton during the pre-
crisis period, the consequences were far reaching.

Pressure from the CNC, the state government, and the international cotton companies resulted in the government absorbing th
agriculturalists' debts to the international companies. In exchange the companies promised to remain in the Valley. The government wanted the transnationals to remain to handle credit, processing, and marketing of cotton. Two companies did not accept th
government offer, but the largest companies, including Anderson
Clayton, did remain. Cotton production continued to fall, however.
In 1966-1967 Anderson Clayton processed 179,383 bales of cotton; by
1970-1971 it processed only 33,646 bales. Between 1966 and 197
the company lost 76,167,000 pesos (Gamboa n.d.). At this point
Anderson Clayton, along with most of the other companies, pulled
their major operations out of the Valley.

Despite the success of the Mexican government in achieving an
accord with the United States to reduce the salt content of water
passing into Mexico, much of the Valley land had been ruined. The
national government faced the decision of either abandoning the
region or making a major, expensive commitment to rebuild it. It
opted for the latter because the region was politically mobilized,
located on the border, and had the potential to again become a
productive center of commercial agriculture. A loan for more than
6000 million pesos was obtained from the World Bank in 1967. The
project began in 1968 and was not completed for ten years. It
included the leveling of 175,638 hectares of land, lining canals

with concrete, improving 533 wells, and building 2,000 kilometers of new roads. The organization of the district was restructured giving the government greater control over water permits and the productive process.

Equally important was a major increase in credit to agriculturalists, from 7.6 million pesos in 1972 to 34.9 million pesos in 1977. The credit was critical because the private sources of credit, the transnational companies that handled the cotton ginning, were no longer operating on a large scale in the Valley. By the end of the decade, the government was the largest source of credit in the region.

The federal government also funded the development of large cooperatives to gin cotton, handle the sale of fertilizers and pesticides, store wheat, and coordinate the raising of cattle for meat and milk. While private cooperatives were also developed during this period without the support of the government, the largest and most powerful cooperatives were those controlled by ejidatarios through the two peasant unions -- the CNC and the CCI. Because it is the largest union, the CNC holds the most offices on the cooperative boards. The creation of the cooperatives under the control of the peasant unions has transformed the power structure of the Valley. The cooperatives provide a critical resource that is controlled by leaders of the peasant unions. Through a multilevel set of patron-client relationships, union leaders choose associates to be members of the cooperative boards.[5] They are paid salaries, but more importantly, they in turn have the power to help appoint other union members to positions in the cooperatives. The result is a highly structured pattern of relationships between people who have special access to the centers of power within the agrarian sector and those who are marginalized. Once one is part of the network, loyalty and complete support is expected.

Economically the cooperatives have helped to transform the Valley. They control an agro-industrial complex that is used by more than 15,000 ejidatarios and has an estimated value of 3,000 million pesos (1984 estimate). They provide direct jobs for more than 300 full-time workers and at least 350 seasonal workers. Along with Banrural, the Secretaria de Agricultura y Recursos Hidraulicos has emerged as the dominant structure in the Valley, replacing the transnational companies.[6]

Ejido leaders from El Tiburón had been active in the politics of the CNC. When the cooperatives were established, several men from the ejido were given important positions; through these men, others received jobs. By 1984 almost twenty percent of the men of El Tiburón had jobs in the cooperatives. Equally important, the ejido received a loan from the government to start a dairy program and a beef-cattle raising program. Cotton is no longer grown on the ejido. Wheat is the major crop.

Growing wheat reflects the latest stage in the transformation of the agricultural sector. To raise wheat, a farmer must get government approval to plant wheat, use the water, and to get credit. The pesticides and fertilizer are bought from government cooperatives and stored at the cooperative. The price for the wheat is set by the government and can only be sold to CONASUPO, the Compañia Nacional de Subsistencias Populares (National Staple Products Company). Access to water, credit, and market are all controlled by the government. On the other hand, the government has made an immense investment in the region to rehabilitate the land and to make commercial agriculture possible. While the process gives the government tremendous control over critical means of production and the power over the agrarian sector, it also reflects a successful effort by agriculturalists to get services from the government. The Valley has been restructured with one form of political and economic control replacing another.

CONCLUSION

We began this essay by suggesting that a political economy approach can be useful not only in conceptualizing the nature of linkages but also in systematizing the examination of social change. The expansion of capitalism and state power were critical processes that led to the transformation of life in the Mexicali Valley. In our analysis, we used an historical approach to trace the emergence of state capitalism as government took increasing control over the means of production and exchange. In the process the state developed its own mechanisms for appropriating value from the agrarian sector.

The Mexican state may become involved in local or community level problems, such as the salinity crisis, when state elites feel their interests are threatened, or when they perceive an opportunity to expand their power. The salinity crisis attracted the attention of national leaders for both reasons. People in Mexicali were aware that the problem could not be resolved locally. As a result they mobilized and exerted pressure through the CNC, CCI, the state governor, PRI, and federal representatives in Congress, in order to get the national government involved. The solution was negotiated between the two nations. Once the salinity crisis was resolved, the informal and formal linkages that had developed during the crisis were used by Mexicali leaders to secure massive credit for rehabilitation and developing the region.

From the perspective of the agriculturalists in El Tiburón, the transformation of the Valley has had multiple implications and contradictions. They have a paradoxical relationship with the government. In contrast to peasants or agriculturalists in many parts of Mexico, the ejidatarios of the Mexicali Valley gained access to low interest state credit, subsidized irrigation water, and state agricultural services. But in the process they lost some of their freedom from state control. The state now set the conditions for access to the means of exchange. On the other hand, the state was replacing the role previously occupied by foreign capitalist enterprises. As a result the state and PRI have coopted the agrarian organizations. In the recent elections, the agrarian sector of the region, in contrast to the urban populations, strongly supported PRI.

State policies and programs are often implemented through intermediary structures -- particularly government bureaucracies.

In the Mexicali case the bureaucracies control key resources and
are subsequently centers of power. The degree to which the resources of these agencies can be controlled by any one group or
network, and how these networks are linked to particular ejido
communities, are major factors influencing patterns of distribution
of resources in the Valley. Because the people of El Tiburón were
active participants in a network that captured control of the CNC,
and at different times leadership positions in Banrural, the state
legislature, the national cotton growing association (which controls export permits), and the cooperatives, they were able to
obtain jobs and support for ejido projects that otherwise would not
have been available to them. Despite the formal nature of the
intermediary structures, the informal networks that linked distinct
people competing for resources and power are the key to understanding how the formal structures function and determining who in
the region receives which resources and services.

NOTES

1. This chapter is based on research carried out by the two
authors in Baja California. The research was made possible by
dissertation research grants from the Women in Development Program
and the Center for Advanced Study of International Development at
Michigan State University, the Mexico-United States Border Research
Program at the University of Texas, a Research Fulbright Fellow-
ship, the Mellon Foundation, the Midwest University Consortium for
International Assistance and the Center for United States-Mexican
Studies at the University of California San Diego. The chapter is
a product of research projects that were designed specifically to
examine processes operating at different levels. The authors contributed equally to the writing of the chapter. They would like to
thank Joseph Spielberg Benitez, Sergio Quesada, William Derman, and
Billie DeWalt for their comments on the chapter. Marcela Gutierrez
and Anne Patterson made a major contribution to the research. "El
Tiburón" is a pseudonym for the ejido described in this paper.
2. The political economy approach emerged, despite not being
clearly defined, as useful for anthropologists studying social
change. Researchers began studies of macrolevel processes that
changed the social environment in which people make decisions about
issues ranging from mobilization to migration. Examples of publications which reflect this change include Long and Roberts
(1978), Whiteford (1981), Wasserstrom (1983), and Roseberry (1984).
3. Ejidos are peasant communities corporately organized by
the government. Individual members of the ejido have access to
ejido land but the land cannot be rented, sold or mortgaged. The
ejido holding in Mexicali are among the largest in all Mexico.
More than eighty-four percent of ejido plots in Mexico are under
ten hectares (Hansen 1971:61).
4. The CCI was originally formed by the <u>Movimiento de Libera-
ción Nacional</u>, a coalition of major leftist organizations. The
leaders of the MLN felt it was important to form a peasant organization that would be independent of PRI and the national govern-

ment. When the CCI was formed as a national organization in 1963, leaders of the CNC tried unsuccessfully to take control of it. The Mexicali branch of the CCI was led by Alfonzo Garzón Santibañez who organized the break from the CNC. A powerful leader, Garzón developed great support in the Mexicali Valley. The government systematically attacked the organization undermining its support by excluding members from patronage and government programs. To make this approach work, the government had to include other peasants in programs. Part of the reason for the massive government investment in Mexicali may have been a response to the threat of the CCI. The CCI joined the Pacto Ocampo agreeing to support the government agrarian policies in return for a place in the political system and access to government services for its members. It is believed by some in Mexicali that the Mexican government used Garzón and the CCI to focus peasant pressures for change away from CNC and PRI toward the United States. When the situation changed, the CCI was incorporated into the system under the control of PRI.

5. In contrast to peasants in many parts of Latin America where government programs are less important than they are in Mexicali, agriculturalists in Mexicali have a vast body of information and folklore about how bureaucratic systems work. Government is an important part of ejidatarios' cosmology or world view. The ejido communities were established by the government which still serves as the patron for most ejidatarios.

6. Landless farm workers are systematically excluded from the CNC or CCI. Furthermore, the employees of the cooperatives are exclusively ejidatarios and their kin. In Mexicali the number of landless agricultural workers fluctuates between 8,000 and 15,000. Of those that remain all year in the Valley, many live in squatter housing along the Colorado River or along irrigation canals. This population receives no protection from the government, although the government has established a minimum wage. The labor of this segment of the population provides value for state capitalist enterprises as it did for the private capitalist companies.

BIBLIOGRAPHY

Adams, Richard N. 1970. Crucifixion by Power. Austin: University of Texas Press.

Carlos, Manuel. 1981. "State Policies, State Penetration, and Ecology: A Comparative Analysis of Uneven Development and Undevelopment in Mexico's Micro Agrarian Regions." Working Paper in U.S.-Mexican Studies No. 19. Program in United State-Mexican Studies University of California, San Diego.

Corbett, John and Scott Whiteford. 1983. "State Penetration and Development in Mesoamerica, 1950-1980". In Heritage of Conquest: Thirty Years Later. Carl Kendall, John Hawkins, and Laurel Bossen,eds. Albuquerque: University of New Mexico Press, pp. 9-33.

Gamboa, Eduardo. 1972. "Estudio Sobre La Incontestabilidad de La Operacion Industrial de Anderson Clayton Company." Unpublished Company Report.

Grijalva Larrànaga, Edna Aide. 1983. "Los Primeros Intentos de Apoderarse del Valle". In Panorama Historico del Baja California, David Pinera Ramirez,ed. Mexicali: Universidad Autònoma de Baja California.

Grindle, Merilee. 1977. Bureaucrats, Politicians, and Peasants in Mexico. Berkeley: University of California Press.

Hansen, Roger D. 1971. The Politics of Mexican Development. Baltimore: John Hopkins.

Long, Norman and Bryon R. Roberts,eds. 1978. Peasant Cooperation and Capitalist Expansion in Central Peru. Austin: University of Texas Press.

Mumme, Steve. 1981. Groundwater in U.S.-Mexican Resource Relations: The Prospect for International Development. Ph.D. Dissertation. Tucson: University of Arizona.

Oden, Peter R. 1984. "A Whole Lot of Reminiscing at Dedication." Brawley News Feb. 21, 1984, p. B-1.

Ortner, Sherry R. 1984. "Theory in Anthropology Since the Sixties". Comparative Studies in Society and History 26:1:126-166.

Oyarzabal-Tamargo, Francisco. 1976. Economic Impact of Saline Irrigation Water: Mexicali Valley, Mexico. Unpublished Doctoral Dissertation. Colorado State University.

Roseberry, William. 1984. Coffee and Capitalism in the Venezuelan Andes. Austin: University of Texas Press.

Smith, Carol A. 1984. "Local History in Global Context: Social and Economic Transition in Western Guatemala". Journal of Comparative Study of Society and History 28:193-228.

Villarreal, Humberto J. 1971. El Valle de Mexicali. Published by the Secretaría de Recursos Hidraulicos. Direcciòn General de Distritos de Riego. Direcciòn de Estadistica Estudios Economicos.

Wallerstein, Immanuel. 1984. The Politics of the World Economy: The States, The Movement, and Civilizations. Cambridge University Press.

Warman, Arturo. 1976. "Introducciòn". In, Elena Azaola Garrido and Esteban Krotz, Politica y Conflicto. Mexico City. INAH - Secretaria de Educaciòn Publica.

Wasserstrom, Robert. 1983. Class and Society in Central Chiapas. Los Angeles: University of California Press.

Wells, Miriam and Jacob Climo. 1984. "Parallel Process in the World System: Intermediate Agencies and Local Factionalism in the United States and Mexico." Journal of Development Studies 20(4):151-170.

Whiteford, Scott. 1981. Workers from the North: Plantations, Migrant Labor and the City in Northwest Argentina. Austin: University of Texas Press.

8
Microcosmic and Macrocosmic Processes of Agrarian Change in Southern Honduras: The Cattle Are Eating the Forest[1]

Billie R. DeWalt

INTRODUCTION

A human geographer has made an illuminating comparison of the similarities and differences between cultural geography and anthropology. One of the points that surfaced in his analysis was that, although in geography issues of scale are a paramount issue, because "...most anthropologists work at the micro scale, the scale problem does not arise" (Grossman 1977:138). While issues of scale or levels of analysis may not be frequent topics of discussion for the discipline, there have nevertheless been persistent attempts to deal with different levels of analysis (see the introduction to this volume). Anthropologists have made considerable contributions with their research at the macro levels of analysis. Geertz' (1963) classic study of Agricultural Involution, Adams'(1970) national study of Guatemala and the many subsequent studies that have been done from various materialist, Marxist, and/or political economy perspectives are prime examples. What has been missing from much of this research, however, is a clear understanding of the dynamics of local-level situations taking place within the constraints imposed by the broader system being studied (see Smith's criticism that dependency theory neglects the internal dynamics of the periphery [1978:577]).

The purpose of this paper is to examine the processes of sociocultural and ecological change occurring in southern Honduras. These processes, as I will show, are closely linked with events that are shaping the global agricultural situation. Accordingly, it is difficult to understand what is happening at the microlevel without simultaneously coming to grips with the more macrolevel processes. The purpose of this paper is to address this problem of linking micro and macro data by demonstrating some pragmatic theoretical and methodological strategies that can be utilized by social scientists in coming to better understandings of the linkages of micro and macro processes.

BACKGROUND

Recent trends in worldwide agriculture raise considerable cause for alarm. After several decades in which world grain production rose substantially (per capita production rose thirty-one percent between 1950 and 1971), gains in output in the last decade have barely kept up with population growth. In addition, Brown has reported that increased production is now possible only by cultivating marginal lands, by annually cultivating grain crops thus increasing the need for fertilizer inputs and increasing the rates of soil erosion, and by "mining" irrigation sources such as underground aquifers that took millions of years to form. Much of the world now depends on North American grain to meet deficits in domestic production. Brown believes that the general expectation for U.S. and Canadian farmers to produce increased surpluses, and even to continue to produce current amounts, is more and more unrealistic given the nonsustainability of their agricultural systems (1981a, 1981b).

What is even more disturbing about the situation is that more and more countries are becoming food importers. As Brown has said:

The world wide movement of countries from export to import status is a much traveled one-way street. The reasons vary, but the tide is strong: no country has gone against it since World War II. Literally scores of countries have become food importers, but not one major new food exporter has emerged (1981b:997).

Conventional wisdom suggests that the major reason for these trends is the uncontrolled population growth of Third World countries. While population increase definitely plays a role, there is a great deal of evidence that there are other factors at work (see Murdoch 1982). One obvious question, for example, is what happened to the thirty-one percent per capita increase in grain that Brown reports was produced between 1950 and 1971?

The present case is designed to shed light on some of the other factors that are accounting for the worldwide problems in agricultural and food systems. Honduras is a good case in which to examine these trends because, on the surface, it conforms to the trends identified by Brown. The country's rate of population increase, for example, has been one of the fastest in the world, averaging 3.3 percent per year from 1970-1978 (World Bank 1980:142). In addition, it is a country that has recently become a food importer instead of a food exporter. Yet there are other important trends occurring in Honduras that help to better explain its food deficits and its high rates of malnutrition.

The general objective of my research in southern Honduras was to look at contemporary farming systems and resource utilization, particularly in terms of how these have developed, how they are related to the larger national and international scene and what future prospects exist for the region. Accordingly, this research was carried out using an ecosystemic or cultural ecology of development approach (see DeWalt 1984). Here,

It is recognized that the relationships between the physical, biological, and sociocultural variables in an ecosystem are reciprocal and feedback processes are at work. Thus, we can ask how human behavior affects biological and physical variables within the ecosystem and vice versa. Recognizing the interplay of these factors also enables us to examine the adaptive significance of human behavior, that is, whether the behavior of a particular population enables it to maintain a viable relationship with its environment (Grossman 1977:135).

The advantages of such a systems and evolutionary approach include the following:

1) It enables the researcher to place due emphasis on the unity of nature and to attempt to incorporate concepts and variables that have traditionally been analyzed separately because of disciplinary boundaries (see Grossman 1977:135).

2) It enables us to understand the dynamics and complexities of whole systems rather than simply modelling parts of them.

3) We are encouraged to view the system in its historical and future dimensions -- that is, to understand how the system developed, what its future directions might be, and what the ultimate evolutionary viability of the system might be.

4) Finally, we are encouraged to investigate both the micro and macro processes that are occurring and to look at how these processes affect and are affected by one another. Thus, we do not view the dynamics of local systems presuming that the larger context is stable, nor do we view the dynamics of larger systems assuming that these will create uniform responses at the micro level. This cultural ecology of development perspective will be used to delineate the processes causing change in southern Honduras.

ENVIRONMENTAL AND HISTORICAL SETTING OF SOUTHERN HONDURAS

Southern Honduras (roughly the Departments of Choluteca and Valle) is quite different from the tropical rainforest environs that we typically think of with respect to Central America. The coastal plain on the Pacific is not extensive and has had very little intensive agriculture until relatively recently. Most people live in the highland areas that are composed of inactive volcanic mountains that rarely reach altitudes as high as 1400 meters. These mountains, however, are extremely steeply sloped and form many narrow, relatively isolated little valleys. The region is quite hot all year round with the maximum temperatures sometimes reaching 105 degrees in March, the hottest month. The most significant climatic feature, however, is the separation between the wet season and the dry season. Almost all rainfall is concentrated in the months of May through November, although in July and August there is frequently a dry period. From December through April little or no rain falls, making the landscape parched, dusty, and hot. Average rainfall is about 1600 millimeters although this is quite variable and drought conditions are not uncommon in southern

Honduras.

The south is quite densely populated. Although the region comprises only about five percent of the national territory, it contains approximately eleven percent of the population of Honduras. There are very few Indians left in the nation as a whole and the people in the south can be classified as mestizos.

Since colonial times, large cattle ranches have occupied the large valleys and the coastal plain. Cattle were marketed locally and in neighboring Central American countries. Historically, the majority of the people were subsistence farmers growing corn on the steep hillsides and many gathered indigo for sale as a source of cash. About a hundred years ago, synthetic dyes led to the demise of indigo gathering but at about the same time sorghum was introduced into the region. Sorghum was quickly added to the subsistence repertoire of the south because of its great tolerance for drought. It did not supplant corn, which was still the preferred food staple, but was grown with it as an insurance crop. In years of poor corn harvests, sorghum grains could be added to or substituted for corn in the making of tortillas.

The improvement of transportation links during the 1950s and 1960s has speeded up the changes in the agrarian structure of southern Honduras. The Pan American highway that runs through the region was completed in the late 1950s and was eventually joined by a paved road running north to Tegucigalpa, the capital. Port facilities on the south coast were also improved. Concomitant with these improvements as Boyer (1983) and Stares (1972) have shown, came an increase in coffee, cotton and cattle production in the south. All of these factors resulted in a process that pushed subsistence peasants off the lands that they had been cultivating so that agrarian capitalism could expand (see White 1977 and Boyer 1983 for documentation). The data that I will be discussing relates to the most important of these areas of expansion -- the growth of the cattle industry and the concomitant spread of pasture in southern Honduras.

THE CATTLE ARE EATING THE FOREST

Table 8.1 summarizes the changes that have taken place in the number of beef cattle, total production, net exports, and per capita consumption of beef for Honduras. As the table shows there has been a fairly rapid increase in the number of cattle in Honduras over the period. Total production has more than trebled (from 18.5 thousand metric tons in the 1959-1963 period to over sixty-one thousand metric tons in 1979). This process has not been limited to Honduras, however, and I have included data for the other Central American countries as well. In every country, the number of cattle has been increasing rapidly and production of meat has skyrocketed. Compared with twenty years ago, Central America now has eighty percent more cattle and produces 185 percent more beef. This increase in beef production has produced corresponding changes in use of land resources as well. Parsons has noted that:

TABLE 8.1. Changes in the Production, Exportation, and Consumption of Beef in Central America. (from U.S.D.A. Foreign Agriculture Circulars, "Livestock and Meat" 1959-1979).

	# of Cattle (millions)	Percentage Change from 1961-1965 Average	Total Production (000 tons)	Percentage Change from 1966-1965 Average	Net Exports (000 tons) 1961-1965	Percentage Change from 1961-1965 Average	Per Capita Consumption (Pounds)	Percentage Change from 1961-1965 Average
Honduras								
1959-63	1.3		18.5		6.6		16	
1972	1.6	+23.1	41.1	+122	23.2	+252	14	-12.5
1979	2.2	+69.2	61.3	+231	39.9	+505	12.8	-20.0
Guatemala								
1959-63 av.	1.2		37.4		3.3		19	
1972	1.9	+58.3	72.2	+ 93	24.6	+645	15	-21.1
1979	2.7	+125.0	96.4	+158	22.4	+579	23.3	+22.6
El Salvador								
1959-63 av.	.9		18.5		---		17	
1972	1.2	+33.3	23.8	+ 29	3.9	+ 62	12	-29.4
1979	1.3	+44.4	39.5	+114	6.3		14.5	-14.7
Nicaragua								
1959-63 av.	1.5		27.8		9.4		29	
1972	2.3	+53.3	68.7	+147	39.1	+316	19	+10.3
1979	2.4	+60.0	81.3	+192	48.7	+418	32.6	+12.4
Costa Rica								
1959-63 av.	1.1		24.2		8.0		27	
1972	1.7	+54.5	49.1	+103	33.5	+319	19	-29.6
1979	2.2	+100.0	81.8	+238	46.5	+481	37.2	-37.8
Panama								
1959-63 av.	.9		21.8		.7		42	
1972	1.3	+44.4	40.7	+ 87	4.5	+543	52	+23.8
1979	1.6	+77.7	40.0	+ 83	1.4	+100	51.7	+23.1
Totals								
1959-63 av.	6.9		148.2		28.0			
1972	10.0	+45	295.6	+ 99	124.9	+346		
1979	12.4	+80	400.3	+170	158.9	+468		

Substantial parts of Central America and Panama have undergone
a dramatic change of aspect in recent years, the result of
accelerated forest clearing and enormous expansion in the area
of artificial or planted pasture (repasto). At times it seems
that the isthmus is on the way to becoming one great stock
ranch. Twenty years ago the Pan American highway route passed
through extensive tracts of tropical forest. Today its entire
paved length is through cropland and potrero, even over its
3700 meter summit in Costa Rica (Parsons 1976:121).

This change in land use is illustrated by data from southern
Honduras (through which the Pan American highway passes). Table
8.2 shows the changes in land use patterns in southern Honduras
between 1952 and 1974. Over these two decades the amount of land
in pasture in Honduras has increased from 41.9 percent of the land
in 1952 to 61.1. Precipitous declines are evident in both fallow
land and the amount of land in forest. Both of these are important
for subsistence crop production because they are part of the shifting cultivation cycle. Thus, land devoted to raising cattle is
displacing forest land and fallow land. Although there has been
some increase in the amount of land sown in annual crops, some of
this increase (3,181 hectares) is due to cotton cultivation and not
to expanded food production.
The cattle are eating the forest but it remains to be shown
how this process is taking place. That is, what are the human
dynamics of the situation in terms of how forest is converted to
pasture? What are the benefits and consequences of this shift in
human terms as well as in ecological terms? And finally, what are
the larger outcomes that might be expected as a result of these
processes and what, if anything, can be done to have a positive
effect on these outcomes? These questions are best answered by
considering the data from the microlevel, especially by examining
the contemporary farming systems in one part of the south.[2]

FARMING SYSTEMS IN THE SOUTHERN HIGHLANDS

The agriculture practiced on the steep mountain slopes in the
south is usually some form of shifting cultivation (although see
Boyer 1983 for a description of some communities where there is no
fallowing cycle). The brief descriptions below are based on data
from Pespire, the municipio (roughly equivalent to an American
county) in which my research in 1981 and 1982 was based.
Fallowing periods on the steep slopes around Pespire are
generally five to six years. After this amount of time has passed,
farmers believe that enough fertility has returned to the soil so
that it can be cultivated again. Although the type of cultivation
that is practiced by small farmers in southern Honduras is usually
described as slash and burn agriculture, the way that a field
enters the cultivation cycle is more accurately described as a
slash and mulch system. Here, the secondary forest growth is cut
down, but rather than being burned it is left lying on the ground
to serve as a mulch for the grain crops that are planted.

TABLE 8.2
Changing Land Use Patterns in Southern Honduras: 1952-1974

		Southern Region*		Pespire**	
		Number of Hectares	Percent of Total	Number of Hectares	Percent of Total
Annual Crops	1952	42,980	14.9		
	1974	51,148	16.8	2,776	14.3
Perennial Crops	1952	9,531	3.3		
	1974	8,937	2.9	195	1.0
Fallow	1952	40,802	14.1		
	1974	16,964	5.6	976	5.0
Pasture	1952	121,266	41.9		
	1974	186,018	61.1	11,110	57.3
Forest	1952	74,593	25.8		
	1974	41,395	13.6	4,226	21.8
Totals	1952	289,172	100		
	1974	304,462	100	19,383	100

* Taken from data presented in Jefferson Boyer, Simple Commodity
Production, Agrarian Capitalism and Rationality in Southern
Honduras (draft copy of Ph. D. dissertation, University of North
Carolina).
** Dirección General de Estadística y Censos, Censo Nacional
Agropecuario 1974, Tomo III, Uso de la Tierra, Tegucigalpa,
Honduras, 1978.

There are three types of slash and mulch systems. The first is used in planting only corn. The corn is planted at the end of August and is harvested in December when it has dried. The yields are small but this corn can be stored longer than the crop harvested during the middle of the rainy season because it can be dried much more effectively. The second slash and mulch system is used to plant a monocrop of sorghum. Here, the sorghum is broadcast sown, the brush is cut down and the sorghum is left to germinate and find its way through the dead vegetation. This sorghum can be planted in July, August or September but still matures in December (because it is photoperiodic). Sorghum yields are about two or three times as large as corn yields. The third slash and mulch system also is used with sorghum but in this case the sorghum is grown for animal fodder. The crop is broadcast sown just as in the previous system but it is planted in October. It does not fully mature by the time it is harvested in December, but this is what the farmer wants because the whole plant can be uprooted and stored to be fed to the animals during the long dry season.

It is during the second and third years that slash and burn cultivation takes place (see Figure 8.1). This most frequently utilized farming system can be seen as a compromise between the clear cultural preference for corn that is the staple of the peasant diet and the climatologically better adapted sorghum that is the less risky crop. Fields are slashed and burned in April and corn and sorghum are interplanted. From an agronomic point of view this system seems odd because these plants compete for the same nutrients in the soil. From the farmers' point of view, however, the system makes a great deal of sense. The corn is a rapidly maturing variety that can be harvested in between sixty and seventy days (around the middle of July). This is the period of the year when the previous year's grain harvest has been depleted and, although corn yields are small, they do serve to sustain the farmer for a few months during the remainder of the cropping season. The corn is harvested but the sorghum is left standing in the field because it does not mature and is not ready to harvest until December.

The parish priest in Pespire said that "sorghum is the salvation of the peasant" in the south and this sentiment was echoed by many other people. Sorghum is so important in the region because of its drought tolerance and because it is a multi-purpose crop. The grain is primarily thought of as a food for animals and a substantial portion of the harvest is sold to truckers who sell it on the national market for use as animal feed. Animals also graze the leaves from the dried plants left standing in the fields and some sorghum is grown so that the whole plant can be fed to animals (called _guatera_). In addition, sorghum can be and is used as a replacement for corn in making tortillas, the staple food of the peasants in the south. Poorer people who are not able to raise enough corn and who do not have enough cash to buy corn in the market use a substantial amount of sorghum for their own consumption.

The poor, landless peasants in the communities we studied in the Pespire region had relatively little trouble renting land to

Fig. 8.1
Fallow and Alternative Cropping Cycles from Pespire in 1981

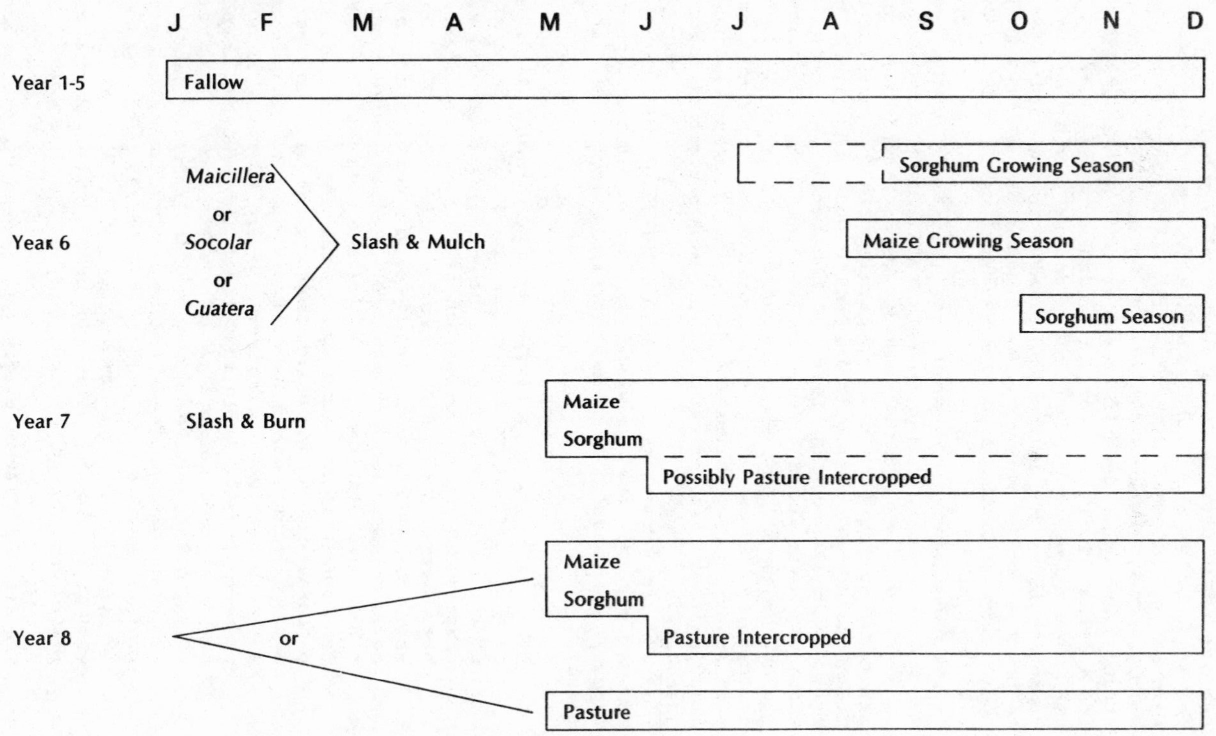

174

produce their crops. For example, almost half of the fifty-two
people interviewed in three small communities in the municipio of
Pespire in 1981 were either renting land or cultivating borrowed
land (see DeWalt and DeWalt 1982 for a description of the sampling
strategy and other details of the research). Perhaps most surprising was that the rental cost of one manzana (equal to 1.7 acres) of
land in 1981 was only about eight dollars and an agreement by the
renter to leave the haulm (crop residue) in the field. While haulm
to be used for grazing by animals in the dry season could be worth
up to fifty dollars per manzana, rental costs still seemed relatively cheap.

It was soon discovered that there was another reason why
landowners were willing to rent their land so cheaply. Their
objective was to have their land cleared so that they could plant
pasture. Rather than have to pay laborers to cut the brush and
trees, landowners rented their land for the growing of subsistence
crops by the landless. Part of the rental agreement was that
pasture grasses would be sown in the field between the rows of corn
and/or sorghum so that when the subsistence crops were removed the
landowner would be left with a new pasture. My estimates are that
such an arrangement saves the landowner at least one hundred dollars in labor costs of establishing each hectare of pasture (zacate
jaragua).

Why are landowners more interested in growing pasture to feed
livestock rather than growing basic grains or some other crop for
export? Parsons, writing about Central America as a whole summarized:

> With price ceilings imposed on most basic commodities it has
> not been attractive to the farmer to intensify his efforts to
> produce rice, maize, beans or yuca. And the market for the
> traditional export crops such as coffee, bananas and sugar has
> been notoriously fickle and unreliable. With beef it is
> another matter, especially since the opening of the U.S.
> market some twenty years ago. Profits have been good and
> risks low. Moreover, grass is the easiest of crops to grow.
> It takes less resources in capital and management to develop
> pasture than to intensify cropping efforts, and it is simply
> easier, requiring less work and effort. In some cases the
> shift to cattle may reflect a desire to avoid labor problems,
> or perhaps recognition that the tired land has been pushed to
> the limit and needs a rest. In the drive to diversify ex-
> ports, government has encouraged an expanding cattle industry,
> and international agencies have given further support. Espe-
> cially decisive has been the availability of low cost credit.
> In Costa Rica, for example, nearly half of all agricultural
> credit in recent years has been to the livestock industry
> (Parsons 1976:126).

The availability of credit for livestock projects has not just
been confined to Costa Rica. The World Bank's agricultural credit
operations in Latin America and the Caribbean have been heavily
oriented toward the livestock sector. Between 1948 and 1973,

thirty of the fifty-five agricultural projects, 71.3 percent of the total of 738.4 million dollars, were for the livestock sector. Only 28.7 percent of World Bank funds were for such areas as crop development, irrigation, fisheries, forestry, and integrated rural development (World Bank 1975:80-1).

Many of Parsons' points about the whole region of Central America can be shown to be operating in Pespire and southern Honduras. First, it has not been attractive for farmers to intensify their production of grains. Table 8.3 shows the range of production costs and the potential range of the value of production that may be derived from raising one manzana of corn and sorghum. In the table, I have provided ranges because the inputs depend on the type of technology used, the type of land, the quality of the labor input, and other variables that differ among farmers and their fields. The value of production assumes what would be an average yield in the Pespire region, then provides data on ranges of the value of production that depend largely on when the farmer sells his product. Grain sold immediately after the harvest would be valued less than grain held until several months after the harvest. The market prices given really do not show the full range of market value because some farmers have to sell their harvest while it is still in the field (vender en agua), in which case they typically receive about half of the lowest market prices (i.e. the price the farmer would obtain by selling grain to a trucker or merchant).

The main point to be made about this table is that in comparing the potential return on investment from one manzana of grain with the cost of production, there is a good chance that a farmer will not make any profit (also see Secretaria de Recursos Naturales 1980: 63). In the scenario of the "best case" (i.e. where the market price is highest and the inputs are lowest), a farmer would be able to make a profit of only about seventy-five dollars. This potential profit is not enough to entice most farmers who have land to produce grain beyond what they require for their own consumption. Those farmers with small landholdings or those who are landless do have an incentive to produce their own grain. Many of the man-days put into the production of crops is their own labor; thus their own cash outlays are relatively minimal. In addition, if they had to purchase grains at retail prices, this would involve a significant outlay of cash.

While subsistence crop production is worthwhile for the landless and land poor individuals, for the wealthier landholders there is a much more lucrative option available in raising livestock. (I should note that, in the larger picture, none of the farmers in the three communities we studied in the municipio of Pespire can be considered a really large landowner. The largest landowner in our sample controlled only fifty-six manzanas). Several of the relatively well-off landowners with whom we spoke reported that they had little interest in planting sorghum and corn because they were not profitable crops. They said that market prices were too low, labor costs had climbed to two dollars a day and laborers no longer worked as hard as they did in the past, and the weather, insects, and other natural forces made grain harvests too unpredictable. As a result, all of the twelve largest landowners in our sample had

TABLE 8.3
Production Costs for One Manzana of Corn and Sorghum

Activity	Date	Number of Person Days	Cost (in Lempiras)
Fence repair	February, March	2	8
Land clearing	April	3-8	12-32
Making firebreaks	April	2-3	8-12
Burning	April	4-6	16-24
Sowing corn & sorghum	April-May	2-4	8-16
(Sowing corn)	(April, May)	(2)	(8)
(Sowing sorghum)	(April, May)	(2-3)	(8-12)
Herbicide application (First weeding)	June	1-2 (20-28)	4-8 (80-112)
Harvest corn	July, August	3-4	12-16
Transport corn	July, August	1-2	4-8
Shelling corn	August	3-5	12-20
Second weeding	August, September	7-15	28-60
Bird scaring (4-6 hrs/day)	December	12-15	48-60
Harvest sorghum	December, January	4-8	16-32
Transport harvest	December, January	3-6	12-24
Threshing and winnowing	January, February	3-5	12-20
	TOTALS:	48-75	200-340

Other possible inputs:

10-20 pounds of corn seed	L. 2.40 - 4.80
5-10 pounds of sorghum seed	.80 - 1.60
1 quart of herbicide (Hedonal 720)	5.00
950 grams of insecticide (Dipterex)	5.00

RANGE OF TOTAL COST OF INPUTS (Lempiras): 208.20 - 356.40

Value of Production	Market Price	Retail Price
3 cargas (600 pounds) of corn	55-93	100-144
8 cargas (1600 pounds) of sorghum	112-168	209-256
Haulm (crop residues)	50-100	50-100
RANGE OF TOTAL VALUE OF PRODUCTION:	217-361	359-500

* Two Lempiras are equal to one U.S. dollar

begun converting significant portions of their land into pasture. They rented their land to landless farmers who, as part of the rental agreement, sowed zacate jaragua (Hyparrhenia rufa) in between the subsistence crops they were growing.

Perhaps paradoxically, the modest agrarian reform program that took place in Honduras in the early 1970s may be hastening the conversion of land into pasture. Even some of the small landowners with whom I talked expressed fears about the government expropriating their land to be redistributed. One way that farmers felt they could be assured of retaining their land would be to demonstrate that they were productively utilizing it. Forest land, even if it is fallow and will be cultivated in the future, appears not to be in use. So some farmers reported that an additional incentive for planting pasture was that it showed that their land was being used in case another series of land reform programs were promulgated.

In addition to the substantial amount of land being devoted to pasture, another twenty-three of the fifty-two individuals in the sample had begun to plant sorghum solely for use as a dry season food for livestock (i.e. planted guatera). Maintaining livestock during the dry season has been one of the limiting factors in expanding livestock production in Central America (see Parsons 1976:129) but farmers in southern Honduras have found the solution with sorghum. This crop can be uprooted, stored in a dry place, and fed to the animals throughout the dry season.

A ready market for livestock is provided by seven meat packing plants that were established in southern Honduras between 1958 and 1971 (Boyer 1983). Several of these packing plants were established with the assistance of U.S. capital and/or are owned by American corporations and their products are largely for export markets (Slutzky 1979). One reason why packing plants are being established in such places as Honduras may be that historically the meat packing industry has had low earning rates compared with other U.S. industries (see McCoy 1979:192).

The Pespire region is not one of the larger suppliers of animals for the packing plants. The importance of cattle raising for farmers in the region, however, can be gauged from the number of sales of animals recorded in the year prior to our research by the fifty-two individuals we sampled. There were thirteen individuals who had sold cattle and a total of thirty-seven animals changed hands. These animals were sold for amounts ranging from 250 to 500 Lempiras each ($125-250). Profits from selling even one animal thus exceed the total amount of profits that might be gained from cultivating several manzanas of grain.

The result of these forces is that data on the municipio of Pespire are similar to southern Honduras as a whole (see Table 8.2). Pasture land is increasing while forest and fallow land is disappearing. Although the amount of land in annual crops seems to be holding steady, it cannot be assumed that this land is being used to produce subsistence crops. As we have seen, sorghum for fodder and even a large amount of sorghum grain, which show up in census reports as annual crops, are being grown for animal consumption rather than for human food. What are the implications of this process in both human and ecological terms?

IMPLICATIONS -- DEVELOPMENT OR DESTRUCTION?

Richard Adams has written that

Development...becomes meaningful evolutionarily if seen as a sequence of changes a society may undergo that are advantageous to that society: it refers to events that will not only be specifically different for different societies, but which must, at some point, also become conflicting and competitive. If evolution is the universal process whereby life becomes more complex, development is the specific means whereby a given viable entity successfully improves its position with respect to its environment. If evolution involves cooperation and competition, natural selection and random variation, adaptation and destruction, then development also involves these very same processes (1970:42).

Seen in these terms, development implies destruction of natural resources and of portions of society as well as beneficial change for certain species and for certain portions of society.

The processes by which pasture is replacing forest in Honduras as well as other parts of the world (see Parsons 1972; Gomez-Pompa, Vasquez-Yanes and Guevara 1972), is a good illustration of Adams' point. In the alteration of the ecosystem that is taking place, jaragua grass and sorghum, both African introductions (see Parsons 1972), are taking over primarily at the expense of the forest species. There have been warnings that this process of forest destruction will not be without far-reaching consequences for humans and the environment (see Gomez-Pompa et. al., 1972). Other individuals, however, are not so alarmist and believe that, with the proper management, the negative ecological consequences may be avoided (see Parsons 1976).

On the human side, the picture is complicated as well. In the short run, the process seems to be quite beneficial for the landless as well as the landowners. Landowners recognize that production of livestock is a much more profitable enterprise than production of grains and they have discovered an efficient and cheap way of converting their land to pasture. The poor have available to them, for the time being, relatively cheap land to cultivate the basic grains they need to support their families. At the same time they recognize that forest land is becoming scarcer and that eventually there will be no land for them to farm. Livestock raising provides few employment opportunities. Permanent and temporary migration for wage labor is already quite a common strategy for many families in the Pespire region. Unfortunately, as we might suspect, the industrial and commercial agricultural sectors in Honduras have not been creating jobs at a rate to absorb the stream of migrants from such rural areas as Pespire (see DeWalt 1985b).

The production of livestock benefits those who have access to land in places like southern Honduras, but what does this increased production of high quality protein mean for the country as a whole? Unfortunately, it appears that the production of beef is not bound for the estimated fifty-eight percent of Honduran children under five years of age who suffer from identifiable malnutrition (INCAP 1969). Referring again to Table 8.1 we see that although the total production of beef has increased 231 percent in Honduras since the 1959-1963 period, per capita consumption of beef has actually declined by twenty percent. Similarly, the large increases in beef production in other Central American countries have not been accompanied by large increases in per capita consumption, and in El Salvador, just as in Honduras the per capita consumption has de-creased. The main reason why Central American populations are not benefitting from the expansion in number of cattle can be seen by looking at the "Net exports" column of Table 8.1. There it is apparent that exports of beef have risen much more rapidly than production. The 185 percent jump in production over the twenty year period has been accompanied by a 500 percent increase in exports. In Honduras this increase in exports has been 505 percent. Thus, the beneficiaries of the conversion of land from forests and grain crop production to pasture are the landowners, the owners of the meat packing plants, and ultimately the consumers in wealthy nations who have access to cheap Central American beef for their hamburgers and pet foods.

The situation for those individuals who do not have land on which to produce their living and who do not have cash incomes large enough to share in the consumption of beef products is deteriorating in other ways as well. The conversion of large amounts of land to pasture has led to shortages of grain in Honduras. Since 1976 Honduras has become a net importer of corn, rice, sorghum and beans, thus joining the ranks of many other developing countries that have become dependent on the large grain producing countries like the United States for their food staples. Although part of the reason for having to import these basic foodstuffs is related to an increase in population, another reason is the competition for resources between livestock and people. We have already seen that substantial amounts of land in places like southern Honduras are used for pasture rather than food crops for people. Much of this is the most fertile land available so that food crop production is increasingly being relegated to the most marginal land. In addition, considerable quantities of corn and sorghum are being fed to livestock. It has been estimated, for example, that forty-six percent of the sorghum and sixteen percent of the corn produced in Honduras is used for animal feed (Secretaria de Recursos Naturales 1980:38, 58). Thus, for this nation, the foreign capital that is being generated by the export of beef is already beginning to be offset by the importation of basic food grains (cf. DeWalt 1985a for similar trends in Mexico).

The implications of the conversion of southern Honduras into a vast pasture for export oriented cattle production for individuals like those in Pespire are the following. First, in the long run, fewer individuals will have access to land on which to produce their own subsistence crops. Employment opportunities in the local region will decline because livestock raising is less labor intensive than grain crop production. The permanent and temporary migration that these processes produce can only exacerbate the already explosive social, economic, and political situation that exists in Central America.

The directions that are being taken in Honduras are similar to those occurring all over the Third World. Poor countries turn precious cropland into facilities to produce goods and commodities desired by the developed countries. Dependent on developed countries as markets for the goods produced, they also become increasingly dependent on these same countries as providers of their basic foodstuffs. The wealthy countries obtain the commodities they desire, in the present case cutter-and-canner grade beef, while food supplies in poorer countries become scarcer, unemployment increases, and the land and other resources are increasingly degraded.

The process that is occurring in the world system is analagous to the ecological concept of the food chain. The poor in developing countries are in a relatively low position on this food chain and the foods they consume are relatively low on the chain. The major portion of the population survives by eating basic grains and the local foodstuffs they can obtain. An increasing number of Third World countries, however, are now producing commodities such as cattle that are relatively high up on the food chain for export to the people in the developed world who are at the top of the food chain. Most distressing is the fact that, as in Honduras, local populations have to compete with the animals that are lower on the food chain for the locally available resources. Table 8.4 shows that, despite the fact that the United States produced almost twenty-five percent of the total beef in the major producing countries (over three times the amount produced by any other single country), it also imports over twenty-nine percent of the beef in the world, more than twice as much as its nearest competitor, the United Kingdom (U.S.D.A. 1981). Imports would probably be even higher if it were not for the Meat Import Law of 1964 that established import quotas to protect domestic producers (McCoy 1979:366).

RESEARCH AND METHODOLOGICAL STRATEGIES

The analysis of any particular situation such as that of southern Honduras is just one historical case study unless we can draw some larger methodological or theoretical significance from it. To be sure, the Honduran case is an addition to the literature showing how the internationalization of capital (see Barkin 1983) is transforming regions like southern Honduras or what the consequences of delocalization are (see Pelto 1973). Rather than focus on these, however, I would like to discuss some of the methodological implications of the research. My focus will be on suggesting some productive ways for integrating micro and macro analyses of change.

As Adams (1970) has pointed out, there is really no shortage of concepts that can be utilized to effectively link different

TABLE 8.4
Relative Importance of the U.S.A. in Beef Marketing of the World's
Major Producing and/or Trading Countries

	United States	World	U.S. Percent of Total
Number of Cattle (000)	110,869	935,199	11
Total Beef Production (000 metric tons)	9,924.7	40,168.6	24
Total Beef Imports (000 metric tons)	1,102.7	3,785.0	29
Total Beef Exports (000 metric tons)	77.6	4,356.7	2
Total Beef Consumption (000 metric tons)	10,974.3	39,606.8	27

Source: U.S.D.A. Foreign Agriculture Circular, Livestock and Meat,
FLM 2-81, February 1981.

levels of analysis. The few relevant anthropological examples that
we have that integrate different levels of analysis use these
linking concepts as central elements of the analysis. Thus, Adams
has used power, Leslie White and others have used energy, Wolf has
used the notion of culture broker and a number of Marxist-oriented
anthropologists have used the notion of class. Another possibility
for a more topical way of integrating levels of analysis is to use
a commodity focus. Although this is a much-used strategy for
delimiting parameters for research efforts in the agricultural
sciences and in economics it has not been used frequently by anthropologists (see Sharp 1952 and Cook 1982 for some exceptions).
Part of the reason for this, of course, is that anthropologists are
more interested in people than commodities and we are usually
interested in how production, distribution and consumption of a
large number of commodities are inter-related. To be sure, this
focus must be used with caution but in the present case I believe
that it has been quite useful as a starting point for the research.

In the case considered here, there were actually several different commodities being analyzed because of their interrelationships. Despite the fact that my research was funded by a commodity
specific project (the International Sorghum/Millet Program), my own
research interests quickly expanded beyond sorghum when it became
obvious that (1) it was interplanted with corn that is the preferred subsistence crop; (2) pasture was the predominant cultigen
in the region; and (3) the pasture was being fed to cattle. Although the focus in this paper is predominantly on cattle, the
tracing of linkages with these other commodities is an integral
part of the analysis.

What does the commodity focus allow the investigator to do?
In the present case, it led me to focus on the role that these
various commodities play in the local, regional, national, Central
American, and world levels as well as the interconnections that
exist among these levels. Understanding the place of grains and
cattle in the larger systems aided me in interpreting the processes
at the microlevel, in understanding why decision makers in small
communities in the municipio of Pespire were making the choices
they did. Although the process by which land is being converted to
pasture undoubtedly differs somewhat in other communities, what we
are seeing is one of the adaptive responses being made by individuals to a changing regional, national and world situation. Regional data from southern Honduras and from Central America as a whole
show that processes similar to those identified in Pespire are
occurring throughout the wider area. The cattle are eating the
forest all over Central America (as well as in such far-flung
locations as Brazil, Papua New Guinea, various parts of Africa and
other regions of the world), and the reason for this is because of
the rapidly-expanding demand for meat within the developed world as
well as among the middle and upper classes in developing countries
(see Ehrlich, Ehrlich and Holdren 1977:313-5; DeWalt 1985a).

Tracing the commodities from the producer to the ultimate
consumer through some of the data from different levels of analysis
that I have presented in this paper shows who is benefitting from
this "development" process and also suggests who some of the vic-

tims might be. As with so many other cases of delocalization, the consequences for local populations are that inequalities appear to be increasing, the nutritional status of a part of the population is suffering, people are becoming dependent on the world system for their survival, and resources are being used unwisely.

Finally, by looking at these commodities in terms of what they imply in evolutionary terms, we can foresee some of the potential long-range consequences of their interrelationships. Although Brown and others may try to convince us that the increasing world population is to blame for turning developing countries into food importers, Honduras is another case that shows that the real problem is decisions about how resources are to be allocated and used. Along with the rest of Central America, Honduras has become a large cattle ranch for the developed countries, principally the United States. It has done so at the expense of grain production. This process creates greater unemployment, a lower standard of living for a part of the population, and a role as the purveyor of cheap beef to people who can afford to eat high on the food chain (and whose pets can eat there too). If the goal were to create a sustainable agricultural system that would have the potential to continue to feed the nation's population, then those who control such decisions in Honduras have made the wrong choice.

A commodity focus must be supplemented with other conceptual tools and research strategies, but it does offer considerable utility for demonstrating some of the linkages between phenomena at the microlevel and at the macrolevel. In the present case, utilizing a commodity focus within a cultural ecology of development perspective has allowed us to understand some of the differential distribution of costs and benefits of development and underdevelopment in southern Honduras and Central America.

EPILOGUE

Beef consumption in the United States reached a peak of about 133 pounds per capita in 1976. During 1977, the United States consumed about 12,660.5 thousand metric tons of beef (USDA FLM 2-81 1981:24). Since that time, beef consumption has dropped precipitously due to rising prices, greater health consciousness, and other factors. In 1981, consumption per capita had dropped to about 105 pounds per person (USDA FLM 5- 81 1981:3) and the United States used only 10,831.9 thousand metric tons of beef (USDA FLM 2-81 1981:24).

The importance of these trends for the present analysis is that the United States is importing less beef in recent years. In Honduras, the effects have been devastating. By late 1982, five of the seven meat packing plants in the country had stopped processing cattle. Prices paid to producers by those plants that continued to operate were substantially lower than they had been. Most producers who did not need cash were holding their animals off the market waiting for higher prices, or were smuggling their animals into El Salvador or Guatemala where higher prices were to be found.

To a large extent, these recent events just demonstrate again

what we already know -- the cattle business is no less subject to
the boom and bust cycles that affect other export commodities. The
events surrounding the cattle and meat packing industries in Honduras are similar to those that affect cotton, sugar cane, coffee,
and other products. The biggest difference, however, is that
landowners investing in cattle have affected much more land. As we
have seen, over sixty percent of the land in southern Honduras is
dedicated to pasture for cattle. When this commodity ceases to
have much value on the world market, the human and ecological costs
that cattle engender are even more difficult to justify.

NOTES

1. The research reported here was supported by the International Sorghum/Millet Collaborative Research Support Program
(INTSORMIL) through contract #AID/DSAN-G-0149.
2. I should note here that what I have been calling the
"micro" and "macro" level are actually composed of many different
levels of what Richard Adams has called "operating units" (see
Adams 1970:39-55).

BIBLIOGRAPHY

Adams, Richard N. 1970. Crucifixion by Power. Austin: University of Texas.
Barkin, David. 1983. The Internationalization of Capital and the Spatial Organization of Agriculture in Mexico. In Frank Moulaert and Patricia Salinas eds., Regional Analysis and the New International Division of Labor. Boston: Kluwer, Nijhoff Publishing. pp.97-109.
Boyer, Jefferson. 1983. Agrarian Capitalism and Peasant Praxis in Southern Honduras. Unpublished Ph.D. dissertation, University of North Carolina.
Brown, Lester. 1981a. Building a Sustainable Society. New York: Norton.
_____. 1981b. " World Population Growth, Soil Erosion, and Food Security". Science 214:995-1002.
Cook, Scott. 1982. Zapotec Stoneworkers. Washington: University Press of America.
DeWalt, Billie R. 1984. "International Development Paths and Policies: The Cultural Ecology of Development." The Rural Sociologist (in press).
_____. 1985a Mexico's Second Green Revolution: Food for Feed. Mexican Studies/Estudios Mexicanos. 1:29-60.
_____. 1985b The Agrarian Bases of Conflict in Central America. In, Kenneth Coleman and George Herring, eds., The Central American Crisis: the Sources of Conflict and the Failure of U.S. Policy. Wilmington, Delaware: Scholarly Resources Press.
DeWalt, Billie and Kathleen DeWalt. 1982. Farming Systems Research in Pespire, Southern Honduras. Lexington, KY: University of Kentucky Department of Anthropology.
Ehrlich, Paul, Anne H. Ehrlich and John Holdren. 1977. Ecoscience: Population, Resources, Environment. San Francisco: Freeman.
Geertz, Clifford. 1963. Agricultural Involution. Berkeley: University of California.
Gomez-Pompa, A. C., K. C. Vasquez-Yanes and S. Guevara. 1972. "The Tropical Rain Forest: A Nonrenewable Resource." Science 177:762-765.

Grossman, L. 1977. "Man-environment Relationships in Anthropology and Geography." Annals of the Association of American Geographers 67(1):126-144.

Instituto de Nutricion de Centro America y Panama. 1969. Evaluacion Nutricional de la poblacion de Centroamerica y Panama. Guatemala City.

McCoy, J. 1979. Livestock and Meat Marketing. A.V.I. Publishing Company, Inc.

Murdoch, William. 1982. The Poverty of Nations. Baltimore: Johns Hopkins University Press.

Parsons, J. 1972. "Spread of African Pasture Grasses to the American Tropics." Journal of Range Management 25:12-17.

_____. 1976. "Forest to Pasture: Development or Destruction?" Revista de Biologica Tropical 24 (Supplement 1):121-138.

Pelto, Pertti. 1973. The Snowmobile Revolution. Menlo Park, CA: Cummings.

Secretaria de Recursos Naturales. 1980. Los Granos Basicos en su Aspecto Economico. Tegucigalpa, Honduras.

Sharp, Lauriston. 1952. "Steel Axes for Stone-Age Australians". Human Organization 11:17-22.

Smith, Carol. 1978. "Beyond Dependency Theory: National and Regional Patterns of Underdevelopment in Guatemala." American Ethnologist 5:574-617.

Stares, R. C. 1972. La Economia Campesina en la Zona Sur de Honduras 1950-1970: su Desarollo y Perspectivas Para el Futuro. Informe Presentado a la Prefectura de Choluteca, Honduras.

U.S. Department of Agriculture. 1981. Foreign Agriculture Circular: Livestock and Meat. Washington, D.C.

White, Robert A. 1977. Structural Factors in Rural Development: The Church and the Peasant in Honduras. Unpublished Ph.D. dissertation, Cornell University.

World Bank. 1975. Agricultural Credit: Sector Policy Paper. Washington: World Bank.

World Bank. 1980. World Development Report -- 1980. New York: World Bank.

9
Methodology in Macro-Micro Studies

Pertti J. Pelto and Billie R. DeWalt

INTRODUCTION

Growing interest in the study of microlevel/macrolevel linkages calls for the development of suitable methodologies to guide empirical research. Heretofore, the approaches and methods employed in sociocultural data-gathering have been suited to the study of relatively small-scale, localized communities, within which the means for gathering data on broader scale phenomena are often quite limited. The basic model of community-based research in anthropology needs considerable expansion if we are to develop more sophisticated analyses of interactions between local/regional phenomena and the broader systems with which they are in constant interaction. We feel that there are two basic methodological tasks required for developing this kind of research:

First, the conceptual models and systems of postulated relationships among levels need some clearer delineation, in terms of empirical, observable social units. These include the "actors," "scenes of activity," and "process events" about which anthropological generalizations can be formulated (see also the paper by Bennett in this volume).

Second, we need clear definitions of the <u>rubrics</u> of intersystem linkage. By "rubrics" we mean better operationalization of the descriptive labels and other key words in the <u>data language</u>, including the explanatory constructs, used to describe and discuss particular kinds of intersystem processes. Such <u>rubrics</u> provide guidelines for empirical research methods. For example, economic processes at various levels are seen as operating through mechanisms of "price," "supply and demand" and related economic constructs. Of course a major aspect of any economic system is observable in the actual transfer of goods and services from one location to another. Religious movements, on the other hand, reach out and touch peoples' lives through proselytizing, travelling evangelists, religious messages by radio, TV and other mass media, and special "revival meetings" (see Gerlach and Hine 1970). These rubrics -- including "price," "supply and demand," "proselytizing," etc. -- are often evident in the day-to-day language of the actors whose activities are directly concerned with micro/macro inter-

actions. Yet scholars have been largely unable to determine met
odological strategies for utilizing these rubrics to more effe
tively relate microlevels and macrolevels.

The major point to be made is that we do have a variety
rubrics in anthropology and the other social sciences that spar
spectrum of microlevel/macrolevel linkages. What we do not ha
are operational ways of relating these rubrics to empirical obse
vations. In the following pages we will discuss some examples
such operations.

RUBRICS IN SPACE, TIME AND CAUSALITY

As we pointed out in the introduction, micro/mac
relationships may be involved primarily with the spatial dimensic
chronological progression, causality in hierarchical systems,
combinations among these three spheres. Sharper methodologic
tools are needed for clearly distinguishing the interrelationshi
among these dimensions. Surprisingly, it is perhaps the archaeol
gists who have done the most work with this methodological issu
Among archaeologists, terms such as "sequence," "horizon," a
"diffusion" are generally given quite clear operational meaning
relation to observable spatial/temporal data from excavations.

In an earlier era of anthropological research, the "age-are
hypothesis" provided a similar model by which anthropologist
attempted to directly infer chronological information from spatia
relationships. Thus widespread cultural features such as girl
puberty rites were seen as having greater antiquity than cultura
features with very narrow geographical distributions. Whatever th
problems with this formulation, at least the basic "rule" fo
translating spatial data into time sequences was reasonably clear.

Rubrics concerning time and space are often intended to b
primarily descriptive. They draw our attention to the patternin
of empirical observations, without the provision of "causa
mechanisms." Strictly speaking, "causality" is largely absent fro
concepts that refer to empirical observables. It is therefor
useful to remind ourselves of the logical resources generally use
to infer causality. Basically, co-occurrence in time and space
coupled with appropriate time sequence, remains the essential an
primary means for inferring cause.

The conceptual language of micro/macro linkage, particularl
farther up the ladder of abstraction and explanation, ofter
contains the inference of causal mechanisms. Terms such as
"infiltration," "dumping," "protest movement," and "politica
favoritism" point to movements of people, goods, or information
They also suggest something about the forces or motives involved i
these processes.

Scrutiny of terminologies concerned with micro/macro linkage
is likely to demonstrate that most of our language of causality o
theoretical explanations refers to complex concatenations of lowe
level concepts. Thus, terms such as "marginalization," "regiona
exploitation," "agricultural involution," "delocalization," "th
internationalization of capital" and "foreign capital hegemony" all

require accumulation of complex data concerning a number of empirical referents. These are terms that encompass the articulation of
a variety of microlevel/macrolevel processes. Yet they do not
result in "testable" propositions and hypotheses precisely because
the rubrics of linkage or articulation are not made explicit. (The
contribution by Cancian in this volume is designed to begin to make
sense of the rubrics of linkage among the concepts of class, power,
and status). That is, what are the empirical observations, the
interrelationships among phenomena, that constitute marginalization? Unless we can answer such questions, then such a term will
remain in the realm of a descriptive label (albeit, one that
"carves at the joints") rather than a theoretical concept with a
great deal of explanatory significance.

It is our belief that the first methodological task is to
develop ways to identify the empirical observations needed for the
lower-order terms, from which the higher-order causal and explanatory statements are constructed. This is not to say that the
process is fundamentally inductive. Although we do often lack the
tools for directly documenting or testing our formulations we do
frequently have clear theoretical frameworks and hypotheses in the
middle range. We will illustrate in the following sections.

MICRO/MACRO LINKAGE IN POLITICS: AN ILLUSTRATION

National political campaigns are, in many respects, excellent
situations in which to study the articulation of diverse levels,
because their activities are clearly marked in both organizational
structure and communications "events." (See Eidheim 1963, Mayer
1966, Nicholas 1965, for examples of local politicians and elections illustrating some "rubrics of political linkage" in peasant
societies). Political campaign managers speak a great deal about
"mass media saturation," "TV imagery," and on the other hand,
"grass roots organization." In the United States, as in many other
countries, presidential campaigns commonly include hosts of "volun-
teers" who carry the macrolevel messages to the local level in
"door-to-door campaigns," organized in part by local representatives.

Equally visible are the intensive "fund-raising" activities
connected with presidential electioneering. These may be national
level mailings and national level organization of "political action
committees," as well as state level and local level "fund-raising
events" such as $100-a-plate dinners. Presidential election orga-
nizations (in theory) have clear hierarchical structures, with an
overarching national committee, plus state organizations and
regional/local campaign groups and organizers.

The nature of election campaigns is intrinsically very public,
because the object is to attract positive attention, to get votes.
Thus the "rubrics" of inter-linkage between macro and microlevels
are often quite clear. Political organizers often measure their
impact at local levels in terms of "name recognition" (the per-
centages of voters in particular areas who recognize the name of
the candidate). At the local and state levels political organizers

seek to enhance the candidate's position through "events" -- especially visits of the candidate, speeches for selected groups, attendance at ethnic celebrations, and other occasions that engender local publicity.

A researcher concerned with political events in a particular region or community would identify all the pathways or channels through which political messages and influences (and campaign finances) pass between the local/regional scene and the larger political system. After identifying these channels, a next research step is to find ways to observe these phenomena farther up in the hierarchy, for example at the state level. At that point the researcher may find it useful to focus on ways in which state-wide organizations relate to the local/regional site. The researcher would seek out key actors and events, using the clues in the rubrics of political language identified at the local level.

A full national level analysis of micro/macro relations would also require study of the central campaign headquarters of at least one "exemplar" candidate. At the central level one would pay special attention to the lines of communication (and the messages that flow along them) to state and local levels.

The microlevel/macrolevel linkages in the political arena are particularly interesting because of the highly developed concern among political practitioners about their own "rubrics of linkage." Although the local level actors in political campaigns may often feel that the central leadership is "out of touch with the grassroots," the national headquarters people are likely to make great efforts to maintain their levels of information concerning state/local issues and turns of political events. Great effort is generally expended in "briefing the candidate" about key local persons and political issues in each region the candidate visits. The political concern about microprocesses is also visible in the kinds of public opinion polling contracted by the candidates. Instead of simply asking "Who would you vote for?"; the campaign managers seek data on age, sex, education, residential locations, occupation, ethnic group, and positions on key local and national issues concerning their voter populations. Public opinion polls, whether simple or sophisticated, serve as one important feedback of influence from local communities to the macrolevels of political activity. The feedback from state level primaries and state/local caucuses bring about sharp changes at the macrolevel, as "front runners" may get increased financial support and attention, while lesser candidates drop out of the race.

This brief sketch of political campaign rubrics points to some research tactics and suggests some of the ordinary public language that aids in identifying key points of data-gathering. We have not, in this example, identified specific hypotheses for testing, as our objective is to lay out some of the general descriptive terrain across which the anthropologist moves in developing full-scale analysis of a complex system. Analogous systems of communication and linkage could be explored in other topical domains, as suggested in Table 9.1. This table presents a preliminary sketch of some sectors of macrolevel/microlevel linkage, with examples of some rubrics that apply to these major domains. It is not intended as a definitive nomenclature, but rather as a preliminary inventory around which data may be organized for research purposes. A researcher's theoretical background and practical interests will of course suggest certain focal areas for research, but we feel that exploration of the rubrics of discourse "out there" in the empirical world also provide important methodological guidelines.

Many other domains or topics could be charted out in this manner. The methodological elements -- including descriptive/theoretical rubrics, types of linking persons, media of exchange, units of analysis, and linking events -- are only a small sampling of the framework one would use for full-scale micro/macro analysis. The point is that the researcher must search for some workable analytic model in which "forces," "impacts" or other kinds of information flow are traced in their movements from one system level to another (for examples of such research on migration see DuToit and Safa 1975; Kemper 1977).

Such heuristic models of the rubrics of intersystem linkages should contain enough information and features to identify points of observation and data-gathering. The following paragraphs present another illustrative example, using elements identified in Table 9.1.

SAMPLE CASE: STUDY OF A COMMUNITY HEALTH PROGRAM

The focus of the research is a study of a health care program in a developing country, here referred to as Fictonia. Noting the elements in the table, our first research task is to identify the "structures" of administration, in terms of individual administrators, and the "programs" with which they are involved. Health programs such as the one we are studying are imbedded within an administrative structure -- often, but not always, the Health Ministry of the nation. In Fictonia, as in practically all nations, any program -- including a community health program -- is embodied in written protocols, including perhaps legislation, at national or regional levels. The written protocol is likely to include general statements of program philosophy and objectives, as well as descriptions of the intended administrative structures and activities at lower levels, reaching down to the primary sites of implementation. Often such protocols are relatively vague about the administrative linkages in the middle levels. On the other hand, if the community health program has been introduced by a foreign aid program or non-governmental organization, we would expect to find written agreements between the organizers of the program and high level administrators. (Scrimshaw's paper in this volume illustrates a case in which a national policy [concerning abortion] has rather little relationship to actual events and practices at the local level, among health practitioners and their clients).

The regional and local levels of community health projects should be evident in specific components (health centers, personnel, and activities) identifiable in individual communities. The sites of actual implementation -- in community settings -- are the locales with which anthropologists are most likely to be familiar.

TABLE 9.1
Elements of Macrolevel/Microlevel Research Methods

TOPIC/ DOMAIN	RUBRICS OF DESCRIPTION AND THEORY	TYPES OF LINK-ING PERSONS
Political elections	vote patterns, political power, political parties, campaigns, political issues	candidates, campaign managers, regional/state coordinators, "powerbrokers"
Art/ritual religious forms	diffusion, proselytizing, innovation, stimulus diffusion	performers, artists, impresarios, evangelists, missionaries
Migration (both rural/urban and international)	economic pressure, political pressure, religious persecution, wage labor, head taxes	labor recruiters, kinship links
Economic transactions, Commerce	price mechanism, supply/demand, consumerism, exploitation, economizing behavior	corporate agents, vendors, wholesalers, truckers, shippers, buyers, brokers
Political administration	bureaucratic principles, struggle for power, factionalism, class struggle	administrators (all levels), political brokers, party officials
Health care	epidemiological principles, peoples' health, decision-making, inter-relations of traditional/modern health programs	administrators, providers, medical vendors

TABLE 9.1 (cont'd)

"MEDIA OF EXCHANGE"	LINKING EVENTS	TOPIC/ DOMAIN
contributions, endorsements, votes, "media exposure"	rallies, fundraisers, primaries, elections	Political elections
art objects, ritual acts, techniques, paraphernalia, sacred texts	art shows, gospel meetings, solo performances	Art/ritual religious forms
number of migrants, letters, communications, money remitted	departures, arrivals, reunions	Migration (both rural/urban and international)
commodities, services, cash, prices	sales, shipments, transactions, market days, deliveries	Economic transactions, Commerce
political favors, administrative acts, legislative acts, political information, public works, protests	meetings, committees, hiring, firing, programs, projects, political ceremonies, directives	Political administration
patients, morbidity, mortality, medical supplies, referrals, cases, health facilities	clinical encounters, treatments, hospitalization, home visits, immunizations, childbirths	Health care

Anthropological studies of local/regional health programs generally focus on the operations of health centers and community-based health workers, although some include discussion of the regional hospitals or other levels of referral and administration in the national medical care system.

Local health centers or community health projects are usually situated within a provincial, state, or departmental system. Unfortunately, the intermediate level administrative systems are often being glossed over by field workers, perhaps for lack of time. Nonetheless, intermediate administrative levels usually have powerful influence in mediating macrolevel policies and processes "down" to local levels.

In the following discussion, "intermediate level" refers to any and all administrative offices in the direct "chain of responsibility" between local, operational levels and the national policy-setting ministries. Usually such intermediate administrative offices are to be found in provincial, regional or "state" capital cities. In complex systems there may be two, perhaps even three, intermediate levels intervening between local and national levels.

In studying aspects of a community health program (with attention to the operation of the program in a particular set of communities, the following questions focus attention on the intermediate levels of linkage:

1. What intermediate level administrative offices are responsible for the program?
2. What are the geographic characteristics of the region? If we have begun observations of the community health program in a particular set of communities, how do they relate, physically, to the intermediate administrative centers? Is our microlevel locality far from the administrative center of the region? Is it a culturally or economically "different" sub-region within the administrative area?
3. What other administrative units in the province, state, or department also relate to the community health program? (e.g. Department of Education; Agriculture Dept. etc.)
4. What kinds of persons (and messages) come to the local health centers from the regional headquarters? What reports (and other messages) are transmitted "upwards" to the regional headquarters?
5. In physical terms, how far away is the intermediate regional administration, and how do persons and messages travel between those offices and the local (community) health centers?
6. Does this community health program have direct links to the national levels? If so, to what offices? How do they communicate with the local level operations?
7. How are funds and supplies transmitted to the local level operations?

Based on the items listed under "media of exchange" and

"linking events" (Table 9.1), we can pursue the study of a community health program at the microlevel through observations of
"patient-provider interactions," special events such as group immun-
izations, health education meetings, and case-finding by means of
a survey process. Some of this local level data-gathering can make
good use of epidemiological methods and concepts.

All of these data-gathering processes depend on the specific
theoretical and practical objectives of the research project. If
the primary aim is to examine the extent and effectiveness, at the
local level, of nationally developed policies mandating community
participation in health programs, the following questions and (hypothetical) data provide a framework for research in a local
(microlevel) region in Fictonia:

> Question: What structural forms of community participation are
> suggested or mandated by the national health policy, and are
> any of these structures apparent in the research region?
> Data: There are local health committees, mother's clubs, and a
> training program for community based health workers. (There is
> actually an entire manual on community participation and train-
> ing). In the research area there are (according to key inform-
> ants) all of these features.
>
> Question: What observable events embody the "community parti-
> cipation" of these local committees, mothers' clubs, and other
> features?
> Data: There are weekly meetings, as well as projects initiated
> by the mothers clubs, including health education sessions, and
> training sessions for community health workers.
>
> Question: Do they actually meet on a regular basis? Is there
> attendance by the expected individuals? Are projects actively
> being pursued?
> Data: "Yes and no." The Health Committees meet weekly (in
> most communities of the region), but attendance is erratic.
> Only about thirty percent of the membership attend regularly.
> The mothers' clubs in four of the five subcommunities meet
> regularly and are active, but only about forty percent of
> eligible-attendees seem interested and active. Local health
> workers are being trained, but two of the ten selected indi-
> viduals have dropped out; four health workers attend only
> irregularly; the other four are enthusiastic and always attend
> the regular sessions.
>
> Question: What explanations are given by local people for lack
> of participation?
> Data: The explanations given include: lack of knowledge of
> the program, transportation difficulties, chores and duties at
> home, and a number of other reasons.

After establishing certain features of community participation
(as articulated by national policy), as well as certain weaknesses
or failings, it is time to turn our attention to the role of

intermediate level administrators in implementing the program. It would be useful to have some impressionistic information about the operation of the intermediate level administrators from both the national level and the local level, including names of the key persons (whom we may have met in the initial, negotiation, phase of research). Before going to the regional or provincial (or state-level) offices, we should already have some idea of when the inter-mediate level officials last visited the local region, and what kinds of communications they maintain, by telephone, mail or other means, with the communities.

Our visit to the intermediate level officials might include the following sequence of questions:

Question: What information (and impressions) do the interme-diate administrators have concerning progress in implementing the "community participation mandate"?

Data: The program seems to be going well in most areas, including the one on which we are focussing, although there are some marginal areas where nothing is happening. (The adminis-trators are eager to hear our opinions and data about community programs in the research area).

Question: What means do they use to develop, monitor, and encourage community participation in their various regional centers?

Data: Instructions and supporting materials have been sent to each Health Center in the area. Visits have been made to some Centers, including one in a nearby rural region in which a foreign (Country X) technical assistance team is giving support to the program. (NOTE: This is the first time we had informa-tion on the presence of the foreign technical assistance team in the region. It will definitely be worth visiting them, to expand our base of information resources. They may even have research focussed on our main question).

Question: What problems or obstacles seem to be the major ones impeding progress in the community participation program, in the opinion of the administrators?

Data: Among the answers are resistance and "urban elite orien-tation" of health professionals, ignorance and illiteracy of local people, some opposition from "political extremists," and poverty.

Question: What kinds of communications and resources from the national level influence program activities?

Data: There is very little communication, except for the original directives, and the bundle of "instructional mate-rials" that were sent out to the various Health Centers. How-ever, Dr. RR in the "Human Services Division" of the Health Ministry is "very interested" and has promised to visit this province in a month or two.

Question: Have reports been received from the various Health

Centers of the Province?
Data: Yes, they have all sent reports (we may look at them if
we wish), but these are brief, perfunctory statements, all of
which claim that all aspects of the program are being implemented fully. Some reports include statistics of participation, but the provincial administrator assures us that the
statistical statements are mainly fabricated by politically
ambitious local administrators at certain Health Centers.

Question: How do funds flow to support the local participation
and programmitic efforts? Have they in fact received financial
support in accordance with program procedures?
Data: Yes and no. Communities that fail to send in reports and
requests don't receive supporting funds. Only about forty-five
percent of the communities of the province have been active in
these aspects of the program. The communities in Region Y (the
area of our field site) are somewhat above average in levels of
activity, and they have received funds.

Question: What other provincial agencies or offices gave
concerns or interests affecting this program?
Data: Other important agencies include the Office of Agricultural Development; Education (school system), and a special
"Family Planning Task Force" -- all of which are supposedly informed of this program; all are supposed to be cooperating with
the overall project, but they are actually not very active or
interested ("because the original initiative was entirely
Health Ministry, without cooperation at top levels with other
ministries").

These are just a small sampling of the kinds of initial research questions, and possible turns of data-gathering, relevant to
understanding the intermediate (provincial) level of implementation. Continuing along these lines, we are likely to discover
administrative complexities, political and economic cross-currents,
and other middle level factors affecting the community health
program from above. Back at the local level, we will expect to
find various cultural and economic factors affecting the successes
and failures of the nationally-mandated program. These local level
factors, however, often take their particular forms through interaction with the processes initiated from intermediate and national
levels of the system.
Some of the main elements in the research strategy illustrated
here are the following:

1. Entry to the research action generally requires that we
   have some sort of "clearance" and relationships with administrators at the national and regional levels of the
   governmental hierarchy.
2. After developing relationships with administrators at the
   relevant levels, initial review of "the system" often begins
   at the macrolevel -- basically to identify the general scope
   and aims of the relevant program from the national perspec-

tive.

3. A provisional explanatory model is postulated, based on
    one's original abstract model (developed "back home") but
    now loaded up with concrete details of a specific health
    system. This model is still quite incomplete and tenta-
    tive.
4. "Rubrics of discourse" are examined from the national level
    perspective, and throughout the system as one moves to
    identify actions and processes at the local level. These
    rubrics are encountered in key informant interviews as well
    as in written documents.
5. Field work in local communities involves both qualitative
    and quantitative observations (including participant obser-
    vation) and quantitative methods.
6. Often the quantitative materials (e.g. structured inter-
    views, health center case reviews, etc.) focus directly on
    giving operational meaning to the rubrics identified ear-
    lier.
7. Ideally, both qualitative and quantitative research is
    carried out at every level of the relevant administra-
    tive/political hierarchy.
8. The broader explanatory/causal concepts in our provisional
    theoretical model are given operational meaning through
    relationships to specific "rubrics" of linkage at the em-
    pirical level.
9. The provisional model of interaction processes and linkages
    is filled in and revised in the light of the new data.

CONCLUSIONS

The main purpose of this chapter has been to suggest some
methodological approaches for furthering anthropological work on
microlevel/macrolevel relationships. In particular, we have
suggested here the necessity of paying greater attention to the
rubrics of linkage, the rules for studying and demonstrating articulation of different levels in terms of space, time and causality.

The methods suggested here are based on the premise that
anthropological research will continue to have one foot in
community-based observations (hence, usually including microlevel
phenomena). We also assume that many of the major research tools
of anthropology, particularly those involving detailed, open-ended
interviewing and direct observation of events, are applicable to
significant portions of data-gathering on macrolevel processes.

At the same time, study of macrolevel phenomena almost always
requires considerable attention to written documents -- published
and unpublished historical materials, production statistics, price
lists, governmental reports, census data, and so on. Survey data,
involving interviewing of at least moderately large samples of
householders, or perhaps special categories such as "community
leaders," "health practitioners," or "representative entrepreneurs," are also important methodological components.

Some very important micro/macro research is carried out

through careful analysis of existing archival materials. Smith's chapter concerning Guatemala is an excellent example. Most interesting in her analysis of political/economic processes over the past five centuries is the way in which the interpretation of historical materials requires ethnographic (community level) information from relevant periods. Broadbrush historical analyses have often fallen short if sufficient microlevel data were lacking. In the case of Guatemala, Smith made substantial use of extensive community-based ethnographic works, in addition to older sources that provided glimpses of local level phenomena of earlier centuries.

Anthropologists have acquired credible expertise in the study of macrolevel political, economic, and other kinds of data. Jointly with scholars in other disciplines, our theoreticians have in recent years developed more and more sophisticated models for analysis of the complex processes of world-wide sociocultural change. These macrolevel processes, and the models that seek to explain and understand them, are only now beginning to be related to the small-scale, community-based phenomena of anthropological field work. The exploration of linkages between the large-scale and the microlevel models in anthropology requires solid, innovative field research. Theoretical models may be constructed and reconstructed, and rubrics of linkage may be proposed, but these require empirical testing. Our suggestions in this chapter have been intended to explore this middle ground.

Several of the chapters in this volume, especially those of Cancian, DeWalt, Scrimshaw, and Whiteford and Montgomery were based on empirical research that included methodological strategies along the lines suggested in this discussion. These researchers explored ways of dealing with those "intermediate structures" that provide connections between, for example, national socio-political processes and the daily activities of people in local communities. This is an important area for anthropological work, and is being approached with the eclecticism (i.e. utilizing concepts from a variety of disciplines and perspectives) usual in our discipline.

The paper by Cancian on stratification systems directed our attention to three highly significant rubrics -- rank, class, and power -- as carriers of interdigitation across the micro/macro continuum. These key concepts involve different kinds of empirical data and they are expressed in quite different, though related, dynamic processes. Whiteford and Montgomery's discussion of the Mexicali Valley also suggests some of the rubrics of linkage, including key organizations (governments, unions, and others) that have a variety of different relationships to micro and macrolevels.

While our theoretical models have become more sophisticated, as the authors in this volume have shown, there is increasing evidence that we need to build in more complex feedback loops between microlevel and macrolevel systems. The theoretical discussions of Adams, Bennett, and others provide frameworks and rubrics that require complex, multilevel empirical data placed within a dynamic setting.

Much of the literature dealing with national and world-wide

processes is focussed on political and economic issues, but it is
self-evident that practically all topics and aspects of human
culture have macrolevel, as well as local level, expressions. We
should recognize that the _rubrics_ of linkage, and therefore the
research modes for studying them, can differ substantially. Not
everything in the world travels along lines of commerce and government. We hope that future anthropological research will fill in,
with a rich panorama of models and explanatory frameworks, the
intermediating "middle ground" that appears at the moment to be
only lightly sketched in anthropology.

BIBLIOGRAPHY

DuToit, B. M. and H. Safa. 1975. <u>Migration</u> <u>and</u> <u>Urbanization</u>.   The
    Hague: Mouton Publishers.
Eidheim, H. 1963. Entrepreneurship in Politics.   In F. Barth,ed.
    <u>The</u> <u>Role</u> <u>of</u> <u>the</u> <u>Entrepreneur</u> <u>in</u> <u>Social</u> <u>Change</u> <u>in</u> <u>Northern</u>
    <u>Norway</u>. Oslo: Universitetsforlaget.
Gerlach, L. and V. Hine. 1970. <u>People,</u> <u>Power,</u> <u>Change:</u> <u>Movements</u> <u>of</u>
    <u>Social</u> <u>Transformation</u>. Indianapolis: Bobbs-Merrill.
Kemper, R. V. 1977. <u>Migration</u> <u>and</u> <u>Adaptation:</u> <u>Tzintzuntzan</u> <u>Peas-</u>
    <u>ants</u> <u>in</u> <u>Mexico</u> <u>City</u>. Beverly Hills: Sage Publications.
Mayer, A. 1966. The Significance of Quasi-groups in the Study of
    Complex Societies.   In M. Banton,ed. <u>The</u> <u>Social</u> <u>Anthropology</u>
    <u>of</u> <u>Complex</u> Societies. <u>A.S.A.</u> <u>Monograph</u> <u>4</u>. London: Tavistock
    Publications.
Nicholas, R. W. 1965. Factions: a Comparative Analysis.   In M.
    Banton,ed. <u>Political</u> <u>Systems</u> <u>and</u> <u>the</u> <u>Distribution</u> <u>of</u> <u>Power</u>.
    <u>A.S.A.</u> <u>Monograph</u> <u>2</u>. London: Tavistock Publications.

Index

Aberle, D.F., 13
Abortion, induced, 15, 16-17,
    121-143
  case studies of, 128-130
  government attitudes toward,
    138-139
  health care system attitudes
    toward, 139-141
  incidence of, 131-135
  methodology for collecting
    data on, 121-128
  methods of, 135-137
  a population perspective on,
    131-141
  women's attitides toward,
    130-131, 137
Abortion, spontaneous, 132,
    (table), 135
Access-making, model of, 148
Achievement value-orientation,
    33-34
Activity, scenes of, 187
Actors, 187
Adams, Richard N., 6, 10-11,
    13-17, 73,98, 165, 178, 180,
    182, 199
  Crucifixion by Power, 10
Adaptation, 23, 39-40, 42, 46
Adaptive behavior, 3, 4, 16,
    48, 73, 167, 182
Adaptive device, 58, 60
Adaptive system, 41
Affiliation, degrees of, 4
Africa, 27, 28, 31, 37, 38,
    40, 43, 182
  See also East Africa
Age-area hypothesis, 188
Age of Reason, 49
Agricultural Directive Com-
    mittees, 154
Agricultural economics, 28
Agricultural Involution
    (Geertz), 165
Agricultural involution, 188
Agricultural sciences, 182
Agriculture, types of, 26,
    93, 170, 172

Agriculture, types of (cont'd)
  See also Farming; Farming
    systems; Plantation
    agriculture
Agro-industrial complex, 159
Alamo Canal, 150, 154
All-American Canal, 154
Amerinds, 24, 32
Amnesty International, 105
Analysis
  of complex systems, 189-198
  levels of, 7, 10, 13, 15, 16,
    165, 182
  units of, 2, 27, 31, 43, 147,
    191
Analytic-abstract Approach (AA),
    42-44
Anthropology, 7, 8, 28, 47, 122
  applied and development, 5,
    24, 46-47
  community focus in, 44-45, 69,
    83-84, 187, 198-199.
    See also Community
  and history, 5-6, 27, 109-110
  and sociology, 27, 29, 43, 48
  micro/macro issue in, 8, 23-
    24, 46-48, 165, 188, 198-200
    See also Methodology for
    micro/macro research; Theory
Anthropology of the Nation State
    (Fallers), 28
Anthropology Resource Center, 48
Apollonian style, 31
Arabs, 27
Arana Osorio, Carlos, 107
Archaeology, 69, 188
Arizona, 44, 156
Articulation, 73, 78, 79(m6),
    147
  levels of, 10, 13, 157, 189,
    198
Ascription value-orientation,
    33-34
Asia, 37-38
Asociación Algodonera, 155
As You Sow (Goldschmidt), 26

203

210

Theory
  analytic-abstract(AA) and
    historical concrete(HC),
    42-44
  in anthropology and
    sociology, 23, 27-29, 32,
    43, 46, 48, 50
  need to link micro and
    macro approaches, 5, 6-7,
    11, 198-200
Third World
  capitalism in, 86, 166,
    180
  economic development in,
    26, 41-42, 46
  local/external interaction
    in, 32, 38, 47
Time scale
  See Micro and macro, time
    scale of
Tonnies, Ferdinand, 29
Totonicapan (Guatemala), 99,
  100, 108
Tribe, 24-29, 31-32, 43, 49
Tributary mode of production,
  78
Triggers, 64
Trobriand Islands, 29
Typologies in anthropology,
  27-35

Ultimate cause, 4
Unions in Mexicali Valley,
  157-158
United Kingdom, 180
United States
  and beef production in
    Honduras, 166, 174, 177,
    180, 181(table), 183
  and contraception in
    Ecuador, 16, 138
  and economy of Guatemala,
    93, 98, 104, 108
  and irrigation development
    in Mexico, 149-158
  and metacommunication, 63
United States Agency for
  International Development
  (USAID), 26, 108
Universalism value-orienta-
  tion, 33-35
Urban studies, 32, 122-123
Urban systems in Guatemala,

  96, 103, 104
Value-orientation components,
  33-35
Valle, Department of
  (Honduras), 167
Veblen, Thomas, 88
Vidich, Arthur J., 25
Wagley, Charles, 91, 99
Wallerstein, Immanuel, 41-42,
  69-70, 71, 73
  The Modern World-System:
    Capitalist Agriculture
    and the Origins of the
    European World-Economy in
    the Sixteenth Century, 69
Wasserstrom, Robert, 86, 98
Watanabe, John, 99
Weber, Alfred, 30
Weber, Max, 33, 72, 77
Wells, Miriam, 148
Wellton-Mohawk Project 156,
  · 157
Wheat production, 149, 153,
  159-160
White, Leslie, 182
Whiteford, Scott, 14, 15, 16,
  199
Whyte, William F., 29
  Street Corner Society, 29
Wilson, Margo, 4 ·
  Sex, Evolution, and
    Behavior, 4
Wolf, Eric, 48, 84-85, 75,
  77-78, 182
  "The Mills of Inequality:
    A Marxian Approach," 77
  Peasant Wars of the
    Twentieth Century, 75
Work, 59, 62-63, 65
World Bank, 26, 159, 174-175
World Court, 157
World Ethnographic Atlas
  (Murdock), 13
World systems, 60, 180, 183
  and anthropological approach
    to suprasystems, 40-46
  and history of local com-
    munities, 83-86, 109-110
  and interaction with local
    communities, 5, 7, 15,
    16, 17
  and interaction with local
    stratification systems,